John Gittings

Real China

From Cannibalism to karaoke

POCKET
BOOKS

LONDON · SYDNEY · NEW YORK · TOKYO · SINGAPORE · TORONTO

First published in Great Britain by Simon & Schuster, 1996
First published by Pocket Books, 1997
An imprint of Simon & Schuster Ltd
A Viacom Company

Simon & Schuster Ltd
West Garden Place
Kendal Street
London W2 2AQ

Simon & Schuster Australia
Sydney

A CIP catalogue record for this book is available from the British Library

ISBN 0 671 51651 5

Printed and bound in Great Britain by
Cox & Wyman Ltd, Reading, Berkshire

Acknowledgements

Many people in China have helped me write this book, often without knowing they were doing so. The older values of friendship and helpfulness to strangers survive better in Middle China than in the new developed areas where making money comes first. Long distance travel provides a chance for frank conversation. On leisurely strolls through back streets it is possible to stop and chat. A visitor seeking to understand China's history is usually welcome – with a bit of discretion. Individual names are hard to mention but Zhu Xianhua and friends deserve special thanks.

This is an opportunity to express my admiration for Yang Xianyi and Gladys Yang, Bill Hinton, David and Isabel Crook, Chen Han–seng and Su Shaozhi, in Beijing or formerly so, and my gratitude to two respected teachers and scholars, Professor Jerome Ch'en and the late Professor Wu Shihch'ang.

China specialists in England are a small but supportive group: my particular thanks to Elizabeth Croll, Harriet Evans, and Stephan Feuchtwang for years of friendship. I used the excellent libraries of the School of Oriental Studies (London University) and the Universities' Service Centre (Chinese University of Hong Kong). Essential material came from Human Rights in China and Human Rights Watch/Asia.

Without inspired advice from Michael Simmons at the *Guardian*, this book would never have been knocked into shape. Aelfthryth Gittings and Helen Lackner also read the text and made very useful suggestions. I am grateful for help on various points to members of the China Study Committee at Inter-Church House, London, also to Hao Wang. Danny Gittings eased my way through Hong Kong on many occasions. This book is for him and for Tom, Joe and Max.

My research benefited considerably from several visits to China on behalf of the *Guardian*, and parts of chapters 7 and 8 are based upon articles published on 16 January and 27 November 1993. Part of chapter 6 is based on an article which appeared in the *London Review of Books*, 5 August 1993. The poem quoted on page 83 is from Arthur Waley's *170 Chinese Poems*, reproduced by permission of Constable Publishers. The poem by Su Dongbo on page 93 is copyright Lin Yutang, reproduced by permission of Curtis Brown Group Ltd, London. The poem on page 123 is from *Journey to a War* by W. H. Auden and Christopher Isherwood, reproduced by permission of Faber and Faber Ltd. The extract from 'Dawang' on pp. 176–77 is from *The Chinese Earth* by Shen Tseng-wen, reproduced by permission of HarperCollins Publishers Ltd.

The maps were drawn by Finbar Sheehy.

Contents

Chronology

Imperial China (selected dynasties)

SHANG	c. 16th–11th century BC
CHIN (QIN)	221–206 BC
HAN	206 BC–AD 220
TANG	618–907
SUNG (SONG)	960–1279
YUAN (Mongols)	1279–1368
MING	1368–1644
CHING (QING)	1644–1911

Modern China

OPIUM WAR	1839–1841
TAIPING REBELLION	1850–1864
SELF-STRENGTHENING MOVEMENT	1861–1895
REFORM MOVEMENT	1895–1898

BOXER REBELLION	1900
NATIONALIST REVOLUTION	1911–1912
WARLORD PERIOD	1917–1927
NATIONALIST RULE	1927–1949
WAR WITH JAPAN	1937–1945

Communist Revolution

BIRTH OF PARTY	1921
BIRTH OF RED ARMY	1927
LONG MARCH	1934–1936
YANAN PERIOD	1937–1945
CIVIL WAR	1946–1949

People's Republic

NATIONAL DAY	1 October 1949
KOREAN WAR	June 1950–May 1953
HUNDRED FLOWERS	1956–1957
GREAT LEAP FORWARD	1958–1959
SINO-SOVIET SPLIT	1963
CULTURAL REVOLUTION	1966–1976
MAO ZEDONG DIES	9 September 1976
DENG TAKES POWER	1978
DEMOCRACY WALL	1978–1979

SHENZHEN SEZ FOUNDED	1980
RURAL REFORMS	1978–1985
INDUSTRIAL REFORMS	1984
HU YAOBANG SACKED	January 1987
DEMOCRACY MOVEMENT	January–June 1989
BEIJING MASSACRE	3–4 June 1989
DENG GOES SOUTH	January–February 1992
ECONOMIC BOOM	1993
DENG IN DECLINE	1994–1995

I

Journey to Middle China

There are two Chinas in the 1990s. One is the China of the expanding cities, the coastal boom, and the entrepreneurial ethic promoted by Mao Zedong's successor and veteran political survivor Deng Xiaoping in his final years. This is the China with which Mr Deng tempted his people and appeased foreign outrage after the Beijing massacre in and around Tiananmen Square in June 1989. The second China lies further inland, in the provinces away from the coast, and within each province in the more remote rural areas away from the towns. Here millions of Chinese peasants continue to live at the mercy of their traditional enemies: flood, drought and official corruption which has returned recently to plague them. Here the effects of modernisation and change are patchy and uneven, widening the gaps between urban and rural China, between rich and poor.

The difference between these two Chinas is illustrated by the single word 'gold'. It is the difference between those who purchase gold and those who produce it, between the shops with neon lighting where it is sold and the dark and dangerous tunnels where it is mined. When I first visited China during the Cultural Revolution (1966–76), the only gold to be seen was in the haloes painted around saintly portraits of Chairman Mao. Two decades later, in the China of Deng's economic revolution, gold has become

1

the most highly prized purchase – soft yellow 24 carat gold, the traditional hedge against inflation. Domestic gold production grew by five times between 1990 and 1992 to 181 tons, and almost twice as much again was imported. In Beijing alone, there are now more than four hundred jewellers' shops. In 1993, the government almost doubled the state purchasing price of gold to stimulate domestic production and reduce smuggling from abroad. In Guangzhou, gold has become a culinary talking point: the Guangzhou Restaurant now serves dishes decorated with 24 carat gold leaf to its new rich clients. The menu includes abalone, shark's fin, crocodile and clams sprinkled with gold leaf. Even the humble beancurd can be transformed by its addition into a dish of 'golden unicorn beancurd'.

To satisfy the gold fever of urban China, there is a gold rush in many parts of rural China where illegal mines are burrowed into the mountains, often with drastic results. During 1992 in Guangxi alone, more than seven thousand people were caught mining illegally in 179 sites. The next year in Hunan, a gold rush in the Banbian mountain area near Liuyang brought thousands of hopeful prospectors – and a crime wave which terrified local peasants. The official trade paper *China Gold* reported that 'Armed robbery, brawling, murder and other serious incidents occur frequently, so not even the chickens and the dogs feel secure!' In the same year a mountainside in the centre of Henan, undermined by hundreds of illegal shafts, collapsed killing ten prospectors. (The tragedy, said *China Gold*, should teach all unlicensed gold diggers a lesson!) City touts have invaded gold-producing areas to buy cheap gold in collusion with local Communist Party officials. There are stories of gold bars being smuggled out by live 'corpses', carried by accomplices in coffins.[1]

This second China – where the gold is produced but not consumed – is less accessible and has been studied less in recent years than the glossy, alluring China of the great cities, the coastal provinces and the Special Economic Zones. I call it Middle China because it is physically, politically and culturally China's heartland. Much of it has been so for two or even three millennia. Middle China was the earliest home of Chinese civilisation; it was the source of the greatest Chinese literature and painting; it was the thoroughfare for mobilised armies and the origin of great peasant rebellions. In coastal China and the most advanced cities, the pace of development is so fast that the past already seems obliterated. Middle China is also changing, but not so rapidly and more unevenly. Past, present and future jostle in awkward juxtaposition. Here is the real test of the policies of the 1980s and 1990s which have introduced capitalism ever faster, lightly dusted with socialist rhetoric, across the nation which once worshipped the Thought of Mao Zedong. Yet for most people, Middle China remains a blank on the map.

This is the blank that I seek to fill here. After the Beijing Massacre I have rarely returned to the capital, not only because of the memory of what I had seen there but because Beijing no longer seems so relevant to the questions about China which need to be asked. Instead I have made a series of ten visits to five provinces of Middle China. From north to south these are Henan, Hubei, Hunan, Guangxi and Hainan. (Guangxi was a province until 1958 when it became the Guangxi Zhuang Autonomous Region. This had no real effect and I shall continue to refer to it as a province. Hainan, formerly part of Guangdong, only became an independent province in 1988.) Together with coastal Guangdong – with whose amazing transformation their own less spectacular 'progress' can be compared – they formed the Central-South Region, which was established in 1950 after the communist victory. Each province has provided one or more themes which form the core subject-matter of this book. Though based on the province in question, these separate topics are also discussed in a more general, national context. In a country still largely under centralised control, local themes continue to reflect national trends although often in a special or accentuated form.

Henan province, where I begin, was the birthplace of the rural Great Leap Forward where Mao first declared that the collectivised People's Communes Were Good! Now it is one of the main reservoirs of unemployed and exploited peasants, who clog the railways seeking cheap labouring work in the towns. Their plight only began to be discussed cautiously at least four years after it emerged. Across Henan and other central provinces, millions of peasants have turned for comfort to old and new religions. The phenomenon is rarely mentioned in the Chinese press except to condemn those who preach outside the officially sponsored churches and their followings.

The next province is watery Hubei. Here the future development of the middle reaches of the Yangzi river is dominated by the enormous Three Gorges Dam scheme, first endorsed by Mao himself in a famous line of poetry. The dam continues to be challenged on environmental and social grounds by a few brave critics whose arguments in recent years have only been published abroad. Meanwhile in Hubei's capital city, Wuhan, thousands of workers have protested against economic reforms that threaten their jobs, again with hardly any official acknowledgement. While Hong Kong companies promote their grand plans for prestige developments in Wuhan, the city's crumbling infrastructure continues to deteriorate.

South of the Yangzi, Hunan is not only Mao's birthplace but the home of many other brilliant Chinese writers and political figures. Neither Mao's role nor theirs can yet be evaluated properly beyond the fulsome or perfunctory judgements of the official press. To find out more, we must visit their birthplaces and talk with the people who remember those days. Further south we come to Guangxi, scene of the most severe factional fighting, slaughter and (as we shall discover) even worse in the early years of the Cultural Revolution. Guangxi is changing fast though patchily under the influence of dynamic Guangdong to the south and Hong Kong beyond, but those who suffered most in those years are still unable to 'settle accounts' with their persecutors. Across the narrow straits from the mainland, Hainan island has been a home for exiles – officials and poets who had fallen from favour – since early imperial times. In the 1960s it became the destination for thousands of young Red Guards, 'sent down' to work alongside peasants, clearing the hills for new rubber plantations. Now it is the promised land for a new wave of voluntary exiles from the mainland, all seeking to make their fortunes on the wild frontier of China's largest Special Economic Zone. The social costs, which include one of the biggest crime waves in China and the most blatant prostitution, remain uncounted. After a brief look at booming Guangdong, once part of Middle China and now the model to which it aspires, I conclude by posing some essential questions: Where is all this leading, and what sort of system is replacing the one previously called 'socialism'? Is it going to produce a different result from the developmental mix of modernisation and backwardness, luxury and squalor, so widely encountered elsewhere in the Third World?

The map of Middle China is marked by ink-spots of modern development, and its provincial capitals and main cities possess at least one western-style shopping precinct, a new hotel and several luxury housing estates. There are new 'development zones' seeking to attract foreign investment, new highways with Western-style filling stations – and the ubiquitous karaoke bars. Economic and social change is most noticeable along the small number of east-west routes which cross the main north-south axis of Middle China, and particularly along the Yangzi River which is becoming the new highway to the interior. Yet the atmosphere in much of this region still remains much closer to Mao's China than could be imagined from Beijing. There is no political debate (dissenting voices are quickly silenced) and very little cultural life. Newspapers in Middle China remain the same stultifying four or eight-sheet affairs filled with long official speeches and stories of economic success. For every young entrepreneur in small-town Middle China who manages to 'plunge into the sea' and make his or her own way in life, there are a dozen young people condemned to a dull job with no prospect of escape – or to unemployment.

In many ways our partial perception of China has not improved so significantly since the last century. Then too the Western powers concerned themselves mostly with the court politics of Beijing and the economic development of the 'treaty ports' along the coast. The great interior was left for missionaries, botanists and antiquarians to explore. This was less surprising in an age of extremely poor communications, when a good day's travel inland might at best cover ten or fifteen miles by cart or sedan chair. Communications are relatively developed now, with a network of railways reaching every single Chinese province or region except Tibet, national highways throughout the country and paved roads to most villages. Yet by the higher standards of the late 20th Century, travel is still painfully slow away from the main routes. A different world can be found by deviating only a few tens of kilometres. The rural hinterlands and the mountainous areas which usually lie on provincial boundaries far away from their capital are uncharted territory. Off the main tourist and business thoroughfares, foreigners (except for Overseas Chinese returning to visit friends and relatives) are still rare.

Where China – a quarter of the world's population and Asia's largest power – is heading must be of critical importance for all nations, yet our attention remains fixed on the immediate events and the nearest parts of China. For 40 years after the Communists succeeded in 1949, it was what happened in Beijing which seemed to matter most. Those who watched and analysed events in China were actually called 'Pekinologists'. (Should they now, with our adoption of Chinese *pinyin* spelling, be called Beijingologists?) In the last decade, since the economic reforms which followed the death of Mao Zedong, this single focus has been broadened to include the Chinese coastal zone from north to south. This is the famous 'gold coast' most affected by the reforms and most easily surveyed from the vantage point of Hong Kong or Tokyo. The speed of change and the apparent success of shifting to a market economy in this zone has been hailed, uncritically, by too many Western politicians, economists and China-watchers as a new 'China miracle'.

It has also been greeted with a great deal of relief. For a while, the Beijing Massacre obliged Western governments to express disapproval of Chinese human rights abuses which they previously sought to ignore. Yet China remained an important player on the international scene as well as an immensely tempting market. There was at first a conflict of opinion as to whether China should be isolated or wooed. But over the five years after the Beijing Massacre, the trend was to normalise relations with Beijing, to seek its cooperation on international issues, and to downplay any evidence that its economic progress might be flawed or tarnished by persistent human rights violations.

Immediately after the Massacre the economic over-heating and price inflation which fuelled the popular protests had given way to policies of tight control and the future of the Chinese economy for a while looked bleak. This combination of political repression and economic decline, administered by an ageing leadership which had forfeited the confidence of most of its people, seemed to indicate very serious trouble ahead for the Party. During 1989–90, the atmosphere remained tense and unstable. The successful anti-communist revolutions in East Germany, Hungary, Czechoslovakia and before long the rest of Central and Eastern Europe, together with the rapid weakening of the Soviet regime, appeared to increase China's isolation.

However these external changes before long began to work to the advantage of the Chinese leadership. The end of the cold war and of US-Soviet bipolar domination gave China, as a permanent member of the United Nations (UN) Security Council, a stronger voice in international affairs. This was soon demonstrated in the Gulf crisis of 1990–91 when, after Iraq had invaded Kuwait, the US-led allied coalition sought Chinese consent to wage war on Saddam Hussein in the name of the UN. In the critical Security Council resolution to use 'all necessary means' against Iraq, China obligingly abstained instead of using its veto. Meanwhile, the political chaos and monetary inflation which followed the break-up of the Soviet Union enabled China to claim greater wisdom for its own policy of 'putting economic ahead of political reform'. The revolutions of Eastern Europe, far from inspiring Chinese dissidents to fresh efforts to overthrow their own regime, had only inspired gloom. 'If even Romania can get rid of Ceauşescu,' said one student leader, 'we must be very backward'. The new conflicts in these countries, which in Yugoslavia led to the break-up of the federation, also prompted many Chinese to fear the consequences for their own national unity of radical change.

International considerations were then reinforced by the lure of China's revived economy. At the end of 1992, Deng Xiaoping was chosen by the *Financial Times* as Man of the Year, against the strongest contender, US president-elect Bill Clinton. Deng's election rested, the newspaper explained, on the hypothesis that 'in 1992, the flowering of Chinese capitalism that he fostered became irreversible; that, despite the manifest flaws of its political system and the worries about its stability, China is becoming a political, economic and commercial force with which the world will increasingly have to reckon'.[2] China's new leap forward was both impressive in itself and as a major component of the surging East Asian economy where per capita incomes had nearly quadrupled in the past quarter of a century. The explosive growth of southern China was becoming a new focus of study by western economists, along with the more familiar successes of the four 'tigers' (South Korea, Taiwan, Hong Kong and Singapore) joined recently by the three 'cubs' (Malaysia, Thailand and Indonesia). Western economies now accepted the inevitability of seeing production transferred to take advantage of cheaper Asian labour. Even the original East Asian leader, Japan, now felt threatened by the new 'Asian miracle'.

China was billed as 'the next superpower' in cover stories by several of the glossy international and regional periodicals.[3] Western opinion was further encouraged by a promise from Vice-premier Zhu Rongji, Deng's chief henchman for economic reform, that 'the only way to go [for China] is to accelerate the mechanisms of the market'. This was followed by a World Bank report which saw the 'Chinese Economic Area' as the 'fourth growth pole' of the world economy.[4] A new study from the International Monetary Fund (IMF) claimed that conventional statistics for China's economic growth had understated the real figure by more than four times. A different measuring system for China's gross domestic product (GDP) would show that in 1992 China produced almost $2 trillion worth in goods and services, instead of less than $500 billion. This would put the Chinese economy at only slightly smaller than that of Japan! (The IMF's calculation was rejected by China, not because it disclaimed great power status but because it would lose access to low-interest international loans if it was no longer regarded as a developing country.[5])

The West's new love affair with China was offset, before long, by concern that the boom might get out of hand. A new cycle of economic 'over-heating' and inflation was set in motion by Deng Xiaoping's initiative. In mid-1993, Zhu Rongji was obliged to launch an austerity programme with advice from the World Bank, but the spate of wasteful investment projects by businesses and financial institutions proved hard to control. Too much was invested in speculative building in the cities and along the coast, too little in agriculture and essential infrastructure in the interior. Powerful provinces like Guangdong openly declared that they were doing so well that they were entitled to exercise less restraint. The Western view became confused and inconsistent. China was hailed by *Time* magazine (10 May 1993) as the world's 'next superpower', but the same report warned that regionalism was steadily weakening the central government and that Beijing would have to deal with 'inequality and social ferment'.

Yet the appeal of the Chinese market remained irresistible. Throughout the 1950s and 1960s Washington had sought to 'contain' Communist China with vociferous support from the 'China lobby' which championed Chiang Kai-shek's regime on Taiwan. The policy was only reversed in 1972 when President Nixon opened a dialogue with China in order to isolate the Soviet Union. Under Deng Xiaoping, the Chinese market – lost to the US when Chiang was defeated – began to offer lucrative prospects, creating a new and more powerful 'China lobby' with very different aims. By the 1990s it included the wheat growers for whom China was now the number one cash customer, the aircraft and oil industries selling jet-liners and exploration equipment to China, and the wholesale suppliers of shoes, toys and other consumer products who had shifted production bases to China[6]. The issue around which they mobilised was the renewal of China's Most Favoured Nation (MFN) trading status with the US. What chance did the human rights lobby, pointing to the thousands of political prisoners, and hundreds of thousands of ordinary Chinese detained every year without trial, as well as the widespread use of torture and exemplary execution, have against these forces? In June 1994, five years after the Beijing Massacre, President Clinton finally de-coupled the renewal of MFN from any conditions on improving human rights. US companies from IBM to General Motors now prepared to engage in the Chinese market more aggressively, and sanctions were also lifted on the export of high technology. Market surveys identified China as one of the fastest-growing consumer economies. The geographical disparities in income were acknowledged but not regarded as a problem. The advice was to target the coast and the more prosperous urban sector, leaving the interior and the countryside alone. 'Here comes the boom', proclaimed a survey from DRI/McGraw-Hill:

> China's size and diversity call for smart marketing strategies. Segmentation should begin with geography, especially along urban versus rural lines, since there are great disparities in spending power between the two, and across regions in general. For example Shanghai, China's richest province, has per capita income of four times the national average, about equal to the average income in Thailand . . .
>
> Only a small percentage of Chinese can purchase imported luxury products, but a small percentage of a big population translates to millions of affluent Chinese. China now has 34 million urban residents in the top 10 per cent urban income bracket; this will increase to 41 million by 2003. Also, the income gap between the poorest areas and the national averages will narrow. As growth spreads from the coast toward the interior, today's 'second cities' should provide excellent consumer markets.[7]

The vast differences between the different regions have long been appreciated within China. Modern Chinese geographers start by dividing the national map into two roughly equal halves – this was first done by the social geographer Hu Huanyong in 1935. His purpose was to distinguish between the vast, still sparsely inhabited interior and the central and coastal area where most Chinese live. Hu drew a line, covering 3,500 kilometres, from Heihe on the northern frontier with Russia to Tengchong in Yunnan province (later extended to Ruili on the Burmese border).[8] On the continental side lie the mountains and deserts of a vast region, which we may call Western or Imperial China, occupying 57 per cent of the Chinese landmass but containing only 5.9 per cent of the population. The greater part of this territory, including Tibet, Xinjiang and Inner Mongolia is and was inhabited by non-Chinese races who were only conquered by the Han Chinese in times of dynastic strength. On the other side of the Heihe-Ruili line lies, by contrast, nearly all of China's agricultural land and fertile river systems, occupying 43 per cent of the landmass and containing 94.1 per cent of the population. This we may call Eastern or Classical China, for it includes all the areas into which the Han Chinese have spread permanently over the past two to three thousand years. Also, by contrast with the high mountains and desert plateaux of Western China, 80 per cent of Eastern China lies below 1,000 feet above sea-level – nearly half of it below 500 feet. Thus, it mainly occupies the third and lowest 'step' in the geological 'staircase' which descends from the Himalayas to the China Seas. This Eastern half can be sub-divided in turn into Middle and Coastal China (see Map 1).[9]

Middle China is the substantial intermediate zone, roughly egg-shaped in appearance, in the central-south of Eastern China. To the north lie the cities of Beijing and Tianjin, the surrounding province of Hebei and the industrial north-east of former Manchuria. To the east are the booming provinces of Coastal China and to the west the impoverished highland provinces bordering on Western China. To the west too lies

Sichuan, the fertile land-locked province of more than 100 million people, so large as to almost constitute a separate country.[10]

The five provinces of Middle China on which I have focused occupy 812,000 square kilometres – just under 20 per cent of the land mass of Eastern China and containing 22 per cent of its population. In 1993 this amounted to 259.9 million Chinese, equivalent to the combined populations of Germany, France, Britain and Italy or the entire population of the former Soviet Union. This area presents a younger, more fertile demographic profile than the China of the great cities and the coast. All except Hainan showed a much higher net annual population increase (at least 17 per thousand) than the national average (14.7) for the period 1982–90. All except Hubei have a lower than average median age (under 25) and a higher percentage of population below the age of 14 (from 28 per cent in Hunan to over 33 per cent in Guangxi). Population density is 318 per square kilometre, less than the average density of Eastern China as a whole (387) which includes heavy urban concentrations, but vastly more than that of Western China (11.8). It is also nine times the world average!

The statistics for per capita gross national product (GNP), resources, agricultural and industrial output, retail sales and similar indices of economic growth are only slightly below the national average in these provinces. Extreme degrees of poverty in mountainous and other deprived areas are masked in the figures by the relative prosperity of the rich river valleys and large towns. But the gap between Middle and Coastal China is visible and widely felt, as in the case of landlocked Hunan and its prosperous neighbour Guangdong. Hunanese recall that during the Cultural Revolution those with relatives in Guangdong would keep them supplied with food to supplement their poor diet. Now at least 2.3 million ex-peasants from Hunan work in Guangdong, remitting funds to their families at home. In 1985 peasant incomes in Guangdong were already 25 per cent higher than in Hunan; by 1990 the gap had almost doubled.

How to tackle the disparities between different Chinese regions, and between the regions and the central authorities, has been a critical question throughout Chinese history and continues to be so today. There has been a succession of contradictory policies since 1949 seeking to answer the difficult questions raised by regional differentiation. Should the backward areas be given preferential treatment to assist them to 'catch up', or should the most developed areas be encouraged to 'get rich first'? Which is more important: to equalise the differences between rich and poor, worker and peasant, town and countryside, or to stimulate efficient and profitable production in some areas in the hope of improving the economy as a whole? Or is it possible to avoid this stark choice altogether by an integrated programme which encourages specialisation and interdependence, developing the 'strong points' of each region? Should China seek economic 'self-reliance' to avoid dependence on the outside world – the policy of the 1960s which tended to favour the 'backward' regions? Or should China seek to join fully the global economy so as to make the best use of its comparative advantages and avoid being left behind – the policy of the 1980s which assigned the main role to the 'advanced', mostly coastal regions?

The arrival of Western trade, enforced by Western gunboats, in the mid-19th Century led to the establishment of Treaty Ports along the coast of China and to the growth of China's early industries. Coastal China continued to expand after the 1911 revolution, while the internal provinces were devastated by civil war in the 1920s. Japan's invasion in the 1930s forced a shift away from the coast to inland areas where both Chinese Nationalists and Communists established their wartime bases. After Japan's defeat the coastal cities briefly regained their dominance together with the new economic base built by the Japanese in the north-east. But the Communists, after 1949, while retaining the coastal industries, sought to tilt the balance towards the interior. Two-thirds of the main 'backbone' industrial projects in the First Five-Year Plan (1953–57) were established in non-coastal provinces. This was partly to avoid concentrating investment at a time of Western hostility along the vulnerable seaboard, but the redistribution of economic assets to the less favoured interior was also seen as politically desirable. This combination of strategic and social argument in favour of diversifying industrial development inland was carried much further in the Great Leap Forward (1958–61).

All areas of China were expected to seek self-sufficiency by promoting local industrialisation. Many of these small-scale efforts collapsed with the Great Leap, but the strategic argument was strengthened by China's isolation from the Soviet Union, as well as from the US, in the early 1960s. This led to massive secret investments in a region known as the 'Third Front', deep within China, from the mid-1960s to the early 1970s. This region covers the south-west fringes of Middle China, Sichuan province and part of the north-west extending into Xinjiang. During this period two-thirds of industrial investment went into an area containing less than 40 per cent of China's population. The regional pendulum only swung back to Coastal China slowly after Mao Zedong's death and the easing of international tension. This was underpinned by an ideological shift in which it was argued that since China was only at an early stage of 'socialism', the prime task was to develop the national economy as fast as possible. The quest for local self-sufficiency would divert effort from this task and lead to waste and duplication of resources: those areas with economic advantages should be allowed to 'get rich first'.

In the Seventh Five-Year Plan (1986–90), Coastal China

would for the first time receive more than half of total investment in fixed assets. Central China (including most of the north-east) would receive less than a third, and Western China only one-sixth. The Plan still envisaged a rough division of labour between the Coastal, Central and Western regions and proposed special links between them. However the Special Economic Zones and 'open ports' along the coast which offered tax concessions and other advantages to foreign investors were designated as China's 'window to the world', leading the way to prosperity which was then supposed to filter through to the inland regions. This strategy led directly to the economic 'over-heating' of 1988, mounting popular protest and the political backlash which resulted in the Beijing Massacre.[11]

The coastal boom resumed after a recession lasting less than two years. In 1992 Deng Xiaoping made his famous 'southern expedition' to visit the SEZs in Guangdong. There he praised their achievements and urged in effect that the semi-capitalist approach of the Zones, including large tax incentives for foreign investment, should be copied throughout China. Market forces should be encouraged to the full without being labelled as 'capitalist'. Socialism was redefined as any policy which raised the productive forces and contributed to the people's well-being, under the control of the Communist Party. In theory, everywhere was now equally free to 'get rich first'. Those areas such as the SEZs which already possessed significant advantages were worried that these would be acquired by other regions which would then rival their appeal, offering even cheaper labour. By the mid-1990s, new pockets of high-technology development and high-consumption society had multiplied inland, particularly in the 'second cities' – mostly provincial capitals – of Middle China.

Though there are still significant differences between the coast and the centre (and even more the west), the most significant phenomenon has been the widening of differentials *within* each region and the resulting growth of social tension. In the more backward, remote or disadvantaged areas, the new policies are more likely to stimulate corruption and unrealistic development schemes. Deng's green light to get rich first encouraged increasingly blatant corruption and diversion of funds by local officials. By 1993–94 this led to a second round of economic over-heating and a new wave of inflation, which resulted in a fall in real income for some urban dwellers and many more in the countryside. In 1994 the State Statistical Bureau reported that 'the gap between China's cities and countryside has exhibited a widening tendency since 1985, growing most rapidly over the course of 1993.' From 1985 to 1992 the ratio of urban to rural incomes widened from 1.72:1 to 2.33:1. There was also 'a widening chasm in education': the percentage of illiterate or semi-illiterate persons aged 15 or above was nearly three times more in the country than in the cities.[12]

Middle China awaits exploration, but where should we start from and how should we proceed through it? My attention had been caught, in the early 1980s, by reports of a new railway line which cuts through Middle China from north to south, running parallel to but inland from the familiar route from Beijing to Guangzhou. Its construction had been a state secret in the 1960s and 1970s, and it might as well still be a secret today. Not one tourist in a hundred thousand knows about it, and most Chinese who travel on sections of it are unaware of its full length and strategic purpose. This, I decided, was the route to take into Middle China.

The Second North–South Trunk Line, as it was called on completion, passes through the four provinces of Henan, Hubei, Hunan and Guangxi to end in Guangdong province facing the island of Hainan. For more than two thousand kilometres it sweeps through the central region of rivers, hills and plains which lies between the coastal provinces and the wide regions of the west. It sweeps too through the history of the Middle Kingdom, beginning at the Yellow River near the archaeological sites of Bronze Age China and the sacred Mount Sung. It follows the extension southward over many centuries of Han Chinese culture and power, across the Yangzi and through the highlands of central China to the southern coast. This spread of the dominant Chinese culture continues today: the railway has helped transform rural life in the central and southern highlands, penetrating areas mostly populated by national minorities and poorly served by roads.

The purpose of the Second Trunk Line was both to open up China's central region and to provide an alternative route to the familiar, heavily-used, Beijing-Guangzhou line first completed in the 1930s. It also linked existing lines to the north and south with two lengthy new sections of track. The first of these sections was from Jiaozuo in northern Henan to Jicheng in Hubei province on the Yangzi river (the 'Jiao-Ji Railway'), and the second was from Jicheng south through Hunan province as far as Liuzhou city in Guangxi province (the 'Ji-Liao Railway'). To the north, this linked up with another railway (the 'Tai-Jiao') already under construction, which headed from Jiaozuo towards Taiyuan, capital of Shanxi province. To the south, it connected with an older post-1949 railway (the 'Liu-Zhan') terminating at Zhanjiang, just inside Guangdong province on the coast opposite Hainan island. The whole length from Taiyuan to Zhanjiang was nearly 2,500 kilometres, two-thirds of which consisted of the two new stretches from Jiaozuo via Jicheng to Liuzhou (see maps).

An important strategic argument for the Second Trunk Line was to provide an alternative route in case of war at a time when China was isolated by both superpowers and threatened by Soviet as well as US missiles. The railway became one of the great mass projects of the Cultural Revolution, mobilising more than 1.1 million peasant labourers on the Jiao-Ji section north of the Yangzi alone. Henan province contributed half a million of them, organised on military lines and led personally by the commander of Henan's People's Liberation Army. The proud boast in Henan's provincial history is that, starting in November 1969, they completed clearing and laying track within the astonishing time of eight months. The official railway history notes more realistically that it took another five years to prepare for regular traffic.

The southern section of the Second Trunk Line, through the highlands of Hunan province, required more skilled engineering work and equipment. This section includes no less than 396 tunnels, nearly one-fifth of its total length, as it threads through the central highlands. In the most inaccessible places, the line alternates between tunnel and bridge half a dozen times before reaching open ground, offering a succession of brief, dizzy glimpses into wild country of amazing, precipitous beauty. This Ji-Liao section took eight years to complete from its start in August 1970.[13]

Completion of the Second Trunk Line was announced in 1979, yet it remains largely unknown except for those who need to use it. Stretches of it are used by expresses from Beijing or Shanghai as they head westwards into Sichuan province. In spite of the line's official name there is no through train from north to south: anyone attempting such a journey must spend a laborious three and a half days en route with a minimum of four changes. The similar length of journey from Beijing to Guangzhou can be completed in just 36 hours by through express. Trains on the Second Trunk Line are frequently delayed for hours at a time at passing places, and often arrive half a day late.

While the original purpose of the Second Trunk Line is forgotten, attention is now focused on a brand-new rail link between north and south under construction to the east of the

Beijing-Guangzhou railway. The Beijing-Kowloon railway, scheduled to begin opening in 1995, covers 2,500 kilometres, from Beijing through the port of Tianjin and then through six provinces of eastern and southern China. It too will open up some underdeveloped areas, particularly in eastern Hubei and southern Jiangxi, but its main purpose is to provide a high-speed link between the fast growing areas of north and south China. It should be known as the Third Trunk Line: instead it has usurped the name of the Second which is no longer shown as a through route. The maps in this book show this line will not be found in China! It is the *real* Second Trunk Line which we shall be exploring here.

There are no first-class sleepers with chintz curtains and blue-shaded table lamps on the Second Trunk Line, only the 'hard' wooden or leather accommodation of second class. Standards of food and cleanliness are also far lower than on the élite main line and there can be serious safety problems. On a journey in Hunan – not far from the birthplace of Mao Zedong, on a misty early evening as the water buffaloes were being led home – the window in the next compartment to mine was smashed by a large rock. 'Probably just hooligans,' said the guard, 'I don't think it's bandits on our line. They wouldn't find enough on this train to steal!' But he wouldn't take the chance to stop and investigate. In the same year the Hunan police mounted a special operation to crack down on 'highway and railway crime'. Over two hundred people were sentenced to death or life imprisonment, and more than nine hundred to jail terms of between five and 20 years.

Travelling on the Second Trunk Line, and on most other forms of transport away from the cities, requires patience and physical endurance. Buying railway tickets can mean standing in line for several hours: armed police are often needed to control the queues. The ticket which is purchased often only entitles one to board the train, not to a seat. Trains can be delayed for half a day, sitting without explanation at remote country stations. The carriage floors, swept perfunctorily, are soon carpeted with fruit-peel, peanut shells, cigarette ends and grime. The lavatories become squalid and waterless. It is easier to get a seat on a long-distance bus but the journey can be bone-wrenchingly bumpy, noisy, filled with fumes and painfully slow. The passenger on the next seat may be a basket of chickens or a fat sow. The disturbing sight of burnt-out or wrecked buses by the roadside is only too common. Almost every week the press reports that another country bus has pitched off a mountain road or plunged into a river with the loss of many lives.

Yet this is the way to explore China. On long train journeys the traveller can grasp the contours of China's vast interior as the route traverses entire provinces, crosses wide rivers with unfamiliar names, threads up and down remote valleys and cuts through mountains still far from any road. Fellow-passengers discuss their own affairs and reflect on China's future with a candour they would normally avoid. Travelling by bus is exploration in smaller scale, edging across an anonymous map. There are surprising contrasts between scenes of sudden prosperity and of persistent poverty; between the scars of new industry planted in the countryside and unchanged landscapes of classical beauty. For all of this the wise traveller carries a good stock of water, food and patience. Whether by bus or by train, the average speed of most cross-country journeys is no more than 30 kilometres an hour. But these are the routes which we shall now take from north to south, as we travel the length of Middle China from Henan to Hainan.

II

Peasants in Revolt

HENAN

'Everything has to be done now through the back door. Even to buy half a kilo of meat from a market stand for some festival, you must know someone working there. If you don't, you can't buy good lean pork even if you pay a higher price. If a cadre's relative has a second baby, he goes unpunished. If one of my relatives does the same, they either fine him or have his house sealed. If a cadre does not fulfil his grain purchase quota, the higher officials will turn a blind eye. If we ordinary folk do not do so, they will either confiscate our contracted land or not permit our children to enter school, or refuse to allot land for us to build a house. "People are the masters of the country"? You tell me, what power do we poor folk have? What kind of masters are we?'

(Peasants' complaints, near Luoyang)

Henan is where Chinese history began. Here the peasants have farmed the silt-soil brought down by the Yellow River for thousands of years. Ancient legend tells of the Xia dynasty founded by the Yellow Emperor, and of how his descendant the Emperor Yu tamed the floods and drained the marshes. Remarkably, archaeologists now believe they have found

22

remains of this semi-mythological dynasty (around 2000 BC) near the sacred Mount Song. This mountain, thought by the ancient Chinese to be the centre of the universe, is the seat of the ancient Buddhist Shaolin Monastery – also famous as the home of Kung Fu martial arts. The Xia dynasty was followed by the Shang (around 1550–1050 BC), whose extensive remains have been excavated at Anyang in northern Henan and in the present provincial capital of Zhengzhou. It was already a sophisticated city-state culture, with written records in recognisable early Chinese script. The North China Plain remained the core area of China for over two thousand years, and great dynasties such as the Tang (AD 618–906) and the Northern Song (AD 960–1126) had their capitals in what are now the cities of Luoyang and Kaifeng.

It was in Anyang that I began my researches into Middle China, exploring the rural counties to the west and east of the city, as the new wind of entrepreneurship blew in the early 1990s. But first I paid my tribute to ancient China, visiting the village of Yinxu, site of the Shang dynasty capital. Its remains lie beneath a cluster of small villages and their sandy fields, just outside the city boundary and beyond the railway line, at a bend of the Huan river. Here for centuries local farmers had dug up ancient bones and tortoise shells which were often marked with strange notches and engraved with mysterious signs. Known as 'dragon bones', these were then sold to drug stores to be ground up for medical concoctions. At the end of the last century an eminent scholar in Beijing, examining the ingredients for a prescription to deal with malaria, discovered that the carved symbols were ancient Chinese characters. Thousands more have been discovered since then – part of the archives which recorded the questions put by court priests to the gods. (Heat was applied to the bones and shells, and the resulting cracks were interpreted for the answers.) Many of the inscribed characters are still recognisable, and research shows that the script was already a highly sophisticated mixture of pictures, ideograms and phonetic elements – the same building blocks used in modern characters. All the evidence shows that Chinese was already a mature language over three thousand years ago, and is beyond doubt the oldest written script still in use today.

I walked back across the fields from Yinxu, reflecting on the amazing continuity of Chinese history. Some way along the raised path, I was stopped by a young boy, his clothes stained with the yellow earth. He was struggling to lift an old wooden coffin and balance it on a trolley. He had just dug it up, and was hoping to sell the wood – perhaps for re-use in a new coffin. But when I asked him about it, he uttered helpless, nonsense sounds. He was a deaf-mute. It was a disturbing moment yet one which meshed with the historical sense of the place. In Shang times he might have been sacrificed to the gods. The kings of Shang were buried in much larger coffins, with their horses, charioteers and slaves in adjacent pits – all of them with their throats cut.

Ten minutes later, I was on a local bus riding back into Anyang. This is now a city of nearly half a million, with modern industry and apartments surrounding an older town whose walls have long disappeared. The dictator Yuan Shikai, who destroyed China's first attempt at parliamentary democracy after the 1911 revolution, was buried on the other side of the city in a marble shrine combining elements of a Chinese imperial tomb and a western mausoleum. Yuan's descendants, now living in Taiwan, have recently been allowed to restore the monument in exchange for a large donation to the city. Most of this has been spent on a new shopping street in the centre of Anyang. The shops sell videos, tape recorders and other electronic equipment, shoes and clothing in Hong Kong styles. There are beauty salons, restaurants, dubious bars with curtained booths, and the town's first massage parlour where customers are served with martinis and Scotch whisky.

I was shown around Anyang and its environs by a former airforce pilot with useful connections in high places which allowed him to wear police uniform and own a car. We sat in cafés and discussed the new materialistic philosophy which has replaced the old values of the revolution. 'The grenade is now a bottle of wine,' he joked. 'The bomb is now tobacco smoke.' 'Mao Zedong said that revolution is not a dinner party,' added a friend.

'Today, revolution *is* a dinner party.' Later we drove out on the trunk road to the south, where brightly dressed young women stand outside tawdry restaurants, seeking to entice lorry drivers in for a meal, and more.

Yet away from the city and the main roads, Henan is still deeply rural. Its peasants are described as down-to-earth, stubborn and hard-working but, in times of hardship or upheaval, easily aroused to strong passion. The Boxer Rebellion spread quickly here in 1898–1900 from across the border in Shandong province to the east. Western missionaries feared the anger of the Henanese 'mob'. Bizarrely, the descendants of those same peasants now show unusual interest in quasi-religious cults and movements: China's largest Christian revival has occurred here in recent years (see Chapter III). In the 1950s they had embraced The Thought of Mao Zedong with equal enthusiasm. The first People's Commune was set up not far from Zhengzhou in 1958 and it was there that Mao famously endorsed the slogan that 'The People's Communes are Good!' Yet by the late 1980s, Henanese peasants had become the most vocal in the country in denouncing Communist Party corruption as the benefits of the economic reforms introduced after Mao's death began to wane.

The village of Wangyan Shitun in Liuzhuang District lies a short way north of the Yellow River just off the main road (now being enlarged into a superhighway) between Anyang and the provincial capital of Zhengzhou. This is no marginal land in some remote mountain valley but the rich earth of the North China Plain, deposited over millenia by the changing course of the great river. It is named after a peasant hero of the Song dynasty (the name was changed to Red Guard Village during the Cultural Revolution). The village, one of ten in Liuzhuang District, has a population of 2,244. With its favourable location it should be a model of the post-Mao reforms, but although a few have got rich most of its families still live close to the margin. Their biggest complaint is excessive and illegal taxation. In 1990 they dared to stage a public protest, led by one particularly brave farmer. Here, as he told it to me, is his tale.

As Hu Hai walked to work one grey, dusty morning in the early autumn of that year, the rallying sound of the District loudspeaker system came across the fields, cracked by drought.

'Every citizen has the obligation to pay taxes duly levied according to law,' the announcer began in a youthful female voice – just like the injunctions broadcast on Chinese trains to clean one's teeth and safeguard one's belongings.

'To meet the demands of public education,' she continued, 'every peasant must contribute an exceptional levy of 20rmb (£2). This is in addition to the previously announced Community Tax of 68rmb.'

Hu Hai cursed: 'Damn her mother's . . .!' But the loudspeaker had not finished.

'Fellow county members,' it went on, 'it is your patriotic duty to pay taxes according to law. In pursuance of directives, all citizens of Liuzhuang District are hereby informed: Your children will not be allowed to attend school unless the designated sum is duly paid within ten days! Your property will be confiscated and you will be labelled as a Black Household. Thank you for your civic attention.'

'Damn her mother's . . .,' Hu Hai cursed again, and spat

onto the stunted heads of a maize crop ruined by blight. 'Do they want to tax us to death?' And he vowed to keep silent no longer. His son, Hu Desheng, had graduated from the local school to take his degree at the prestigious Beijing University Law Department and was now working for a legal department in the provincial government. It was Desheng who encouraged his father to protest at the extra education levy, calculating that together with other taxes it amounted to 12.5 per cent of the official figure for average peasant incomes in the village. The maximum percentage allowed by law for such supplementary levies (i.e. excluding the regular grain tax) was only five per cent. Real incomes, he argued, were only half the official estimate which had failed to take into account outgoings for fertiliser, pesticide and so on, so that the levies really amounted to 25 per cent of the peasants' disposable cash. Desheng's explanations of the law aroused the local villagers in support of his father. 'Beijing's rules are good,' they shouted outside the village Party headquarters. 'It's these local bastards who bend the rules, like monks with twisted mouths who distort the true doctrine!'

In May 1991 Hu Hai marched with 40 representatives, elected by more than ten thousand peasants who had signed his petition, to the District headquarters to meet a special 'investigation team' sent down from the provincial capital. The sight of these tough peasants with shaven heads and dusty clothes, jostling noisily in the courtyard of the headquarters, must have deeply disturbed the well-dressed city cadres as they stepped from their curtained official transport. They refused to meet the peasants, only interviewed the local officials, and returned to Zhengzhou to report that all was in order and no illegal taxes had been levied.

Soon afterwards Hu Hai was arrested and was eventually sentenced in December 1991 to three years in jail on the charge of 'violating social order'. He had already been denounced three times in the course of the year at mass meetings called by the District authorities to drum up support for higher taxation. After each meeting Hu was bound with a rope, forced to march through the town and exhibited in the traditional manner on street corners as a criminal. The detailed prosecution indictment left no doubt just how Hu had offended the authorities: he had 'expressed doubt over the Chinese Communist Party's leadership, opposed socialism, organised peasants to visit government departments and report local cadres' corruption so as to disrupt local tax collections . . . They further went to Beijing to protest to the central government.' Hu's worst offence was, in the words of the indictment, to have 'made connections with local malcontents'. The concept of 'making connections' (*chuanlian*) touches a very sensitive nerve. When the Red Guards travelled the length and breadth of China in the Cultural Revolution (1966–68), contacting fellow-students to agitate against local Party bureaucrats, their activities were known as *chuanlian*. Senior communist cadres now still remember how the Red Guards drove them into the streets, forced dunces caps onto their heads, and held 'struggle meetings' against them. If the masses were allowed to challenge authority again, who knows what might happen? A sentence of three years in jail for Hu Hai, local officials claimed, could even be regarded as mild.

However, law-school classmates of Hu Desheng held good jobs in Beijing and a few had gone to work abroad. Details of Hu Hai's protest were circulated widely with photocopies of the relevant court judgements. In March 1992 Desheng tried to persuade an intermediate court in Beijing to accept a civil action against Premier Li Peng, head of the Chinese state in whose name the local cadres had acted. In June Hu Hai's case was adopted by Amnesty International, on the grounds that he was being punished for exercising his constitutional right to complain to the authorities. Amnesty's dossier summarised the essentially political charge made by the local prosecutor against Hu Hai.

> [The prosecutor] started his statement by saying that Hu Hai had always been 'dissatisfied with the Party and opposed to the socialist system'. Referring to the 'raising of funds' for education and water conservancy by the Liuzhuang authorities in 1990, he accused Hu Hai of 'having gone round contacting and inciting people, claiming that the fundraising was arbitrary levy' and encouraging people to sign petitions to go to the provincial capital and Beijing to complain . . . [The prosecutor] concluded that Hu Hai's actions – 'inciting the masses, unreasonably causing trouble, organising others to complain to the authorities and seriously disrupting the normal order of government work' – constituted the crime of 'disturbing social order', punishable under the provisions of Article 158 of the Criminal Law.[1]

A year later I travelled along the broad highway between Anyang and Zhengzhou, guided by Hu Desheng, to visit his family. The village lies less than a mile down a small country road, and at first there is no visible sign of the causes of peasant discontent. The houses of Wangyan Shitun's new rich are built on the edge of the village. They have stone patios, porches and balconies with glazed tiles, and are usually enclosed by a high wall with a wrought-iron gate at the entrance. One particularly fine example has massive twin doors of beaten bronze with the character *fu* for 'good fortune' painted on both sides in gold. Others have black tiled roofs in good repair, solid walls of new brick, and walled gardens with oleander bushes and an overhanging vine. In the main part of the village, down deeply rutted lanes, it is a different story. Here the houses are either made of the traditional packed earth or have been roughly rebuilt with poor quality bricks. There are dense piles of fuel for the winter – brushwood and maize stalks. In the bright spring sun almost every Chinese village looks picturesque, but in the rain the unpaved lanes turn into a sea of mud. Desheng calculated that only five per cent of the village households – less than 30 altogether – could be regarded as rich. I could see that some houses had been extended since the agricultural reforms by building on an extra wing, but they were still very barely furnished.

The main room of Hu Hai's house has four old chairs, one old table, a large cooking-stove with no chimney and a black-and-white TV. A thin partition lined with paper forms an extra room to one side. The walls are bare except for some posters of the scenic south-west city of Guilin, a small wooden rack for chopsticks, and a clock with the figure of a monk who used to strike the hour on a miniature gourd – it is now broken. The floor is made of packed earth. The lavatory is outside in the open, a communal pit facing the neighbouring houses with an encircling mud wall barely high enough to squat behind.

Desheng explained to me the economic basis for the rich-poor divide in his village.

The village head is a rich man. If you want to open a shop or start any other business you have to pay him. He makes a lot of money too out of fines on couples who have too many children. It's 5,000 renminbi (rmb) for the second child: he keeps 2,000 and gives the rest to the District. Of course he's head of the Communist Party here too. The village Party branch has about 35 members. Over half of them are old members who remember the higher standards of public service in the past, and complain about the way things are run now, but they are not listened to. The village head assigns jobs to his relatives who are also wealthy. Some have become teachers at the middle school even if they are unqualified – they often take the day off and send the children home. Twenty years ago we paid four rmb a term for school, which would be 40 at today's prices. Instead it has gone up to 140, or 280 in a year, plus something for 'chairs and tables'. That is another reason why the extra education tax caused such an uproar. The County officials are in league with the local ones. We had elections but people were paid two to vote the right way. Those who did not turn up had their ballots filled up for them anyhow.

Hu Hai's neighbours, who had called in to drink hot water (tea leaves were reserved for the foreign guest) and recount their complaints, nodded agreement. They produced well-thumbed copies of their annual taxation bills, covering the demands from the County, District and village. The County collects the nationally-set grain tax, with extra levies for education and irrigation. The levies for the District include school, militia, support for the families of soldiers away from home, and road maintenance. The village raises funds for accumulation, saving and management. The demand for 1992 presented to Hu Hai's family lacked an official stamp, but the peasants said that made no difference: 'if you complain, the cadres will come and take your TV away'. The total was so high that it was hardly worth farming the land and most of it had been handed back. It now lay fallow like tens of thousands of other acres in Henan.

To my surprise Hu Hai himself was at home, having been been released on parole exceptionally early after only one year at the No. 17 Reform Through Labour Brigade of Henan Province. (It has a public name – Xinxiang Construction Materials Factory – to conceal its real identity.) The Party boss of Xinxiang had scoffed that 'even if the UN Secretary-General pleads for you, it will make no difference'. But his early release must have been speeded by the international protest inspired by his fearless son. Hu Hai is a determined peasant with broad shoulders, wide forehead, a firm handshake, and the clear countenance of someone who knows he is in the right. Stiff-backed but smiling, he told me his story.

> Why did they arrest me? It was a case of trying to 'kill the chicken to frighten the monkey' [so that the other peasant protestors would be intimidated]. I was taken away for 15 days without my family knowing where I was. This was contrary to the rules for detention by the police. They asked me to write a confession. No, I said, I have simply been quoting official documents which forbid illegal taxation. Many others who signed my petition were also arrested – even one who was 80 years old. Some were forced to write that 'Hu Hai organised an illegal demonstration', but they added a note that 'I was forced to write this'. The police said they would bind me with ropes if I did not sign. I still refused. Why? I had the Truth and Righteousness on my side. How could I confess or apologise? What I was doing was in accordance with the law.

This is the language both of traditional Chinese morality and of the peasant revolution which the Party so successfully mobilised in the revolutionary bases of Henan in the 1940s, first against Japan and then against the Nationalists. Now instead it inspires a growing number of peasants to denounce the Party's own misdeeds. Yet it is only a decade and a half since the Beijing leadership regained peasant support by the economic reforms introduced after the death of Mao Zedong. How is it then, as urban China booms, that the peasants on whom its strength and stability still depends have turned so massively against the regime?

The peasants of Henan province are the sons and daughters of the Yellow Emperor, say the Chinese today. Farming the soil left by the river's meanderings, suffering the sorrows brought down by its floods, they have all the traditional qualities of a long-established rural community. As described in a recent Chinese survey of the province, they are 'down-to-earth, thrifty, stubborn but absolutely honest, obstinately optimistic, capable but careful. They may not be as rugged as those to the north, or as shrewd as those to the south, but they carry on the old social virtues of respecting the old, loving the young, and working hard and honestly.'[2]

Until very recently more peasants have stayed on the land in Henan than in most other Chinese provinces. Though the percentage of town-dwellers in Henan has trebled since 1949, the current figure of 15 per cent is still well below the national average. Yet floods, drought and the search for work can drive hundreds of thousands into neighbouring provinces – at least 400,000 in each year of the Great Leap Forward (1959–61) and 840,000 in 1964. In the late 1980s more Henan peasants left the province to find employment in the building trade than from any other province except Jiangsu. Henan's birth-rate has always been near or above the national average, but it was one of the worst affected provinces in the famine year of 1960 when the population fell by 1.2 million – nearly four per cent in one year.[3]

In the age of the people's communes the peasants of the North China Plain on both sides of the Yellow River still lived and worked very simply. In normal years it was a settled and comparatively stable life: incomes were low but so were expectations. Horse or mule carts were the main form of transport for goods: bicycles were prized and those without them walked long distances. Every small town still had its traditional Chinese inn – a large courtyard for the animals with sleeping quarters around it. Three big characters were painted on the outside wall: *Che ma dian* – Horse and Cart Inn. Even near the main railway where the countryside was more developed, a train could travel for an hour and pass only one tractor. Small production groups, members of the same 'team' or village, worked ten hours in the fields with wooden ploughs and hoes. Much energy was expended clearing ditches and channels, and spreading natural fertiliser including wood ash and the scrapings from the ditches as well as human and animal manure. Houses were single storied with walls of dried adobe mud: the paths between them became treacherous lakes of wet mud when it rained. The village shop sold enamel pots and pans, thermos flasks, towels and blankets, and other plain household goods.

A decade later the countryside has been transformed in a frenzy of individualist economic activity. The fields are now farmed in narrow strips by single families to whom farming rights were assigned when the people's communes were abolished in the early 1980s. Chemical fertiliser, for those who can afford it, has increasingly replaced natural sources. Peasants have become much less willing to contribute their 'voluntary labour' for public works. Drainage ditches today are often filled with rubbish or stubble which is then burnt off – once it would have been prudently gathered for fuel. Roadside trees are felled and hillsides over-grazed as warning signs and boundary markers are frequently ignored. The building boom has left large moonscape tracts of once fertile land scarred with excavations and brick-kilns. Many houses in the villages have been rebuilt or enlarged. When a Chinese farmer gets rich, he feels absolutely obliged to build a new, brick two-storey house, preferably with tiled fronts and balconies. Sometimes the upper floor is left empty for show while the old house is used for a barn.

Older Henanese peasants still wear plain cotton clothes and shapeless padded outer garments in winter. Young people are more likely to wear jeans or skirts with bright T-shirts and polished shoes even when working in the field. Peasant markets now sell smart clothes from the south as well as local products. The 'marketisation' promoted by the Chinese government has produced some odd contrasts of goods available and disturbing disparities in living standards. On the street corner of a small county town in Henan not far from Anyang, I saw a stall selling complete packs of Craven A, Hilton, Kent and Marlboro cigarettes, unknown commodities even in the big towns until the late 1980s. The next stall to it sold pitiful dried up oranges, though each was carefully wrapped in protective film. At a third stall sides of fly-covered meat hung unprotected on the roadside, sprayed with dust from the passing traffic.

The main roads are choked now with a raucous stream of trucks, tractors, motorbikes and even a few private cars, although horse and mule carts are still fairly common. On the principal highways, small restaurants, often no more than a brick shack but with showers of coloured light bulbs glowing at night, compete for custom from the truck drivers. Young women in trousers and silk jackets, or shorts and colourful blouses, beckon provocatively towards those who slow down. Yet the Henan countryside has not been evenly transformed, and only a short distance away from the main lines of communication, conditions can still be harsh. Nor has the central problem been solved: how to encourage the peasants to stay on the land and how to pay them a fair price for their produce.

Relations between the government and the peasants deteriorated in the late 1980s as the economic gains of the post-Mao reforms began to dwindle and were unequally shared. The dramatic annual increase in farm incomes during the first half of the decade had slowed down and by the early 1990s was being reversed in many communities by rising inflation. The notorious 'scissors' – the gap between what farmers earn for their produce and what they must pay for fertiliser and other essential inputs – was widening again. So was the gap between average rural and urban incomes as well as the divide between rich and poor within the countryside. These disparities were not just limited to those between the more productive areas, close to urban markets, and the more remote, less fertile regions where living standards had always been lower. Sharp local differences could be found between neighbouring counties (typically containing 200,000–300,000 people), between adjacent districts or even between different villages within the same district. The post-Mao 'get-rich-first' philosophy of encouraging individual entrepreneurship widened income differentials at the very heart of village communities. Families with better education and more business flair prospered, especially if they had benefited when the people's communes were broken up by leasing or being allocated tractors and other mechanical services which they could then hire out to fellow-peasants (so-called 'specialised households'). Better *guanxi* or 'connections' with local Party officials who could give preference for the use of scarce or valuable resources also helped substantially.

After suffering a decline of prestige in the early 1980s, the local Party network acquired new opportunities for patronage and financial gain as central controls weakened. Party-related families could more easily secure licences to open new businesses, or fill vacancies in the local bureaucracies which were required – or deemed necessary – to run new development, environmental, transport and marketing agencies. The police was also a significant growth area, with tempting opportunities to acquire new equipment and exact concessions and favours. This new layer of privilege and extravagance had to be paid for, as did the community services – health, education, transport and so on – formerly funded almost entirely out of collective income. (Individual peasant payments for textbooks and medicine in the people's communes had been nominal.) Local officials therefore resorted like their predecessors in pre-communist regimes to extra taxation, claiming they had no alternative if national regulations and standards of public service were to be enforced. The peasants observed the cadres' conspicuous wealth and had another explanation. As state finance was increasingly diverted to profitable investments in urban China while the funds allocated to rural areas were reduced, local governments began to run short of money to pay farmers for the crops still exacted from them by compulsory purchase, even at the fixed below-average prices they were required to accept. From 1988 onwards, government IOUs known as 'white slips' were widely issued instead of payment in cash, leading to a number of serious riots.

Private agriculture now encourages farmers to compete aggressively for resources, over-farming the arable land and threatening forests, grasslands and water reserves. Unless China can mechanise agriculture and create millions more non-farming jobs, the rural environment will soon be devastated by this chaotic small-scale production. Seven out of every ten Chinese still live in villages or country towns – nearly 850 million out of a population of 1.2 billion – and every year ten million more enter the rural job market. The rapid expansion in rural industry of the early 1980s has tailed off in the less developed areas, with many small factories closing down again as profits became the main criterion. As residence controls are weakened, the lure of urban employment has become more powerful. Originally this was confined to the area of Guangdong province near the Hong Kong border, where from the mid-1980s onwards Hong Kong industry increasingly took advantage of cheap Chinese labour. But by the mid-1990s a 'construction fever' was under way in every city as new hotels, apartment blocks, development zones and shopping precincts were built. Cheap peasant labour now swirls around the country's transport system seeking job opportunities. Though the disruption is deplored by the railway authorities and ordinary travellers, the new boom depends structurally upon this prolific source of human capital. Urban development has also sucked scarce financial capital away from the countryside, where it could be productively invested or loaned to peasant farmers, as entrepreneurs collude with bank officials to secure funds for their own grand schemes. Rural post offices frequently have no cash with which to redeem money orders sent back home by the migrant workers, offering instead their own form of IOUs, the so-called 'green slips', which fuel more resentment.

Outside Zhengzhou railway station on a cold, clear late afternoon in early spring 1993, I found six or seven hundred Henanese peasants queuing patiently for tickets, to head north to Beijing or south to Guangzhou in search of work. Though Zhengzhou was their own capital, all available work there had been monopolised by gangs of peasants from other provinces. The railway network at this time of year was so crowded with rural migrants that the first available train might not be for several days. Hundreds more peasants, having successfully bought their tickets, were sleeping in collective mounds on the stone station forecourt. One group of some 30 peasants, without a single padded coat between them, huddled beneath a noticeboard for shelter from the wind and for warmth, lying or squatting on their bundles and cloth bags. When it was dark they would try to slip back into the station to sleep more securely. Why, I asked, had they left the land? A better dressed older man in a blue cotton Mao-suit answered first on their behalf. It was he who had organised their search for labour and would take a commission on their eventual wages. Such a person was often a former migrant labourer who had developed good 'connections' with potential employers. But the shivering peasants quickly interrupted with their own bitter complaints.

The main protest was the familiar one of excessive taxation. Their village had been hit by 18 separate taxes, including road tax, forestry tax, disabled welfare tax, education tax, poll tax, underground water tax, and anti-pollution tax. 'It all goes in the cadres' pockets!' they said. 'Who grows rich in the countryside? Only the cadres!'

Why didn't they object, I asked? 'We don't dare to object; we only dare to get up and go. If we refuse to pay, the tax will be doubled and our goods can be confiscated. Sometimes the cadres come and take the roofs off our houses.'

Could they not complain to a higher level? 'If we complain it doesn't get through. Even the People's Congress has no power.' Life was better in the cities, they said optimistically, even if the work was hard. 'This way we can look for work and send the money back home. We have families to support because we beget more children to increase our labour power. No, we are not heading for the south. There are even peasants from the south coming up north now! Everyone is going in every direction to look for work.'

The group dispersed nervously as two uniformed militia-men strolled over to check on the excitement. The peasants asked the last question of me: 'Please will you write about our troubles in the foreign newspapers? Do you think our government will finally get to hear and do something about it?'

The flood of peasants looking for work which now clogs China's railway system has worsened in each successive year of the 1990s. Migration is at its height at the Chinese New Year when debts are settled and peasants look ahead to the future. In 40 days around the 1993 'Spring Festival', five and a half million migrants passed through Nanjing station in central China. The whole network carried more than 70 million passengers in 25 days. Guangzhou, which normally handles 30,000 passengers, saw a hundred thousand daily, with a peak of 156,000 on January 28. Some trains were so overloaded that the suspension collapsed. Freight traffic had to be halted while extra passenger trains were provided. The Railway Bureau issued a vain appeal to local government authorities to 'discourage peasants from heading blindly to other areas'. By contrast with previous years, these statistics and the dislocation caused to the railways were reported in the Chinese press in unusually vivid detail.

Every southbound train is jammed with migrant workers from the Chinese countryside. No food can be sold on the train because the dining car is also filled with people. Water is also unavailable ... Similarly lavatories are unusable because each one is packed with six or seven people. Experienced migrants bring along bread and sugarcane, and stuff a towel in the crotch of their pants. When they cannot endure it any longer, they urinate on the towel. The minute the train enters Guangzhou station, an anxious mob of people jump out of the windows, in a trail of foul sweat, stench of urine and foot odour, gushing in a torrent which heads straight for the toilets and then for the bus stations ... The tunnels through which people leave the station are trampled by over 100,000 pairs of feet each day, leaving mud and dirt caked so deep it is beyond cleaning. Naturally the people entering the station are also beyond control and there is no way to check tickets on board the train or when passengers leave the station.[4]

Even when the press reported the exodus it seldom enquired into the causes of this flight from the land. An investigative feature in the *China Youth Daily* was a rare exception. The reporter illustrated complaints of heavy taxation with a revealing tale from one county in Anhui province, sub-titled 'the heavy burden of raising a pig'. To encourage peasants to sell their pigs to the state purchasing agency at less than market prices, the authorities had promised a bonus of 100 rmb (£7.50) per pig. But local officials raised the money for paying the bonus by imposing an extra poll tax. A large family could sell its pig, collect the bonus, and still end up poorer. The same report described how peasants starving in railway stations would offer to work for food and no pay. A group of 40 Anhui peasants had arrived in Shanghai and made for a construction site. The contractor only wanted 20 men, and split the group into two rival factions each bidding for the work. Finally they came to blows and the defeated faction returned to the railway station, cursing their former friends.

Yet these peasants had more sophisticated ideas about the causes of their plight than merely to blame excessive taxation by local cadres. What would they do if they were national leaders, they were asked by the reporter.

'I would stabilise the prices of agricultural materials,' replied one, '. . . annihilate corruption, reduce the peasants' burden, adjust the cost of electricity, get the agricultural technicians to come down to the villages, and raise our level of scientific cultivation.'

'If I was running the country,' said another, 'I would take thought for the peasants, regard their education seriously, bring in some good technical assistance, develop rural industry and economic activities to draw in the surplus labour . . .'

'If I was running the country,' said a third, 'I would go down to the villages to study the situation, and listen to what the peasants have to say!'[5]

Sixty years previously, a team of government investigators had indeed gone down to the villages in Henan to study the situation and, by coincidence, much of their work was done north of Zhengzhou, not very far from Xinxiang County where Hu Hai's village is located. Their report on *Rural Conditions in Henan* contains descriptions of extortion and oppression which could be duplicated today. In a village in neighbouring Huixiang county, they noted the following case:

> Zhao Jian is a good hamlet head. He was upset by arbitrary taxes levied by the district head, a certain Chen, lodged a complaint with the county government and thus gave offence to Chen. The county was in need of cash, and so Chen sent people to Zhao's house with an instant demand for 1,700 catties of wheat. The Zhao family had more than 30 members; they farmed just one-third of a square kilometre of land, which was hilly

and poor. By comparison a friend of Chen called Lu had only four or five to feed, and more than ten qing [65 hectares] of land, yet he was only taxed 1,000 catties. Of course Zhao could not pay, so Chen accused him of tax refusal and fined him 200 yuan [Chinese dollars] plus 200 bags of wheat. Zhao was even less able to pay, so Chen sent people to catch him. Zhao got wind of this and ran away and the result was that his father was arrested as security for him. When the father had been detained for a few days, he fell ill in prison. Zhao Jian then borrowed 1,700 catties of wheat, persuaded someone to take it to the county government and buy out his father. Fortunately he did not have to pay the fine as well. But his father was so upset he became very ill, and died within a few days. Later his mother too died from emotion.[6]

High taxes and naked extortion of this kind were notorious evils under the Nationalist regime before 1949. Special levies known as *juan* or 'extra donations' were a regular source of income for local officials and the tax burden was a source of constant complaint. The Communists by contrast won peasant support by lowering taxes and insisting that their officials should have clean hands. After 1949 they kept alive, in drama and films, the pre-revolution image of rapacious officials who taxed the toiling peasants unendurably, often for years ahead. In doing so the Party was able to make effective propaganda by contrasting 'present happiness' with the 'bitter past'.

Half a century later, the Party has forfeited almost all the trust it earned by establishing higher standards of public morality through the revolution. Though these had already slipped badly in the 1960s and 1970s, it is the economic reforms of the 1980s which have finally destroyed the Party's reputation, as cadres are tempted by the far greater opportunities for personal enrichment. Previous corruption was mostly a matter of accepting a few packets of cigarettes

and taking the best free seats at the cinema. Now it can
mean bottles of Remy Martin, hi-fi equipment, and a free
imported car.

Central Party authorities claim that they are kept in the
dark by local officials about popular complaints. But while
launching intermittent campaigns against corruption among
its own members, the Party remains chronically ready to
regard peasant protest as potentially subversive. Corrupt
cadres can easily shift the blame (as in the case of Hu Hai)
by playing on this fear. The result in many rural areas by the
early 1990s has been a complete breakdown of the remaining
trust between Party and peasants, which had survived even
the upheavals of the Great Leap and the Cultural Revolution.
Travelling in northern Henan in 1991, I came across by pure
chance unusually detailed evidence of this collapse of faith.
The previous occupant of my hotel room in Anyang had left
behind a volume of documents on Party-peasant relations
in a nearby rural county. The book was classified as *neibu*
or confidential and in earlier years its loss could not have
gone unnoticed. In the new laxer atmosphere, I was able to
remove the volume and take it away without enquiry. The
book contained all the confidential material prepared for
a conference called to investigate the breakdown of Party
authority in Lingxian County to the south of Anyang (not
Linxian County, discussed below, where the famous Red
Flag Canal is located). Its conclusion was startling: the Party
had not only lost control of the peasants but of many of its
own members, and 'new contradictions between the masses
and the cadres [were] emerging all the time'.

> In these last years, though the economy has improved
> in many places, ideological and political work has
> weakened. It has gone so far that the remnant strength
> of feudalism and the corrupt remains of capitalism
> have filled the gap. Beating and brawling, feudal
> superstition, thieving and gambling, big profiteering,

licentiousness and prostitution, and other such evils
have all returned from the dead. The existence of
these problems has in varying degrees undermined the
morale of local-level cadres. It has adversely affected
the favourable development of agricultural reform and
enterprise construction and has had a negative influence
on the politics of stability and unity.[7]

There is a wide gap between Party and peasant explanations
for what has gone wrong. While peasants blame official
corruption and the decline of political standards for their lot,
the Party version complains that the economic reforms have
encouraged the peasants to become unruly and insubordinate.
In the old days, explains the Lingxian handbook, the peasants
depended on the 'collective' – the village brigade or team –
for everything, and local cadres could easily discipline those
who stole or shirked their obligations. Peasants today are still
supposed to contribute labour to irrigation works, to grow
part of their crops for state quotas, and to obey a wide range
of local laws including those on family planning. But now
that they produce for themselves, the Party laments, they
can defy the cadres who then either lose confidence or resort
to strong-arm methods. 'The Party has become ineffective,'
the handbook admits, 'and some Party branches play no
role at all ... Problems are especially serious with family
planning, state purchases of grain, taxation, house building,
and planned crop production ... The masses have no respect
for the cadres and retaliate against them. They even abuse the
cadres' families, beat them, steal their crops, cut down their
trees, and threaten their property'.

The Party's aim, according to the handbook, is to establish
a 'new order' in the countryside, which while allowing the
post-Mao system of private agriculture and commerce to
flourish would re-impose its authority in the areas where it
has lost control. 'We must arouse initiative with one hand,'
says one document, 'and confine excess with the other.' Yet

the methods which are recommended seem likely only to lead to a new cycle of cadres' corruption and peasant resentment. Lingxian's new regulations on punishment for those breaking family planning criteria (the 'one-child-only' policy) lay down a punitive tariff of monetary fines:

(i) Giving birth before approved marriage age: 3,000–3,500 renminbi.

(ii) Giving birth after approved age but without permission: 1,800 rmb.

(iii) Giving birth beyond authorised quota: 4,000–7,000 rmb (will be levied even if child is reared by another family within its own quota).

(iv) Two extra births as above: 8,000–4,500 rmb.

National regulations to prevent exploitation of the peasants have been repeatedly issued in the early 1990s but just as regularly ignored at the local level. In 1989 local governments were warned not to repeat the previous year's practice of purchasing the state quotas of crops with IOUs. 'This has seriously dampened the peasants' enthusiasm,' they were told. Yet there was already a shortage of government funds and the same government report admitted that only three-quarters of the necessary cash was available.[8] Misuse of the family planning regulations to enrich local cadres was condemned in January 1991 by Henan's party secretary Hou Zongbin. Cases of 'abusing power for private gain, taking graft and severely undermining the policy, must be investigated and punished,' he said. Yet he also urged cadres to bring down birth figures still further and earn 'the glorious title of red-banner unit in family planning work'. Such an exhortation could only encourage further extortion.[9] The State Council and the Party Central Committee in Beijing issued explicit regulations in 1990 on 'reducing the financial burden on peasants and banning arbitrary collections of

45

charges, arbitrary fines and all kinds of arbitrary levies'. But two years later the official *Beijing Review* admitted that 'for several years the central government has urged local officials to stop collecting unreasonable fees from farmers, but to no avail'.[10]

In the freer political atmosphere before the 1989 repression, peasant protests against the Party in Henan were sometimes openly discussed. A transcript of a meeting between peasants and cadres in Jili district near Luoyang published in the *Peasants' Daily* recorded some vivid complaints. In the old days, the peasants said, the District cadres would 'drop by to say hallo every ten days or so'. Now if officials came to their village, it was only 'to visit the local cadres' homes and eat and drink'.[11] In other provinces out-of-work peasants who had flocked to the city were prominent in the two largest provincial demonstrations (Xian and Chengdu) which supported the students in Tiananmen Square. After the Beijing massacre, peasant protest was condemned for 'causing disorder' and many local cadres seized the opportunity to step up their exploitation.

Three years were lost before a chorus of deputies to the National People's Congress in March 1993 called for attention to 'the grim situation in the countryside'. Peasant protest was particularly severe in inland provinces like Henan with large surplus rural populations. A riot against the police in Renshou County, Sichuan province, which received national publicity, had similar features to the case of Hu Hai. Here too a better educated peasant had encouraged his fellow-villagers to insist on their legal right against over-taxation, after an extra levy was imposed on them. Zhang Dean, who had learnt about the law while serving as a soldier, confronted officials with extracts from the tax regulations when a new 'road tax' was demanded. Fearing that he would win in elections for the local people's congress, the county authorities then sought to arrest him on the charge of withholding taxes.

When the police tried to seize Zhang, 'they discovered that 700–800 peasants had surrounded his house and were coming at them, holding rods, scythes and rocks like a group of angels of vengeance. Before they knew what was happening, fists of fury were raining down, and the police vehicle parked by the curb was engulfed in fire. Their lives were only spared because the kind-hearted peasants decided not to kill them'. An investigation team conceded that Zhang was right and announced that some levies would be reduced. The peasants now raised their demands, calling for repayment of excessive back taxes, and marching on the county town. In a second riot, cadres were beaten up and the police used tear-gas to disperse thousands of demonstrators. Official accounts of the affair sought to distinguish between the original demonstration against the road levy – now admitted to have constituted 'reasonable' protest – and the new riots which raised 'excessive demands'.[12]

Before long the deteriorating social conditions in large swathes of the Chinese countryside were causing public alarm. Official statistics now showed a total of 140 million people underemployed out of a total rural workforce of 450 million, and up to 80 million migrants. The official *Legal Daily* admitted that 'social order is in chaos' and reported 750,000 cases of crime in the rural areas in 1993.

> Activities aimed at seizing [state] properties, which include stealing or looting the facilities of key construction projects, oil fields, power stations, waterworks and other installations, as well as railway and highway materials, are extremely serious.
>
> Incidents of armed fighting by the masses, which were triggered by disputes over land, forests, irrigation, roads, clans and other causes, have increased . . . The forces of rural patriarchal clans have revived in some areas, and reactionary secret societies have gained ground . . .
>
> The ugly social phenomena of practising prostitution, patronising prostitutes and gambling, among others, are

spreading in rural areas, and such law-breaking activities as abducting and selling women and children are very serious too.[13]

Older peasants complain bitterly about the new rural crime wave, recalling the higher standards of the past when 'revolutionary discipline' was maintained by dedicated Party members through local mass organisations such as the Youth League and Women's Federation. My ex-pilot part-time police-chauffeur in Anyang took me to visit his aunt, a 79-year-old veteran of the revolution. We drove east to Neihuang, a county town near the border with Shandong province where communist guerrillas had fought the Japanese and Chiang Kai-shek. Grannie Li was a tough old lady, walking with the help of a knobbled stick but straight-backed and firm of view. She recalled first of all the 'revolutionary justice' handed out to local landlords in the revolution. If they did not reveal where they had hidden their wealth they were hoisted on ropes and beaten with clubs, or forced to stand on a hot stove until the flesh was burnt off their feet. 'No,' she admitted, 'it was not Party policy. But when the Japanese were here, the landlords had hid their food and let us starve. After the war, we were determined to get hold of their riches and their title deeds! We did what the masses wanted!' After Liberation, she continued, life became calm and good order was maintained both by the authorities and by volunteer workers.

> In those days you could put anything in the street; you could leave your door open at night. The police were supposed to keep the people in order: everyone did what they were told. The cadres knew who was poor and who needed help. I looked after a family which had come back begging from Shanxi province. That was our job. Cadres were the first to do the difficult work: they took the lead in building people's houses and going out to the

harvest. The people were well organised. They would share a single glass of water in the true spirit of mutual help. The cadres were good and shared their food.

Grannie Li gestured contemptuously in the direction of the oversized police headquarters in the dusty main street.

In 1957, we had a population of 400,000 in the whole of this rural county, and there were exactly 27 policemen. Now the population has gone up by a 100,000, and there are 600 policemen. Yet every month three or four people are murdered and the police never solve any of the cases. Why? Because they are corrupt, and they fear reprisals against their families.

Now people are scared they will be robbed in the street. Even in daytime, they threaten you with a knife and steal your purse. Too many young workers have been laid off from the local fertiliser factory. The good ones go back to the fields, but the bad ones start thieving.

Commitment to the old standards of 'hard work and collective endeavour' has faded too in Linxian County (to the west of Anyang), whose achievements were once nationally known. Linxian is now right off the propaganda map, suffering the same fate as the former agricultural model, the Dazhai Brigade, in neighbouring Shanxi province. Dazhai was famous in the 1960s and 1970s for its success in 'levelling the hills and filling the gullies' to transform the mountainsides into fertile terraced fields, and for its egalitarian system of rewarding the peasants' labour. It was visited by millions during the Cultural Revolution in a campaign to 'Learn from Dazhai' but fell out of political favour after Mao Zedong's death. Its famous leader Chen Yonggui – a national hero who became a Vice-premier – was also denounced and died in obscurity, although local supporters are now trying to restore his reputation.[14]

Linxian was equally famous in those years for the Red Flag Canal, one of the great engineering feats in Mao's strategy of 'self-reliance'. This contour canal, drawing its water high up in the Taihang mountains, irrigates land for a population of half a million. It took more than twelve years to complete, from 1960 to 1972, cost the lives of 180 volunteers and injured hundreds more. At one spectacular section named the Youth Canal, young men and women abseiled down the mountain from above to cut away overhanging rock. Faded slogans can still be traced on the stones: 'Long live the people's communes', and 'the Party leads everything'. Linxian used to rank with Dazhai and the wartime communist capital of Yanan as places of pilgrimage visited by thousands. Hardly any foreigners visit Linxian now, and only a handful of Chinese each day. This monument to 'hard struggle' often evokes no more than amusement tinged with a vague nostalgia. 'Even if they paid people with Japanese money,' I heard a Chinese visitor say, 'no one would do the work now.'

Veteran canal-builders who run the local exhibition centre take care not to criticise the new system of private agriculture, while asserting that 'we could only have built the canal in the spirit of the people's communes'. The Party still tries periodically to rekindle that spirit. In 1991 a province-wide competition was launched to 'emulate the Red Flag Canal' and senior party officials visited Linxian to unveil an inscription by one of China's elder statesmen, Li Xiannian. The competition was won, unimaginatively, by Linxian county itself and the closest neighbouring county. But within a year a serious incident had shown that the spirit was effectively dead.

When I visited Linxian, the main and subsidiary canals were still being adequately maintained, though the water flow had been reduced and there were continual problems over payment. Under the people's communes each village settled its account collectively with the county water board.

Now that land-use has been privatised, each cultivator has to pay his or her own share on the firm principle of 'cash before water'. This had already led to the illegal opening of sluice gates to avoid payment. Official slogans were widely displayed in metre-high characters urging the population to 'use water according to law'.

The Red Flag Canal carries water diverted from the Zhang river which rises in Shanxi province and flows into Hebei, forming the provincial border with Henan for more than 75 kilometres. Henan peasants had always drawn water from the river but the canal allowed them to tap its resources more systematically – though at their neighbours' expense. The official account of the building of the canal describes how peasants in Shanxi had allegedly given up land with good grace for the first 20 kilometres of the canal. 'Our sacrifice of these few hundred *mu* [two or three square kilometres],' they said, 'will enable Linxian's hundreds of thousands of *mu* of land to produce more grain for the state. Besides, great numbers of our class brothers in that county will no longer have to fetch water from far away places.' No doubt compensation was paid to the Shanxi villagers to supplement their class spirit and to the neighbouring counties downstream in Hebei who lost water rather than land.

Relations seem to have rapidly worsened after the communes were abolished. There was a general decline in cooperation between the provinces: by 1991 the road north from Linxian into the Taihang mountains, adjacent to the canal, included an 80 kilometre stretch of almost impassable highway. Shanxi and Henan provinces could not agree on who should pay for its repair. Disputes over water rights reached a peak in August 1992 in conditions of drought. At 4.30 am on the 22nd, two stretches of the main trunk canal totalling 31 metres were blown up near the border with Hebei. The breaches of the canal wall, which was eight metres high at this point, destroyed houses and livestock and ruined crops in the fields below belonging to Panyang village in Linxian County. A rare report was carried in the *Peasants' Daily* noting that the incident arose because the dispute over water use had been 'unsolved for many years'. The class brothers had finally come to blows.[15]

Little has been heard since Mao Zedong died from Henan's other famous rural model, Qiliying (to the south of the provincial capital), where the local peasants, it is claimed, first coined the name of 'people's commune'. When the Great Leap Forward began, Henan set the pace under the leadership of the Party secretary Wu Zhipu, a former student of Mao's. It had already led the way in a vast campaign for water conservancy and land improvement in the winter of 1957. After visiting Qiliying on 6 August 1958 during an inspection tour, Mao pronounced his famous sentence: 'It is better to run people's communes'. Qiliying quickly pooled its labour to build three new canals bringing water from the Yellow River to irrigate more than 90 per cent of its land. As often happened elsewhere, this caused excessive irrigation, raising the water table and threatening to make the land too saline for cultivation. The struggle then shifted to building drainage canals and sinking wells. Even the official history of Qiliying admits that it was a constant battle.

By the 1970s high yields were being claimed in Qiliying, but since then it has fallen completely out of the news. According to one report it continues to rely, untypically, on the collective organisation of its workforce. Shi Laihe, the commune leader who was once eulogised for his heroic efforts, still represents Qiliying at the National People's Congress. At the 1990 Congress he complained – a lone voice – about the shortage of peasant deputies. China's rural citizens, he argued, who made up the bulk of the population, should have more opportunity to take part in politics.[16]

Qiliying apparently clings in its obscurity to rural values of the Maoist age. There are occasional stories of other rural communities which have rejected the new competitive ethic. It seems more likely to happen when the community is reasonably well off and sees no reason to jettison a collective way of life which ensured fair shares for everyone. The village of Nanjie in Jianying County (not far south from Qiliying) has been reported to maintain a system of 'free distribution' in which all services from birth to the grave are provided, without payment. The total value of such services average over a thousand renminbi annually. Portraits of Mao still have pride of place in peasant houses and his statue stands in the village square. All young people serve for a year in the militia, eating and working together, to learn how to live collectively. 'Why should we not have communism in one small community?', the local Party secretary is quoted as asking. In Nanjie, he claims, people can still leave their doors open at night.[17]

The Nanjie experiment (no doubt idealised in the report quoted here) remains a little-known exception to the new entrepreneurial values of the 1990s. The new rural models are no longer found in the 'backward' regions of the interior, but in the more 'advanced' provinces of the coast. The village of Daqiuzhuang outside Tianjin city, celebrated as China's 'richest village', was said to have been designated as a national model by Deng Xiaoping himself. It has turned itself into an industrial suburb of Tianjin by importing cheap migrant labour to work in more than 280 rural factories, producing parts and semi-finished goods for further processing by industries in the city. The resident population of 4,500 was supposed to enjoy an almost unbelievable average income of 124,000 rmb (US$21,000) in 1992. Many now live in three-storey houses, drive Mercedes and take foreign holidays. (Daqiuzhuang's success was somewhat tarnished in 1993 when its Party secretary and leading entrepreneur, Yu Zuomin, became involved in a murder case. Yu was accused of deploying local toughs to prevent police from investigating the crime. He was only arrested after high level discussions in Beijing where he was believed to have powerful protectors.[18])

China's most famous peasant in 1994 was Zhang Guoxi, a former carpenter in Jiangxi province who had amassed a hundred million renminbi in six years. Zhang used cheap skilled local labour to produce high-quality wood carvings for export, principally to Japan. Zhang employed nearly three thousand workers and had investments in Thailand, Hong Kong and South Korea. He also donated shrewdly to local causes, building a new road bridge for his native Yujiang county. This was by coincidence the very place which had inspired two famous poems by Mao Zedong in 1958 to celebrate its success in wiping out the dreaded disease of schistosomiasis. A mass campaign had eliminated the breeding grounds for the snail and liver fluke parasite which are essential links in the complex life cycle of the disease. A quarter of a century later, schistosomiasis has reappeared. Private cultivation of the farmland makes it harder to organise collective efforts to eliminate swampy areas, and the decline of free medical facilities has hindered preventive treatment. Today in Yujiang, it is the individual and not the collective who achieves fame. A campaign to 'Learn from Zhang Guoxi' was launched in 1994 by the Party committee.[19]

By 1993, a decade and a half after the agricultural reforms began, the Party leadership in Beijing was finally obliged to admit that a new crisis had emerged on the land. Deng Xiaoping endorsed this concern in a widely quoted remark that 'If there is trouble in the 1990s, it is very likely to start in agriculture'. Even the unpopular Premier Li Peng asked publicly why peasant incomes should be falling when output of the main agricultural products was rising. Several lines calling for better treatment of the peasants were written into Li's official report to the National People's Congress in March 1993. The popular Wan Li, outgoing chairman of the Congress's standing committee, complained that Li's remarks were perfunctory and delivered a more outspoken speech (unpublished in the national media). He warned that there was hidden unemployment in 50 per cent of the villages and referred to cases where the peasants had rebelled. This was because the Party had failed to fundamentally 'change the countryside' over the past four decades. The situation in the rural areas, Wan Li concluded, 'is desperate!' It was decided to send 'inspection teams' to villages and farms in all the Chinese provinces to listen to the peasants' complaints.[20]

Statistics from Henan were frequently cited to illustrate the peasants' plight. One survey by the State Council's Research Centre showed that 'farmers' incomes were subject to the vagaries of the weather and all kinds of taxes and levies ... there was a shortage of money in the farm economy to improve warehousing and distribution and raise productivity'.[21] There were also complaints of rural theft and lawlessness. Henanese peasants near Zhengzhou had stolen over 90,000 metres of flood-control communication cables and thousands of cubic metres of sand under a Yellow River embankment. In adjacent Hebei province, peasants' incomes actually decreased by 6.3 per cent in the first half of 1993.[22] A State Council directive listed 80 types of possible levies upon the peasants which were no longer permitted – though another 60 were still allowed. Yet by the end of the year there was little improvement: the *People's Daily* reported that the New Year's 'labourer wave' had started early. 'Ever since October,' the pro-Beijing *Wen Wei Bao* said in Hong Kong, 'the areas around Beijing and Shanghai railway stations have been covered with people, some sitting, some lying down, some standing, some squatting, some male and some female, and virtually all of them peasants from interior provinces heading to the cities in search of livelihood.'[23]

As the peasant problem is discussed more openly in the mid-1990s, a sustained attempt has begun to justify it in economic and social terms. The exodus is no longer referred to as a 'blind wave'. The peasants are after all, it is argued, behaving quite rationally in seeking to improve their lot. A new set of tough-minded propositions is put forward instead.

The peasants leave the land, it is said, simply because of over-population. No system could possibly provide them with enough agricultural jobs. They also leave because they have higher ambitions and are no longer content to follow the leisurely rhythm of rural life 'working the fields for four months, making the New Year last two months, and then sitting back idle for six months'. The policy of encouraging rural industry, it is also argued, cannot work in poor areas which lack capital, resources and outlets for whatever goods might be produced. As for conditions in the cities, the peasant migrants may have a hard time, but many will earn enough to support their families at home. They can also learn new skills of benefit to them and the community when they finally return to the countryside.

The 'scissors' between the cost of industrial and agriculture products had admittedly narrowed in the early 1980s, allowing peasants to invest in new housing, equipment and rural industry. But this cannot continue indefinitely: it is natural and necessary now for the 'scissors' to widen again so that industry can also benefit from the economic reforms.

In the end, the official justification concludes, peasant migration is essential for the country's economic development. By contributing cheap labour to the national effort, they help to create new wealth to the advantage of all. The problem is not how to halt the peasant flow but how to 'regulate' it, ensuring that they move to where there is work, and where they can be properly policed and controlled. Some commentators also advocate relaxing the old restrictions on peasants entering the towns. They point out that residence permits are being sold illegally at inflated prices, and that the barriers are already breaking down.

Yet while urban China needs the peasants from Henan and other provinces of Middle China, it also begins to fear them. Increasingly urban governments are turning to a new policy of 'controlled absorption'. Migrant entry will be limited to the number consistent with the needs of industry and of law and order. At the 1995 New Year, new regulations forbade peasant movement on the railways without special permits, and employers were told to refuse leave to those wanting to go home. The image of the Chinese peasant as heroic, honest and hard-working has dimmed since the revolutionary 1960s and 1970s. No one talks any longer of bridging the gap between town and countryside. Today's peasants are more likely to be regarded with a mixture of envy (for those like Zhang Guoxi who have become rural millionaires) and unease (for the shivering peasants at Zhengzhou station who invade the towns). A worried article in *Beijing Review* sums up the dilemma as seen by urban middle-class Chinese:

> The great influx of low-wage labour can do much to boost economic development in cities. In Shenzhen, one of the country's five special economic zones, migrant labour accounts for at least 50 per cent of the city's total labour force. Local residents, some of whom grumble about the newcomers, seem increasingly dependant on the cheap labour to maintain their higher standard of living. In large cities such as Shanghai and Beijing, about 90 per cent of the street sweepers are migrants.
>
> While it supplies cities with badly needed labour to contribute to the national economy, the mass exodus of young and middle-aged farmers is at least partly responsible for increasing crime, vagrancy and other social ills in urban areas. Beijing has nearly two million outsiders, adding to the city's already swelling population of nine million permanent residents. A survey

in 1993 showed that outsiders were responsible for 80 per cent of criminal offences in the capital.[24]

Travelling on from Hu Hai's village near Xinxiang, north of the Yellow River, I reached the provincial capital of Zhengzhou in less than two hours. The next day I visited Zhengzhou High Technology Development Zone on the edge of the city, one of 27 such zones approved by the State Council in Beijing throughout the country. Spread out over 13 square kilometres, it lies close to the new north–south highway now being constructed from Beijing to Guangzhou. It also lies next to the east–west railway from the coast to Xinjiang, across the border into Kazakhstan and on towards Europe. This is China's high technology future. Optimistic managers at the Zone hope to attract the latest state-of-the-art technology from abroad to make lasers, computers, industrial diamonds and other high value products. Many Chinese government ministers, they boast, have already congratulated them on their progress.

I inspected a scale model of the Zone's future development, and then toured the site. A core of new buildings had already been completed: a few factories, an administration centre, apartments for senior staff – and a hotel complete with banqueting room and a karaoke bar. More buildings were rising on the perimeter. They were being built by intensive labour: dozens of labourers swarmed over the bamboo scaffolding, hauling up their materials by hand. Where did the workforce come from, I asked? Were they by any chance peasants from the Henanese countryside? Not from Henan, was the answer. This is a labour corps from Jiangxi province, organised by a contractor who pays and houses them. The Zone has no need to do more. It is the easiest way – and they work much harder. Our local people are too lazy!

Only a few Chinese will face up – in private – to the brutal logic of scenes like these. Once again, the cities are exploiting the majority of rural areas. Substantial economic gains in the countryside are confined to the more prosperous regions (thus peasants in inland Henan in 1994 earned only half the average income of peasants in coastal Zhejiang). Yet is not this exploitation essential for the nation's economic advance? Not all the capital for investment in development can come from private savings or industrial profits or from abroad. Squeezing the peasant, it is argued, is nothing new. The old system of the people's communes had squeezed them at source, making its deductions at the collective level. The difference today is that the accounts are done by each individual household. The peasants can see for themselves what is being creamed off for the state to spend on its own projects. That is why they complain so loudly. But is there any real alternative to this 'primitive accumulation' of rural funds for urban investment?

This pragmatic argument is not fair to the people's communes. Carried to extremes – as during the Great Leap Forward, or in the hands of incompetent or dogmatic cadres – it was indeed a form of exploitation. But when they worked well, the people's communes (subdivided into the smaller units of the brigade and team) offered the peasants an opportunity to pool their resources for the common good. In this way they created a surplus for investment in local education, health and public works which could be seen to reward their efforts. Nor does the argument address the central causes of peasant unrest: corruption on a much greater scale, low incomes and unemployment, and widespread disillusionment with the Party which once liberated the peasants from earlier forms of exploitation. The poorer the area, the greater the loss of faith. In the disadvantaged provinces of the interior – and especially in Henan – the Chinese peasant is turning away from the Party to worship new gods and rediscover some of the old ones.

III

The Religion Fever

The Buddha is so broad-minded that he can tolerate
   many intolerable things in this world;
His smiling face looks so kind that all mean people
   seem ridiculous.
Although it rains over a vast land, grass without roots
   cannot benefit from it;
Although the door of Buddha is opened wide, wicked
   people cannot go through it.

(couplets in the White Horse Temple, Luoyang)

The Temple of Yue Fei at Tangyin in Henan province is
officially a 'cultural site', not a place of worship. Yue Fei
(died AD 1141) was a general who defended the Song dynasty
in its last years against invaders from the North but was
betrayed by traitors in the imperial court. An hour's drive
south of Anyang, the temple is visited by obedient files of
schoolchildren to be given a historical lesson in the virtues
of patriotism. Giant painted characters invoke loyalty and
service to the nation. There are pavilions and courtyards,
statues of General Yue and his family, and kneeling figures
of the traitors.

There has been no regular worship inside the temple for

several decades: the custodians would chase away anyone seeking to light incense before the General's statue. But over a bowl of hot Sichuanese noodles across the road, I am invited to have a look outside the back wall. Tucked in a corner is a small Buddhist shrine, protected by a low railing. Piles of incense sticks are being sold from street stalls and wedged into tins filled with sand. It is soon after breakfast: babies in their padded jackets are parked in the dust while Tangyin women say a morning prayer before they go shopping. 'These are just the Old Hundred Names [the ordinary people],' I am told. 'On special occasions tens of thousands of believers gather in the mountains to the west' – my informant waves vaguely in the direction of the sacred Mount Song – 'to worship the gods'.

Henan's religious revival is not confined to those who *xin Fo* (believe in Buddha). It has also become famous – notorious in some official quarters – for the recent spread of Christianity, on a larger scale than anywhere else in China. Some time later, on the southern side of the Yellow River at Mengjin, near the ancient capital of Luoyang, I give a lift to an old farmer in a Mao jacket. He says he will show me the road to the tomb of Liu Xiu, first emperor of the Eastern Han dynasty. 'Do you believe in Buddhism around here?' I ask. 'Oh no, not here,' he casually replies. 'Here we all follow the Lord!' (This does not stop him from giving me false directions so that we take him right up to his home, missing the tomb and its cypress grove on the way.) Later I am told that this is one of the areas in Henan most affected by the 'Christianity fever'.

The legend says that Buddhism was brought to China in the first century AD by two eminent Indian monks who came to Luoyang carrying their scriptures on a white horse. That is why the White Horse Temple, resting against the gentle Mangshan hills and facing the Luo River, is known as the 'cradle of Buddha'. The substantial complex of buildings, with courtyards shaded by cypress in between, has been restored by a succession of dynasties, most recently by the current Chinese government in the early 1960s and again after the Cultural Revolution in the 1980s. In June 1991 it was visited by Jiang Zemin, the General Secretary of the Chinese Communist Party brought in to the leadership after the Beijing Massacre to give the Party a new face. Jiang's visit received wide publicity, illustrating the tolerance which the Party officially affirms for religious belief. But the official account of his visit also indicates how disillusionment with its leadership is a significant factor in the turn to religion.

After touring the temple, Jiang and his entourage were ushered to a guest room in the usual manner to rest and drink tea. He was served by a young monk in his twenties: Jiang immediately began to interrogate him. Where was he from and why had he become a monk? The young man replied that he came from Guizhou province in the south-west and had previously graduated from technical college to a good job. 'But when I saw all the corrupt phenomena and malpractices in society, I began to be frustrated. I did not want to associate with corrupt people . . . So I came to the White Horse Temple in search of spiritual emancipation.'

Jiang Zemin, the official account continues, sighed deeply. Every previous Chinese dynasty, he said, had been infected by corruption and the present was no exception. He could not deny that in the past few years some 'unhealthy trends' had emerged in the Party and society, but these would not be solved by becoming a monk! Trust the Party and the government, he urged the young man.[1]

Further north in Wangyan Shitun (Hu Hai's village) where there is very little trust in the Party or government, most villagers have turned instead to 'believe in Buddha'. A new temple stands at the entrance to the village, a solid brick building with a tiled roof supported on columns. When I visited in spring 1992, the statues of the gods were being lovingly decorated in bright glossy colours. Outside two upright stelae recorded the names of those who had helped with its construction, in the manner of temple inscriptions from the imperial past. At first, I was told, the County government refused permission for the temple to open, claiming that it was 'feudal superstition', but the authorities were forced by local pressure to give ground. The worst off villagers were said to be the keenest to help build the temple, hoping that it would bring them good fortune. Hu Hai's son Desheng explained how the construction and maintenance was arranged:

> The temples [there is a second one at the other end of the village] basically cost no money. All the materials, bricks, tiles, cement, wood etc, were donated by the villagers from their own houses. They are looked after by some older people without payment, and any repairs are done by the villagers again without charge. There is no particular class distinction among those who attend the temples, but they mostly consist of people who cannot find happiness or comfort in their present lives, ordinary peasants who have been oppressed.

Small road-side shrines have also been rebuilt in this and many other villages of northern Henan. It should be noted that although local people talk casually of 'believing in Buddha', the gods in their temples are the same eclectic mixture that they were in pre-communist times. The Buddhist Guanyin, goddess of mercy (herself transmuted in Chinese tradition from the male saint Avalokitesvara) may be found next to the Daoist door-god Zhong Kui, expeller of demons, or the figure of a local hero. One or more of the Daoist Eight Immortals (*Ba Xian*) may be grouped with some of the 18 Buddhist models of perfection (*Luohan*). The larger temples, restored at government expense primarily to attract tourism, are not much frequented.

Serious study of Buddhism is popular among urban intellectuals in Beijing and other cities where state-subsidised
Buddhist colleges can be found. Some provincial temples,
supported by funds from Japan, Taiwan or other overseas
Buddhist sources, have also revived as centres of learning.
A small number of Buddhist 'masters', former students of
the 'masters' of previous generations, give instruction to
individuals or private classes, but large public meetings are
frowned on by the authorities. Scriptures and annotated texts
are hard to find even in the cities: in the countryside they
are virtually non-existent. At a hillside temple not far from
Neihuang (home of the fierce Grannie Li) I talked to women
who had never seen a single book of Buddhist scripture and
had no idea how to obtain one. Most rural believers have
only a sketchy knowledge of the simplest prayers, and in
these conditions Buddhism becomes little more than folk
ritual. Thus government restriction reduces it to the level
where it can then be more accurately condemned by the
authorities as 'superstition'.

In 1989 an official commentator in the *Peasants' Daily*
sought to explain why 'believing in Buddha' was on the
increase. A survey of worshippers at the Nanyue shrine on
Mount Hengshan in Hunan province (one of the eight sacred
mountains in Chinese tradition) showed that 75 per cent were
peasants and that one in four were young people. In one case
a primary school teacher had brought his class to pray for
success in transferring to secondary school. He prayed too,
the survey reported, because his own chances of a pay rise also
depended on their examination marks. In another case, a local
official led 200 villagers to thank the Buddha for granting
a good harvest. They marched to the sound of firecrackers
behind a placard with the legend 'Bringing prosperity to the
millions' displayed in large gold characters. Other examples
included a son praying for his mother's health to be restored,
and a young entrepreneur giving thanks for previous favours

from the Buddha by burning 40 brand-new 100 renminbi banknotes (worth £10 each). The *Peasants' Daily* sought to find an explanation for a phenomenon not confined, it admitted, to the rank and file:

> People who have received some education ... should pin their hopes on regional economic development and prosperity and not organise the masses or their students to 'beg protection from the Buddha' ... In the last few years, influenced by the view that 'no one can say explicitly what socialism is', we have slackened off in our ideological and political education in the rural areas ... A small number of people have become greedy and corrupt and have begun advocating that 'ideals means making more money' and 'money means the future', which has resulted in serious ideological confusion among the cadres and people ... This is why there has emerged a 'superstition craze' and a 'worship craze' in some of our rural areas, and why some cadres and teachers have led peasants and pupils to worship the Buddha ...[2]

The revival of traditional Buddhist and Daoist beliefs attracted less critical attention, however, than the parallel upsurge in various forms of Christian worship during the 1980s. These were better organised and more likely to be regarded as subversive, particularly when they took place beyond the control of the officially approved church, the Three-Self Patriotic Movement (TSPM), or when they were encouraged by foreign missionaries. In the towns, surviving members of congregations which had been suppressed in the 1960s emerged to worship again. TSPM churches which had been turned into workshops or storerooms were reopened. For a time they were joined by many young people, curious to get a taste of a new ideology, but by the late 1980s other foreign ideas had become more popular. The urban Christian revival was soon out-stripped by the rapid expansion of the religion in the countryside. Much of this activity took place in unofficial gatherings beyond the control of the TSPM, and had a strongly evangelical character which often led to conflict with the authorities. This remarkable phenomenon was more widespread in Henan than in any other Chinese province.

The rural 'Christianity fever' was much more than a revival among dwindling numbers of the elderly faithful: most adherents were far too young to remember the past and new communities emerged in areas where the official church had not existed in the 1950s (although there may have been some evangelical activity before the communist revolution). The numbers involved were also much higher than before. In 1949 there were between 700,000 and one million Protestants in the whole of China, according to rough and prabably optimistic figures. This would be equivalent to between 1.4 and two million at the population level of the 1980s. Yet by 1988 estimates of the number of Protestant Christians in Henan alone ranged between 830,000 and two million. (Henan Catholics were estimated at 70,000 and had not increased at the same rate.)[3]

The scenes of religious activity in the villages of Henan, witnessed by foreign visitors and sometimes even recorded on video, demonstrate a degree of fervour and enthusiasm which those who remember the rural revolution of the 1950s and the Cultural Revolution of the 1960s can hardly credit. Yet the Christianity fever often seems to arouse a similar spirit to that displayed in these earlier social movements. The following description is based upon photographs and a video taken by a Hong Kong evangelist group, mostly in central Henan, in the early 1990s.

> A farmhouse courtyard is packed with several hundred villagers sitting on the hard earth floor, women to the front and men against the yellow mud walls. A large white cloth with a red cross and a painted landscape of heavenly mountains hangs on the side of the house.

The preacher delivers his sermon with a skipping dance movement to emphasise each sentence. Then an old peasant with shaved head is carried in on a chair. The preacher lays hands on him: he rises up and walks, smiling. The audience shouts 'Alleluia'.

A night-time meeting of church activists is held in a cave behind the village used for storing brushwood and farm tools. It was a secret place of worship, say the villagers, even in the Cultural Revolution. Many of those present are young people with little education who read the sacred texts with difficulty. After prayer and song, they are told that the Holy Spirit is about to fall upon them. The atmosphere becomes hysterical as they hug, sob, and lay hands on their neighbours' heads.

Early in the morning, a group of believers assembles in the village watched by a curious crowd. A small band plays with trumpets and tambourines. The believers dance from one end of the village street to the other and back: some small children form their own dancing circle.

In a school hall, a troupe of young women in green jackets and black trousers performs a synchronised dance with elaborate hand gestures, reminiscent of the song-and-dance routines in praise of Chairman Mao during the Cultural Revolution. One of the 'sisters' begins to speak in a strange tongue; another holds her hand and interprets, sentence by sentence, eyes shut and smiling ecstatically.

At night-time next to a hillside torrent, converts line up to be baptised by total immersion. Two strong peasants with their trousers rolled up dunk them backwards into the stream. The converts include older women and young children, fully clothed. One young man has sensibly brought his swimming trunks.[4]

These scenes of mass, fervent religious activity among the peasants of Henan would have been regarded as literally miraculous by the foreign missionaries who, a century before, had laboured in the area to so little effect. During the Boxer Rebellion of 1900 many paid for these efforts with their lives when, at a time of growing poverty and famine, the secret society of that name attacked and killed foreigners throughout northern China. Conservative officials of the Manchu court – who might otherwise have become the target of the Boxers – had directed their wrath against the foreign missionaries in particular. They were already widely regarded with mistrust and hostility. Their physical presence, often at locations where they insisted on building houses and churches violating the requirements of *fengshui* (geomancy), was protected by treaties imposed on the Chinese government and enforced by diplomatic protest. Christian ritual, especially the act of communion where 'blood' and 'flesh' are consumed, was widely misunderstood. So was the missionary zeal for 'saving the souls' of babies and small children on the point of death. Stories circulated that the missionaries had poisoned wells, stolen gold from underground, and killed orphans to steal their organs for the purpose of alchemy. Missionaries also discredited themselves by internal feuding, not only between Catholics and Protestants but between rival evangelical sects.

Henan was regarded by the missionaries as 'one of the toughest provinces to crack' with a fierce resistance to conversion.[5] When missionaries and their families were murdered by the Boxer Movement in 1900 – 160 of them in Shanxi province alone – those who escaped southwards encountered 'new perils in Henan'. 'We had yet to learn by sad experience that to be quit of Shan-si was by no means synonymous with being quit of danger, or even of Boxer danger. The spirit of that terrible movement has already infected Ho-nan . . .', wrote Archibald Glover of the China Inland Mission. Though at first the country folk gave no cause for serious alarm, experience showed that the mood changed after a couple of hours in one place. 'There were times when we had to hurry through a village or market town in instant fear of the threatening crowds that hooted us'. The following extract describes the scene in a market town soon after Glover's group, under military guard, had entered northern Henan.

> Faint and weary, we sought shelter from the scorching blaze and the oppressive crush under the 'p'eng' [awning] of a small bread shop near by, where we hoped to get some necessary food as well. Our first experience of Ho-nan friendliness was not encouraging; we were driven from the premises, the shopkeeper refusing even to sell us a piece of bread. So, the ladies and the little ones were forced back to the cramped discomfort of the litter in sheer self-defence, the barrier of the poles supplying them with the only relief they could get from the great pressure.
>
> It proved to be one of the most distressing and anxious times in all our experience. For three full hours we were momently expecting an attack . . . The roadway in front of us was blocked. Tier on tier, right away back to the shops, they were struggling, a dense mass of men and lads, to get near us . . .
>
> Noise and jostling were now the order of the hour; and the spirit of something more than rowdiness – a spirit of open hostility – was beginning to break through it. The opprobrious term 'iang kuei-tsi' [foreign devil] came ominously to the front, and told of a distinct rise in the tide of feeling. Coarse jests were flung across at us, and in many eyes we read the racial hatred that found vent in muttered curse.[6]

The highest estimate of the number of Christian converts in China at the time was 100,000, mostly located in the seaboard provinces of Fujian, Zhejiang and Guangdong. Church congregations in Britain and the US were urged to contribute to the rescue of the 'heathen Chinese', and it was claimed that conversion would continue by 'geometrical progression' until Protestantism had a share 'in the government of the country'.[7] Even at this time there were sceptics. The Australian journalist

George Morrison (later famous during the Boxer Rebellion as 'Morrison of Peking') noted acidly that in 1893 a total of 1,511 Protestant missionaries in China claimed to have converted no more than 3,127 Chinese during the year. This was achieved 'at a cost of £350,000, a sum equal to the combined incomes of the ten chief London hospitals'.[8] A far higher claim was made for Catholics in China but many of these were suspected of being nominal or 'rice' converts (i.e. those who agreed to conversion in order to secure regular supplies of food, either as hand-outs or preferably as servants to the missionaries).

Christianity made greater gains in the first half of this century, particularly in the cities and among progressive nationalists. The founder of the Chinese Nationalist Party Sun Yat-sen was baptised as a young man; his successor Chiang Kai-shek was converted to Methodism, though his ruling ideology owed more to Confucian tradition and the influence of European fascism. Rural China remained relatively untouched by missionary activity. 'The urban bias of Protestant missionary work was evident,' writes one historian, 'both in the failure to respond to the social needs of the countryside and in the inadequate response to nurturing the rural church.[9] However, some Chinese Christians resolved to establish an autonomous movement, and a national conference of independent churches was set up in the 1920s. Most of these churches were in Henan and Zhejiang, the two provinces which would lead the religious upsurge of the 1980s. Some of today's groups claim direct descent from independent evangelical groups of this pre-war period. The best known of these was the 'Little Flock' founded by the biblical literalist Watchman Nee. Others included the 'True Jesus Church' and the 'Local Church' movements.

The egalitarian and millenarian aspects of Chinese revivalism had considerable appeal in the troubled 1930s and 1940s when China was afflicted with civil war, social deprivation and endemic economic hardship. The main expression of faith was 'a fervent atmosphere, public confession, emphasis on sin, salvation and faith healing; and spiritual gifts such as psychic phenomena and glossolalia [speaking with tongues]'. Such activities, say the authors of a recent study of Chinese Protestantism, were a natural form of religious behaviour among peasant communities and recent immigrants to cities. 'It is not surprising,' they conclude, 'that at a time of intense social stress they surfaced in rural China.'[10]

The new Christianity fever in rural Henan and other provinces has also emerged in conditions of considerable stress. During the Cultural Revolution churches of all faiths (including Muslim mosques) were closed by Red Guards in the campaign against the 'Four Olds' (old ideas, old culture, old customs and old habits). This created a religious vacuum in which only a few of the autonomous house-church movements could survive underground. When Christianity was again tolerated, it revived slowly in the city churches where some TSPM clergy had survived. But in the countryside it was the autonomous groups, not the official church, which rapidly grew in numbers and appeal. As a Chinese social scientist has observed in a rare study of the 'fever':

> During the decade [1966–76] when religion was prohibited, believers were deeply scarred and these wounds will not be healed in a short period. The fact that for ten years the patriotic [TSPM] religious pastors were on the sidelines meant the spontaneous rise of a whole core of fervent preachers. 'Spontaneous churches' broke traditional moulds, so people became used to small scale and diffuse activities.[11]

By the mid-1980s unapproved house-church activities were widespread in the south and north-west of Henan. Illegal open air meetings, numbering several hundreds or even thousands, were reported. The conservative character of

Henan's peasants encouraged the revival of old beliefs, but many new converts were recruited among disillusioned Red Guards 'sent down' to the countryside in the Cultural Revolution. Many became lay preachers, filling the space left by the persecution of the official church's ministers. (By 1990 there were only 66 TSPM pastors and 140 elders, many of them elderly or infirm, to take care of more than 800,000 Protestants in Henan.) The new evangelists were accused by the TSPM of 'taking advantage' of the situation. They included the leaders of such sects as the 'New Birth', 'Ultra-spiritual', 'Full Range', 'Living Jesus' and the 'Shouters'. The last named group, an offshoot of the Little Flock of the 1930s, contains some Shamanistic folk-religion elements in its ritual, and its worship includes an element of loud repeated shouting. But the term is also used by the official church to brand any group of which it disapproves.

The leader of the New Birth sect, Xu Yongze (a converted Red Guard like other members), is better known than most others because of his chance exposure to the international press in 1988. Arrested in 1982 for organising underground house-churches, Xu escaped from jail after several months captivity, pedalling away nonchalantly on a bicycle. His arrest and escape was followed by a wave of persecution in Henan. By 1988 his sect claimed to have set up more than three thousand independent groups and to have sent evangelists to more than twenty provinces. In April 1988 Xu left his place of hiding – by now in Shaanxi province to the north-west – for Beijing where he hoped to hear the visiting American evangelist Billy Graham preach. He was seized while walking with friends in a Beijing park: Mr Graham told US journalists that he had prayed for Xu's release.

In 1989 the TSPM-approved church in Henan sent teams to contact the unofficial churches and seek to win them back by negotiating with local authorities for funds and land on which to build new places of worship. But the official church admitted that 'it covers an immense area, and its duties are onerous' so that the task of 'replacing heresy with orthodoxy' was almost beyond it.[12]

A survey carried out in the same year by the Shanghai Academy of Social Science provides unusual insight into the Christian phenomenon in Henan. Conducted in Nanyang district in southern Henan, it was based on a sample of 600 Protestant believers most of whom lived in the country areas. The most important finding was that the sample's standard of living was 'universally low', and over 50 per cent had an annual income of less than 50 rmb – less than a tenth of the national average for peasants. About a half of the sample had been converted in the 1980s when 'the suppression and persecution of all religion during the Cultural Revolution brought about a situation where all the pent-up religious feeling from this time [was] released in a great rush'. There was a high degree of literal faith: almost two-thirds believed that 'every sentence in the Bible could be taken to be true'. The large majority became Christians 'in order to solve problems or difficulties in their lives'.

Most of those surveyed had some connection with the official church. Its conclusions would apply with even greater force to the unofficial house church and sect adherents. Henan's rural Christians are overwhelmingly poor and poorly educated, with a tendency to fundamentalist belief. Religion offers hope of transforming a life where recent economic changes have created, for the majority, greater risks rather than greater wealth. Yet why have they chosen this particular faith? The survey also argues that 'the educational and cultural level of many peasants in huge areas of the Chinese countryside is very low and the standard of living is very low, so that it is very easy for evangelists to engage in activities'. There is some truth in this observation: foreign-inspired evangelical activities do appeal predominantly to the poor and the uneducated. However this analysis may also reflect an effort to explain away the appeal to Chinese peasants of a foreign doctrine.[13]

China's Christians, for obvious reasons, have attracted more interest abroad than the believers in Buddhism and other religions. Human rights organisations monitor their treatment and document alleged cases of persecution, while energetic – and sometimes aggressive – foreign missionary activity has resumed in China. Yet the Christians only number a small percentage of believers in one faith or another.

According to some estimates, upwards of 100 million Chinese are 'religious'. Estimates of Christians range between four and a half and ten million. As many as 70 million believe in Buddhism or Daoism. Both exist as mature philosophical doctrines, but with a strong inter-mixture of folk belief.[14] Muslims are reckoned to total around 20 million, composed of Uighurs, Kazakhs, Kirgiz, Tajiks and the so-called 'Chinese Muslim' Hui minority. They are mostly located in the north-west border regions, although there are significant numbers of Hui in other provinces including Henan.

Daoism (or Taoism) is based on the quietist tradition in Chinese philosophy which can be traced back to the school of thought represented by the legendary Lao Zi (Lao Tzu), traditionally believed to be a sixth-century BC contemporary of Kong Zi (Confucius). The Daoist scholars of the Warring States period (453–221 BC) preached belief in the Dao (Tao) or Way of Nature, against the Confucian Dao of government and society. The other source of Daoism was the ancient tradition of shamanism and magic, which peopled the hills and streams of China with demons, spirits and fairies, and told wonderful tales about miraculous happenings and transformations. Daoism today is almost entirely confined to this kind of popular tradition.

The later import of Buddhism (its first recorded arrival from India in China was AD 65) also combines profound philosophical thought with an array of beliefs in magic and the supernatural. Serious Buddhist thinking is very largely an urban phenomenon while the more popular form – which is often hard to disentangle from Daoist belief – is predominantly rural.[15]

Chinese official policy distinguishes between 'religious beliefs', which are protected in the Constitution, and 'superstition' which is regarded as socially harmful and often criminal. In the long run religion, as well as superstition, will in theory disappear as a fully socialist society emerges. But for the time being religion is tolerated, not only because China is still officially at 'an early stage of socialism' but also for more practical reasons. These are to avoid upsetting the 'national minorities' among whom religion (particularly the Muslim faith) is prevalent; to satisfy the psychological needs of people who – it is admitted – do not find material life sufficiently rewarding; and to avoid upsetting foreign countries with an interest in Chinese culture and religion.

The actual handling of religion has varied according to the overall political mood in Beijing, but rural religious activities always tend to be treated more harshly. Popular religious practices outside the established church, in whatever denomination, are more likely to be branded as superstition, though some religious festivals may gain approval as acceptable examples of 'cultural tradition'. The 1979 Criminal Law explicitly prohibits some popular practices such as divination and fortune-telling on the grounds that they will be used to cheat and deceive the masses, and prohibits the spreading of superstitious belief which may undermine respect for the government.

In 1987, after the defeat of the liberal faction in the Communist Party led by Secretary-General Hu Yaobang, there was a clamp-down against 'feudal and superstitious activities' in the countryside. A public security official listed the following problems:

1. Taking advantage of the party's religious policies and the renovation of cultural relics, a handful of superstitious believers have incited the masses to build temples and mould statues of gods.

2. People have made pilgrimages to temples and mountains and prostrated themselves before the image of Buddha or God.

3. Witches and sorcerers have swindled others of money or property by telling fortunes and practising geomancy.

4. Long-banned reactionary secret societies have seized the chance to re-form and recruit disciples.[16]

There is no doubt that religion in the countryside is often used for fraud and trickery by charlatans claiming divine inspiration. A typical example from Henan was reported in 1989. Two women preachers in the mountain community of Tongbai, claiming to be in regular contact with Jesus, had collected donations from over a hundred peasant women. Forecasting that the world was coming to an end, they persuaded their followers to gather on a hillside and wait for a signal to drink poison and ascend to Heaven.

> Twenty of so farmers' wives, who were known as 'ministers of state', dressed in specially made yellow nylon gowns, knelt on the ground, awaiting the arrival of the self-styled 'servant of God', Xiong Chunhua, who would proclaim 'the message of the journey to the Kingdom of Heaven'. On hearing the 'message', they would assemble a hundred or so Christians, who would drink poisoned wine and pesticide and then ascend in a body to heaven. They waited for a long time, but Xiong failed to turn up to proclaim his message, whereupon a dozen policemen who had heard about the event hurried to the spot and prevented the disaster. Xiong and her accomplice, Zuo Guoxuan, admitted that they had been deceiving some rustic Christians and, by taking advantage of their piety, had swindled them out of their money.[17]

Even educated urban Chinese often display a remarkable degree of credulity towards magicians and healers. One famous case in Beijing even involved members of the national leadership. Zhang Xiangyu, a practitioner of the occult art of *qigong* was arrested on charges of deception in April 1990. Zhang claimed to be able to cure illnesses in others by concentrating her *qi* or vital energy on the patient – without actually laying hands on him or her. Zhang was said to have duped her victims out of more than 100,000 rmb: much of this was paid in fees to see her perform. She was eventually sentenced to six years in jail for 'spreading rumours and conducting occult activities'. Zhang had fallen foul of the tougher policy which followed the 1989 crack-down on all forms of dissent. She was said to have sought in vain to buy immunity from prosecution by making a large donation to the municipal fund for staging the Asian Games in 1990. According to Beijing gossip, senior government leaders including Deng Xiaoping invited another *qigong* practitioner Zhang Baosheng to perform for them. On one occasion Zhang is said to have succeeded in moving a pair of jade exercise balls out of the hands of the former general Wang Zhen into another room. Wang is supposed to have remarked enthusiastically that 'Maybe in the future he can steal some nuclear secrets from the Russians and Americans for us!' Mr Deng, the same unofficial account alleges, wrote a special message for him: 'I hope that Zhang Baosheng will do good deeds, not bad deeds.' Whether or not the anecdote is entirely true it illustrates the well-known ambivalence of the ruling élite towards traditional forms of superstition. In 1994 new rumours that the ailing Deng was being treated by *qigong* had to be officially denied.[18]

As the religious fever grew in the early 1990s, so did the government's counter-measures. Christian house-churches were a particular target, both because they rejected the 'leadership' of the official TSPM and because of their frequent contacts with foreign evangelists. Amnesty International and other human rights bodies documented a lengthening list of arrests in Henan, together with other centres of rapid Christian growth such as Anhui, Fujian, Shaanxi and Hebei. Some were charged with 'counter-revolutionary crimes' under the Criminal Law; others were simply sent to re-education-through-labour without charge or trial (this 'administrative' punishment may be imposed for up to three years: in practice it is often extended). The Henan Shouters were a particular target, having already been heavily repressed in the early 1980s. Their belief in the 'second coming' and refusal to take part in political campaigns had led to their designation as a counter-revolutionary movement. The authorities were alarmed by their rapid growth in and around Lushan County in central Henan and many Shouter leaders received long prison terms. By the 1990s, police tactics reflected the new entrepreneurial spirit. Rank and file Shouters were rounded up and threatened with arrest unless they could pay fines which amounted to ransom money. They also had to pay for attending 're-education' classes.[19]

In the summer of 1993, Hong Kong newspapers clashed in a controversy over religious freedom in Henan. The independent English-language *South China Morning Post* claimed that up to a thousand Protestants had been arrested and jailed: house-churches had been broken into and many worshippers were beaten with electric truncheons and forced to pay fines. The pro-Beijing Chinese-language *Wen Wei Po* rejected the story. No private homes had been broken into and no one was persecuted for their religious beliefs. However it was admitted that 'no citizen is above the law' and some Christians had been punished for crimes against the law and 'activities harmful to social order'.[20]

So who would define which religious activities were or were not harmful? Local authorities had considerable leeway in interpreting the various laws and administrative regulations.

Unofficial churches might be left alone for months or years and then raided, often it appeared, simply in order to raise funds for the police. The situation was to some extent clarified in two new decrees issued in January 1994 by the State Council. The first governed 'the religious activities of foreign nationals within China'. This for the first time explicitly allowed foreigners to worship at Chinese 'religious venues', whether temples, mosques or churches and even to preach on invitation. But seeking converts or distributing publications was forbidden with equal clarity, and attendance at a non-approved house-church would also be in breach of the law. The second decree spelt out what was meant by a 'religious venue'. Monasteries, temples, mosques, churches and other 'fixed venues' were all required to be registered for religious activities. Again, this established for the first time a legal basis which had previously been lacking. Once recognised, the venue had the protection of law as long as it was properly managed. But it was also obliged to refrain from activities which 'harm national unity, ethnic unity, or the social order, harm citizens' health or obstruct the national educational system'. Such a catch-all provision would not be difficult to invoke by hostile local authorities. The law also meant that any unrecognised house-church or other venue would violate the law by the simple fact of its existence.

The law was immediately used by the public security bureau in Fangcheng County, Henan, to break up an unauthorised house-church and to arrest foreign missionaries and local church leaders who were present. The missionaries claimed that the police had confiscated cash, video cameras and other equipment to the value of several thousand US dollars. Their leader, the US evangelist Dennis Balcombe, was based in Hong Kong where his Revival Christian Church had for several years openly advertised for volunteers to become 'donkeys for Jesus' and carry bibles into China. Mr Balcombe had previously made a legal investment in the main Fangcheng department store. He also claimed that his arrest under the new law was a ruse to prevent him being paid the money that he was owed from this transaction. This was denied by the Chinese who said that the foreigners were carrying out 'illegal religious activities' – as indeed they were according to the law which had been published without advance warning or discussion just six days before![21]

The 1994 National People's Congress gave local authorities an additional weapon by extending public security regulations for minor offences to cover those who 'organise activities of superstitious sects and secret societies to disrupt public order' or who 'damage people's health' through feudal superstition or religious activity. This meant that ordinary participants could be detained for 15 days without trial and fined up to 200 rmb.

None of these measures have checked the religious fever and the spread of superstitious beliefs which are often peddled for financial gain. Fortune-tellers and geomancers are routinely consulted for any new business venture including those sponsored by local government bodies. Secret societies, both new and old, are becoming a familiar feature of organised crime, particularly in the southern coastal provinces where – as in pre-communist China – corrupt links are forged between them and the police. In June 1994 the *People's Daily* published a despairing account of the spread of superstition which, it said, was actively encouraged by some 'leading cadres'.

> Random construction of temples disturbs people's thinking and leads to the emergence and spreading of feudal and superstitious activities. When someone is sick, he does not go to see a doctor. Instead he goes to kowtow to the statue of a deity and grab some incense ash for use as a medicine. When a locality has a drought, people do not build irrigation channels but ask the god what has happened, divine rain by the Eight Diagrams, and beg the

Jade Emperor for help. Among the people, sorcerers and fortune-tellers have made their comeback, doing what they have done before to harm people and swindle money from them ... The problem regarding the re-emergence of some reactionary societies, cliques and clans is even more serious.[22]

There is nothing new in attempts by the central Chinese government to clamp down on superstition. In imperial times, 'heterodox thought' was regarded with great suspicion, sometimes correctly, as a cloak for subversion by secret societies intent on bringing down the dynasty. Peasant cults, even without a political motive, were strongly disapproved of at times by the Nationalist government as standing in the way of progressive thought. A decree from the new Nationalist regime of Zhejiang province in 1928, for example, announced that 'in the present time of renaissance and scientific enlightenment, these bad traditions not only keep people ignorant but make us a laughing stock among nations'. As the Communists would do later, Zhejiang distinguished between temples with cultural significance which could be preserved, and those where 'evil religions' and cults were practised, which should be confiscated.[23]

But in the modern conditions of the Henan countryside, as the cases described above illustrate, the Party's efforts to suppress illicit religious activism and win the peasants back to official doctrine have relied heavily on the weapons of control and extortion. Thus it is exacerbating the very same social problems which have contributed so largely to the religious fever. Economic inequalities also encourage the fever, but may be relatively less important. Chinese researchers say, in private conversation, that the real stimulus for religious revival is the 'degeneration of people's power and the growth of bureaucracy'. The main contradiction in the poorer rural areas is between the majority of farmers and a 'small handful of corrupt and career-minded cadres'.

The problem is intensified by the vulnerability of peasant families who now farm the land on their own, no longer part of a collective team, and who must shoulder all the financial risk. This increases their insecurity and need for religious reassurance, while making them more vulnerable to blackmail by local officials. Though the religious revival is mainly a rural phenomenon, the problem of disillusion with the Party is widespread. Among the more educated urban population, the gap has been filled to some extent by a new commitment to modernising and entrepreneurial goals, though *qigong* and other fads still offer for many a pseudo-scientific appeal. However the most powerful substitute for the traditional ethic of socialism under Party guidance is the consumer revolution with its imported goods and values. This may hold loss of Party faith at bay in urban China, but can it supplant the new rural idols?

IV

Damming the Gorges

Frail and slender, the twisted-bamboo rope:
Weak, the treacherous hold of the towers' feet.
A single slip – the whole convoy lost:
And my life hangs on this thread!
I have heard a saying 'He that has an upright heart
Shall walk scatheless through the [barbarian] lands of
   Man and Mo'.
How can I believe that since the world began
In every shipwreck none have drowned but rogues?[1]

No one who sails through the Three Gorges of the Yangzi
River can remain unmoved by their colossal beauty, but
until quite recently admiration was usually mixed with
fear. Navigation through the rapids and whirlpools was
a perilous business: one mistake was enough to destroy
ship and passengers together. The poem quoted above was
written by the famous Tang dynasty poet Bo Juyi in AD
818, in self-mocking description of his panic at being towed
upstream.

Today the traveller is likely to reflect on a different kind of
threat affecting those on shore rather than those on board. For
this is now the scene of the largest water engineering project
in China and – in its effect on the riverside population – the

largest in the world. Within ten years, if the Three Gorges Dam Project is carried to completion, more than a million local residents will have been moved from their homes, some over distances of 20 or 30 kilometres, while 13 cities, 114 towns and countless villages and small settlements will be submerged. For some time to come, until the dam is complete, the sheer rock walls will still appear unchanged from the time of Bai Juyi. Yet it is already hard to gaze on them without mentally calculating how they are going to change. The modern traveller becomes amateur surveyor, making a notional mark high up on the rockface where the new water level will reach, 70 metres above its present average height.

A temple which sailors have used as a guide for navigation for centuries will be moved down stream. A whole town, clinging to the side on concrete and wooden stilts, will move uphill. Harder to guess, but perhaps more disruptive, is the fate of the smaller communities which have established themselves with such effort over generations. (Some even brought the soil for their tiny fields long distances by boat.) In harmony with their surroundings, they seem as perfectly composed as the little hamlets in the foreground of so many Chinese landscape paintings. I remember one not far below the great gorge of Wushan with particular clarity – here it is just as I recorded it in my notebook:

> A gully, too small to be called a valley, appears between two descending folds of rock. The river shore is a tumble of boulders and ledges with a small beach beside. Two wooden boats with striped awnings amidships are pulled up on the shore. Another is heading slowly upstream; the boatman rows forward with firm slow strokes. Above the stones, there is a belt of sparse soil, cultivated with spring wheat, which will be awash in the summer when the Tibetan snows melt. A small path winds upwards towards a whitewashed old house with black tiles. The narrow ledge on which it stands has been terraced and planted with vegetables, rapeseed and two rows

of tangerine trees. The path continues above the house until it is stopped at a wall of slanting rock. All this will disappear. Higher up there is no more land to cultivate: here, the peasants must move into town when the dam is built.

Hubei is the land of 'watery villages and marshy towns', the 'province of a thousand lakes', the 'region of rice and fish' in classical Chinese literature. Though over half of its area is composed of mountains and another quarter of hills and valleys, it is the remaining one-fifth, the river plain formed by the Yangzi river and its many tributaries that defines Hubei's central identity: the benefits of plentiful water and the perils of overwhelming flood. Hubei has 1,193 rivers, large and small, with a total length of 35,000 kilometres and over three hundred lakes occupying more than six thousand square miles. The proportion of lake to arable land is as high as one to six. The Yangzi River runs for over one thousand kilometres through the province, forcing its way through the second and third of the Three Gorges (the first is in Sichuan province to the west) before it drives a winding course through the alluvial flood-plain – its own ancient creation – to the provincial capital of Wuhan where it is joined by the also quite substantial Han River.

Hubei is the crossroads of central China, sitting astride the main land route from north to south as well as the great river route from the sea to the west. Historically the area around the middle reaches of the Yangzi formed a distinct political and cultural focus. Here flourished the southern state of Chu which challenged the northern unifiers of China in the third century BC. It was the scene of the great battles of the Three Kingdoms period five centuries later when wise prime ministers devised stratagems to defeat wily generals. Some of China's first commercial towns rose here in the Song dynasty (AD 960–1279), as the centre of China's economic gravity shifted south. By Ming times it was an important source of surplus grain for the empire. In more recent history it became the thoroughfare for the armies of the Taiping Rebellion (1850–63), for the warlords of the early 1920s, the Nationalist armies which reunified China in 1927, and the Japanese invaders a decade later. Far-sighted regional officials in the last years of the Manchu dynasty laid the basis for Wuhan to become China's first modern industrial base. It faltered during the decades of war and division, then regained its importance after 1949 attracting massive new investment. More recently it has again fallen behind, but now in the 1990s there is a new vision. Led by Wuhan, Hubei province seeks to become the key which will unlock the prosperity of the whole of central China. The plan is based both on the renovation of the provincial capital and on China's most ambitious and controversial engineering project: the Three Gorges Dam which will block the Yangzi River soon after it enters the province.

Water and its control have never ceased to be a central preoccupation of the leadership in Beijing. In July 1989, just weeks after the Tiananmen Massacre, the new Communist Party Secretary-General, Jiang Zemin, left the tense political atmosphere of the capital to rally local officials in Hubei. A flood in that year would have been a double disaster. Jiang spent three days inspecting the dykes where 360,000 soldiers and civilians had been mobilised, urging those in charge to 'be vigilant' and 'really help the peasants'. Over 60 per cent of Hubei's population lives on the flood-plain and three-quarters of them – some 25 million – would be at risk if the dykes were breached. The 'once-in-twenty-years' flood predicted by the statisticians was long overdue: it had last occurred in 1954. Even more to be feared was the 'once-in-a-hundred-years' flood which had last hit Hubei over a century before in 1870.

Is there a long-term solution to the flood danger? The official answer, first put forward in the early 1950s but only approved finally in 1992, is the Three Gorges Dam Project. Environmentalists inside and outside China say this is an anachronistic scheme, dating from a period when 'Big Dams' were in vogue around the world, which will create more problems than it solves. Hubei's leaders and many ordinary people cling to the hope that it will not only dispose of the danger of flooding but produce a new abundance of hydroelectric power for industrial development. Hubei lies at the heart of the projected Yangzi Economic Region which will span nine provinces with a population of 220 million. The Yangzi, it is claimed, will be the new 21st Century highway into the interior, with navigation also improved by the higher water levels created by the Three Gorges Dam. Old and new Chinese development ideologies mesh in this vision: the 'Big Project' through which Man conquers Nature is now transformed into a multi-billion dollar enterprise to 'open up' the interior of central China to the world. The case for and against the project has been argued passionately for over four decades with an unusual degree of openness. Mao Zedong and other top leaders were deeply involved in the debate. The Three Gorges Dam has now become an important test of the post-Mao leadership, closely associated with the unpopular Premier Li Peng. If it works, his colleague and Party propaganda head Li Ruihuan said in 1991, it would 'prove the superiority of the socialist system'. He did not say what the verdict would be if it failed.

The Yangzi flooding comes from two sources: the river's own flow from its upper reaches on the fringes of Tibet, swollen by melting snow from the great tributaries which join it in Sichuan province, and secondly from the lower network of tributaries in Hubei, notably the Han River. The natural way of dealing with floods is to let them happen: that is how the fertile plain has been built up over hundreds of thousands of years. Human intervention was until recently limited to simple sluices and dykes used more for irrigation than flood prevention. The Yangzi's population began to increase from the Sui dynasty (AD 589–617) onwards as China's political and economic centre of gravity shifted south. Wars with external neighbours to the north also encouraged southward migration. New waves of colonisation in the Ming dynasty (1368–1643) reached high into the valleys and hillsides of the Yangzi's tributaries in Hunan and Hubei, increasing the silt flow downstream on the river plain and reducing the areas of natural flood retention. This unbalanced equation between nature and human activity has continued to worsen. Chinese statistics show that over the millennium and a half from the Han to Yuan dynasties (206 BC–AD 1367) serious floods occurred roughly once every eleven years. In the 276 years of the Ming dynasty (AD 1368–1643) this rose to one in nine; in the Qing (1644–1911) to one in five. And in the 39 years of the first republic (1911–1949) the floods came no less than 37 times.

Flood statistics offer four measures of human catastrophe: the flow in cubic metres per second; the area of land under water; the number of people affected; and the loss of human life. The figures in the table below are for Hubei and parts of Hunan on the Yangzi's southern bank.[2]

	cu.m per sec	area (sq kms)	no. affected	deaths
1870	110,000	40,000	15m	1,000,000
1931	–	34,000	28.55m	145,000
1935	–	15,200	10.3m	140,000
1954	76,000	32,800	18.8m	33,000
1991	60,800	17,600	26m	177

These were the years of exceptional flood: human losses in 'ordinary' years were usually unrecorded. The Yangzi was generally regarded as less vulnerable to flooding than the Yellow River – notoriously known as 'China's Sorrow' – and the Huai River which lies between the two and for many years had no regular channel to the sea. The people of the Yangzi's middle region regularly suffered less notable degrees of 'water disaster' (the literal meaning of *shuizai* or 'flood') in silence. In March 1883 the traveller Captain Archibald Little came across this typical scene on the left bank below Shashi.

> In many places along the banks the cottages were entirely deserted, nothing but the wooden framework and thatch roofs being left – skeletons stranded on the bank. On hitching up for meals we were at once surrounded by women and children begging; and truly the condition of the people seems most pitiable as they look idly out on the waters under which lie the rice-fields, their only means of subsistence. The greater part of the population seems to have gone off to other parts in search of food and work; the trade of the town is at a standstill, and no attempt seems to have been made to repair the many substantial brick houses thrown down by the flood when the waters stood five feet higher (as shown by the water-marks) than at present.
>
> Curiously enough, this was the first knowledge I gained of the disaster, so little do we know in the '[treaty] ports' of what is going on in the country around us . . .[3]

The aftermath of flooding was often overlooked once survivors had been rescued and the waters had receded. The China International Famine Relief Commission noted in 1926 that 'the immediate loss of life and property is not the only terrible aspect of a flood, but also the wholesale destruction of the growing crops and the slow drainage which often prevents the next planting'. It could take up to three years for the waters of a severe flood, held in by the dykes which they had originally surmounted, to escape completely.[4]

The 1931 Yangzi flood attracted more than usual attention because of the dramatic devastation caused to Hankou (the principal town of the Wuhan conurbation where the Han and

Yangzi rivers meet). Much of the city was under water for four months and junks and sampans sailed freely down the main streets. More than 700,000 residents were affected and large numbers camped out on the railway line and on two small hills. In Hankou alone 32,600 died from flood or the resulting starvation and sickness. Relief work was hampered by corruption and the higher priority given by Guomindang officials to waging war against communist guerrillas. The Chinese government, as the Famine Commission's chief engineer O. J. Todd complained, was not yet 'river-control-conscious'. The rebuilt dykes were not properly faced with stone and were breached again in 1935, so that in the first stage of that year's flood 10,000 people were drowned 'in the space of a few hours'.[5]

The dykes in place in 1949, when the communist armies crossed the Yangzi and drove Chiang Kai-shek out of China, had suffered from years of neglect. The *gandi* or main dyke, maintained by the state, was in places described as 'too narrow for two carrying-poles to pass'. The subsidiary network of *mindi* or people's dykes depended upon communities whose cohesion had been shattered by a decade of war. The new regime quickly identified flood prevention in the middle Yangzi as a critical test of its credentials. By February 1952 the first stage of a new plan had been drawn up – Mao Zedong himself wrote the inscription: 'For the sake of the broad masses, struggle for success in the Jingjiang Flood Diverson Project!' Former General Li Xiannian, then chairman of the Hubei government, took personal charge of a 300,000 strong temporary workforce, and the work was completed in a record one year and 20 days. Existing dykes were raised and strengthened, old channels were cleared, and a vast new retention basin into which flood waters could be diverted was excavated opposite Shashi City. Just a year later it passed the test triumphantly. The flood gate into the basin was opened three times in July and August

1954, the main dyke remained unbreached and the river plain population to the north was saved.

The tributary Han river, which had flooded 15 times in the past 24 years, was the next target. In 1955 a new workforce of 150,000 was mobilised to build the Han's Dujiatai Retention Basin. Its flood gate would be opened in nine of the next 30 years. Massive works in the middle Yangzi continued with only occasional mention in the Chinese press and even less attention abroad. In 1957–59 140,000 peasant labourers were imported to work on flood relief projects. Most settled down in the area. In the 1960s a similar number was imported to straighten out the ox-bow bends of Zhongzhouzi and Shangchewan, shortening the river's course by tens of kilometres. Today up to 300,000 local people are still mobilised every year to guard the main dyke.

To reach the Yangzi Gorges the traveller must first navigate upstream for over 600 kilometres above Wuhan, through the great alluvial plain protected by the main dyke. From the provincial capital the river rises towards the south until it reaches the edge of the Dongting Lake on the borders of Hunan province, then turns west, proceeding in a series of ox-bow and S-bends – not yet straightened out – to the trading port of Shashi. By water this ancient but fast expanding city is more than 450 kilometres from Wuhan, by road less than half that distance. The river then flows more directly another 160 kilometres to Yichang, gateway to the Gorges. The journey is usually regarded as tedious with 'nothing to see', yet this, the section most vulnerable to flood, has a peculiar fascination. The Victorian traveller Isabella Bird (much more observant than male travellers of the same period) gives a vivid picture of steaming for hours between 'high, grey mud-banks . . . gaining little beyond an idea of the vastness of the level country. Little was visible on the banks except for stacks of cut reeds, which grow to a height of 15 feet or more, and are then harvested for use as building, roofing and fencing material as well as fuel'.[6] Almost a century later, I recorded the same sight in my travel diary:

> The waterway is guarded throughout its course by earthen banks, stone-lined and sloping, up to ten metres high, which shut out the land completely. The only visible life is in the foreground. A team of workers unloads a barge of bricks, climbing slantwise up the incline. Their parked bicycles are silhouetted against some distant poplars and the sky. Along the top a buffalo pulls a wooden cart, an old man walks alongside. Ranges of haystacks with tufted tops line the bank for several kilometres at a time. On closer inspection they turn out to be stacked sheaves of immensely tall reeds, protected by a thatch of the same reeds.
>
> The floods have heaved long belts of sandy silt against the embankment, in some places pulling down the stones into muddy piles. The steamer crosses to the southern side where there is no stone left. In the distance the bank seems like a low cliff beside the sea, with bays, bluffs and promontories. Closer to it is just earth and mud, soft and ever liable to slip, nothing else.
>
> The water appears calm and oily as if boiled in a vat and allowed to settle. Travel is at the same time effortless and inexplicably slow, the viscous quality of the water destroying the sensation of movement. But heading upstream the engines throb with effort especially when the boat encounters clusters of small, sinister whirlpools. Even travelling downstream, steamers must increase engine thrust until the entire boat-frame shakes to pass through the danger.

From Wuhan to Yichang by regular passenger steamer takes a slow 36 hours, and it then needs another a day and a half's journey to Chongqing, the Famous city of Sichuan. At Yichang the river steamers pass through the Gezhouba dam, completed in 1982, and continue upstream past the site of the new Three Gorges Dam, to enter the first great gorge, the 75-kilometre long Xiling. The first steamer only successfully navigated the gorges in 1900. Before then, travellers embarked at Shashi or Yichang onto a Sichuan junk or house-boat, specially constructed for the dangerous journey onwards with a shallow draught, broad steering oar at the bows, large projecting rudder, and room for more than a dozen boatmen as well as a single sail. Isabella Bird, entering the Xiling, wrote of 'the change from a lake-like stretch, with its light and movement, to a dark and narrow gorge black with the shadows of nearly perpendicular limestone cliffs broken up into buttresses and fantastic towers of curiously splintered and weathered rock'.[7] The second gorge, the 40-kilometre long Wuxia through which the Yangzi river enters Hubei from Sichuan, is even more impressive. The photographer John Thomson, a contemporary of Isabella Bird, described how the 'confused masses' of mountains rose to a great altitude. The most distant peak at the far end of the gorge resembled 'a cut sapphire, with snow-lines that sparkled in the sun like the gleams of light on the facets of a gem'.[8]

For centuries passage through the gorges in either direction has been a life-threatening business. When he entered the uppermost Qutang gorge in Sichuan – the shortest and often the most dangerous – in AD 1059 to sail downstream, the poet Su Dongpo confessed his alarm:

Entering the gorge, the river seemed blocked in front.
Then from the cliffs a cleft appeared like Buddha's niche.
The swirling waters began to leave their wide expanse,
And narrow themselves into a deep abyss.
The winds bellowed through the cliffs,
And the clouds spewed forth from the caves.
Overhanging cliffs whistled in the high winds,
And twining vines glistened in resplendent green.
Bamboo groves stood over rocks, dripping with cold verdure,
And rhododendrons dotted the mountainside.
Falling cataracts spread a shower of snowy mist,
And strange rocks sped past like horses in fright.[9]

Heading upstream through the Gorges, the Yangzi junks had to traverse a succession of rapids. Teams of 70 to 80 men, hitched by lines to a single straining bamboo hawser, hauled them through each passage. Others swam in the water to clear the rope from submerged boulders. On board a drummer sent signals to the trackers on shore, indicating when to heave and when to cease pulling. A dozen more men stood ready to steer with the great bow-sweep. When the river was in flood trackers were also needed in the gorges between the rapids, using narrow tow-paths cut in the stone or projecting walk-ways. Fatal falls were not uncommon: nor was there any compensation for broken bones. Cornell Plant, who captained the first steamship to reach Chongqing and was known as 'the Grand Old Man of the Upper Yangzi', wrote in 1920 that the annual death-toll of boatmen was at least one thousand. What the crew and passengers feared most was a break in the tow-line. Hours of effort could be wasted as the boat was swept downstream and the boat itself would be lost unless the pilot quickly regained control. 'The Chinese say,' wrote Captain Plant, 'that one junk in ten is badly damaged, and one in twenty totally wrecked, each trip. This is certainly not an over-estimation.'[10]

Navigation downstream was even more dangerous especially in the high waters of the late summer. Minor accidents were less frequent, wrote Captain Plant, but 'total wreck was to be feared' from whirlpools or hidden rocks. A British naval commander described how the river was turned into a seething inferno of 'tumbling, tossing water, whirlpools, eddies, backwaters and sudden vertical "boils"'.[11] Isabella Bird recorded the sudden end of one unfortunate boat. 'I saw one big junk strike a rock while flying down a rapid and disappear as if she had been blown up, her large crew, at the height of violent effort the moment before, with all its frantic and noisy accompaniments, perishing with her'.[12]

Some protection was provided by the 'red boats', the lifeboats of the Upper Yangzi, which hovered at the most dangerous spots and maneouvred through the rapids and whirlpools to the rescue. Their boatmen were paid from public funds for each rescued person – sensibly at a higher rate for live than for dead bodies. Steamers offered more security than junks though there were still some spectacular crashes in the earlier years. After the People's Republic was established in 1949, the worst shoals and rapids were improved by blasting and dredging and the navigable width was widened in the narrowest places. Older systems of beacons and buoys were improved, and signal stations controlled navigation where one-way working was required. In 1958 Mao Zedong is said to have personally ordered the installation of electric signals allowing all-night traffic. In 1981 the newly constructed Gezhouba Dam at Yichang, by raising the minimum water level throughout the length of the Gorges, submerged more under-water obstacles.

By the 1960s almost all traffic had been motorised except for very small craft yet navigation remains hazardous even today. When the river is either low or in flood, there is still very little margin for error. The weather is notoriously fickle: gusts of wind, funnelled between the narrow gorge walls, can change conditions on the water within seconds. Multi-decked luxury tourist cruisers with romantic names from Chinese history convey the impression of complete safety. But when the gorges are filled with mist and rain, they edge and hoot their way as cautiously as any string of coal barges. There is no place for sentimentality about the constant struggle between boat-people and the Yangzi in the past in which so many have died, and there have been many changes for the better over the last century. We may regret the disappearance of the trackers and their songs, yet they led miserable and short lives. Those who live in the Gorges area are as concerned as those downstream in the central plain area that the Yangzi should be tamed. The argument is how to achieve it.

The great debate on the Three Gorges Project has been unique in the history of post-1949 China. First is its sheer length: the argument began in the early 1950s and has continued at intervals over four decades. Unlike other debates on economic policy which could only be perceived by reading between the lines of official speeches, this one was argued out openly in the early years. It re-emerged into the open in the late 1980s and was a contentious issue at two successive National People's Congresses (NPC). It attracted the largest number of negative votes ever recorded against government policy, and remained controversial even after formal approval. These features of the Three Gorges controversy are all the more striking because the project had been endorsed, at the very start of the debate, by Mao Zedong himself. Nor did he do so just in conversation or in a memorandum, but in the much more powerful form of – a poem!

On 19 February 1953 Mao boarded the navy cruiser 'Yangzi' to sail downstream from Wuhan to Nanjing. Standing beneath the cruiser's big gun on the foredeck, Mao questioned Lin Yishan, head of the River Conservancy Commission, on his plans for flood control, then moved to the bridge to spread a map on the chart table. Lin carefully explained the three-phase improvement proposal which the Commission had prepared: to strengthen the embankments in the river's middle and lower reaches; to reduce the scale of flooding by creating retention basins on the plains and in the lake region; and to construct a series of dams upstream on the river and its tributaries where their passage is narrowed by mountains. At this stage the proposal did not specify exact locations but it clearly favoured the 'multi-dam' approach. As Lin later recalled, Mao had a much simpler idea. Drawing a circle near the mouth of the Three Gorges, he asked: 'That's fine, but if you add all your reservoirs together, will they really match up to a big reservoir at the Three Gorges?' Whether Lin had really thought through the problem or was too easily led by Mao is unclear, but he replied without hesitation: 'They won't match it.' 'Then why not build a dam at the central mouth, and concentrate your forces in one campaign?' Mao asked with a triumphant flourish at the map. Though this was only the start of a protracted argument, Mao's intervention strongly tipped the balance of debate.[13]

A big dam in the Three Gorges had first been proposed by Sun Yat-sen, first president of the 1912 Republic, founder of the Nationalist Party, and an impassioned advocate of great schemes for China's 'national reconstruction'. In his 1919 Plan to Develop Industry, Sun envisaged a dam 'so that ships can sail upstream against the flow of the river, and the river can be harnessed for electric power'. In 1944 during the war against Japan a senior design engineer from the US Bureau of Reclamation, John L. Savage, was invited to investigate. This led to an agreement between the Bureau and the Chinese government on a joint design project. The work was interrupted by the civil war: it is not clear whether Mao was ever briefed about the US involvement. After the 1954 floods there was a new sense of urgency. In December Lin was summoned aboard Mao's special train near Wuhan to meet the Chairman again – the line had been cut by flood water for 100 days. He was questioned closely by Mao and Liu Shaoqi: Zhou Enlai, according to a later account by critics of the dam, remained silent. A team of Soviet experts was then invited to advise: a year later (according to a pro-Dam account) Zhou Enlai expressed his preference for the Three Gorges over another site proposed by the Russian engineers further upstream. Zhou's reputation continues to be wrestled over by the contending factions today in support of their respective cases.

Mao now took his first famous swim, or rather three swims, linking the three towns which make up the provincial capital of Wuhan. He had swum against the advice of his doctor, local officials and his chief bodyguard: this unfortunate man was sacked by Mao on the spot for having given his opinion without testing the water for himself! Mao's personal triumph over the forces of nature – for even at Wuhan there are dangerous whirlpools – could be seen as a metaphor for the larger struggle of the Chinese people to transform their environment. It also symbolised Mao's belief (not shared by all his colleagues) that risks should be taken and that progress on the road to socialism should be speeded up. It was after the third swim at Wuhan that Mao wrote his fateful poem which, critics of the dam contend, has ever since distorted the argument in favour of construction.

Swimming

I have just drunk the waters of Changsha,
And come to eat the fish of Wuchang;
Now I am swimming across the thousand-mile Yangzi,
Looking afar to the open sky of Chu.
I care not that the wind blows and the waves beat;
It is better than idly strolling in a courtyard.
Today I am free!
It was on a river that Confucius said:
'Here the whole of Nature flows by!'
Masts move in the river swell;
The Tortoise and Snake* are still.
Great plans are being made;
A bridge** will join north and south,
Turning the deep chasm into a thoroughfare;
Walls of stone will stand upstream to the west
To hold back Wushan's clouds and rain,
Till a smooth lake rises in the narrow gorges.
The mountain goddess if she is still there
Will marvel at a world so changed.

* names of two hills at Wuhan
** then being built at Wuhan

The editor of the magazine *Poetry* in which the poem appeared wrote that 'Swimming' expressed the spirit of the age – the spirit of the builders of socialism. 'Two simple, forceful statements, devoid of metaphor and hyperbole, reveal the essential spirit of the Chinese people since the liberation as they carry out their great plan to build socialism. And these are breath-taking plans. Not only have we bridged the Yangzi but a great dam is to be built in its upper reaches . . .' Even without this gloss, there could be no mistake about Mao's meaning. Whatever the difficulties, there should be a dam in the Three Gorges.[14]

In spite of Mao's endorsement, it took more than 35 years before the Three Gorges project was given a full-scale go-ahead in 1992. Mao himself, though committed to the grand concept, was cautious about its execution and took a close interest in technical problems. He had questioned Lin Yishan closely in December 1954 about the geological strata at the proposed site. Four years later Zhou Enlai personally conveyed a piece of extracted core to Mao to show that the foundations would be sound. This became known in water conservancy circles as the *fangxin shi* or 'Rest Assured Stone'! In 1969 Mao intervened on the side of further delay. This time he was concerned – at a time when China felt threatened simultaneously by both the US and the Soviet Union – that the dam would be vulnerable to a surprise air strike.

The unprecedented scale of the project also required an immense amount of technical preparation and investigation. The decision in 1970 to proceed first with the Gezhouba Dam above Yichang was partly reached in order to gain experience for the still larger project ahead. The height of the dam and consequently the size of the reservoir upstream and its effect upon existing sites of population was a particularly contentious variable. A range of heights was considered over the years from 150 to 210 metres. The hydrological features of the Gorges and the effect of the dam upon river flow at different times of year, upon siltation, rock stability and even climate all had to be studied. Expert opinion came from conflicting sources at different times. In the 1950s China had relied upon its Soviet 'big brothers'; in the 1960s and 1970s Chinese scientists and engineers worked alone; in the 1980s China turned to North American advice including that of the same US Bureau of Reclamation whose Chief Design Engineer had guided the wartime study.

A project of this size was also hostage to the broader state of health of the Chinese economy. Though the first outline decision to proceed was taken in March 1958, within two years the research team set to work had been cut from 200 to 40 members as the extent of the Great Leap disaster became clear. The plan was called a Golden Millet Dream – from the story of the poor scholar who dreamt he was a high official only to wake and find his pot of millet still cooking on the fire! Final agreement on the eventual site above Yichang at Sandouping was only reached in November 1979 – fully 20 years after the original outline decision – when the project was revived in the flush of China's new enthusiasm for economic modernisation after Mao Zedong's death. Full approval was expected at the 1985 session of the NPC, but this was aborted by concern over the 'overheating' of the Chinese economy which followed the first wave of modernisation.

Great projects which seek to regulate the flow of water – the most basic source of life with which the whole of Chinese history has been bound up since mythologoical times – arouse strong feelings and a determination to speak out even when it is politically unwise. There had also been bitter controversy over the earlier building of the Sanmenxia Dam on the Yellow River to plans devised by Soviet experts, which led to disastrous silting up. Expert critics of this scheme had to be recalled from political exile in the 1960s to oversee emergency remedial measures which involved cutting holes in the actual dam to sluice away the accumulated silt.

The Three Gorges debate raged at several levels, between

experts and officials in Beijing, between provinces with conflicting interests, between rival interest groups within the provinces. It began in 1956 in the pages of the professional magazines of the Ministries for Electric Power and Water Resources. Lin Yishan, now in charge of the Yangzi River Planning Office, published a 20,000 character essay setting out the merits of the Three Gorges Dam in the *Journal of Water Conservancy*. This provoked a series of ten critical rejoinders in the *Journal of Hydroelectric Power* edited by Li Rui, then a Vice-minister of the Ministry of Electric Power. Li was a former journalist and biographer of Mao who became his personal secretary for a short while in the late 1950s. The critics took advantage of the Hundred Flowers period when dissenting views were tolerated, calling the Three Gorges Project an example of unscientific 'subjectivism', and quoting Mao himself on the need for 'objective appraisal'. Their articles were even published in book form – Lin refused an invitation to include his own essay.[15]

This was the first of three clashes between Lin and Li in a quarter-century of argument. On the second occasion, in January 1958, they were summoned by Mao to make oral presentations before Party leaders at the high-level Nanning Conference. Both spoke with such eloquence that Mao is said to have commented: 'Glib talk doesn't solve anything. Go away and write it down!' They then accompanied Premier Zhou Enlai on a tour of the Yangzi after which a preliminary and cautious decision to proceed with the project was taken at the Chengdu Conference in March. Li Rui soon fell out of favour for his criticism of the Great Leap and spent the next 20 years doing menial jobs or manual labour with a short spell in prison. Lin survived, attempting in 1970 to promote the Three Gorges project ahead of the Gezhouba Dam. He tried again in the late 1970s with another long memorandum. Li Rui, just back from years of exile in the mountains, replied at once in their third clash. When the debate broke out once more in the late 1980s, Li became elder statesman to a new generation of radical critics. Lin in retirement no longer joined the argument but the project now had new powerful allies.

As industry boomed in the 1980s and power shortages grew, the dam's potential for power generation began to seem more attractive. In the 1950s the critics argued that it would produce *more* power than would possibly be needed. Now they could only cast doubt on its ability to produce *enough* power. The effectiveness of flood prevention measures undertaken with such enormous quantities of human effort in previous decades also began to be questioned. Nor could such an effort be easily repeated in the new less collective-minded economic climate of the post-Mao years. In 1985 an American consortium including the US Bureau of Reclamation proposed to the Chinese government a joint venture to build the dam. A year later, the official Canadian aid agency launched a feasibility study with backing from the World Bank. The pro-dam forces in China had now regrouped behind Li Peng, then a rising political star and a deputy minister of energy who headed the State Council's Three Gorges committee. The foreign experts recommended that the project be 'carried out at an early date' though favouring a relatively low dam height of 185 metres with a normal pool depth of 160 metres.

In the face of this formidable line-up, a new vocal opposition also emerged in the more relaxed political climate of the mid-1980s. The old campaigners led by Li Rui were joined by a new generation of Chinese intellectuals concerned equally by the lack of proper consultation and the effect on the environment. The Chinese People's Political Consultative Conference (CPPCC), set up in 1949 to represent non-Party opinion but silenced for many years, found its voice again in the more liberal atmosphere. A group of its members led by the veteran engineer Sun Yueqi visited the Gorges and produced a counter-report: 'The Three Gorges Project should not go ahead in the short term'. The March 1989 NPC was expected to approve the dam but one tenth of the delegates called for postponement. With signs of division in the top leadership, Yao Yilin, a senior member of the State Council, announced that no plans would be submitted now or for the next Five Year Plan (1991–95). Yao acknowledged that there were 'strong arguments' on both sides. 'I think now we can stop arguing about this project for a while,' he said. The great dam debate had reached stalemate. Then two months later the tanks moved into Tiananmen Square – on Li Peng's orders.

Sponsorship of the project now became part of Li Peng's efforts at image rebuilding after the Beijing Massacre though at first he claimed to be neutral. The dissenting journalist Dai Qing had edited a volume of essays attacking the dam. *Yangzi, Yangzi* was banned and Dai Qing was imprisoned for over a year, accused of 'instigating' the Tiananmen students. Two crusty Party elders from central China, Vice-president Wang Zhen (a native of Hunan) and CPPCC Vice-chairman Wang Renzhong (former Party secretary of Hubei) now called for the 'early and rapid launching' of the project. Wang Zhen denounced Li Rui as a Hunanese 'black sheep' and 'counter-revolutionary'. Government funds were spent freely to escort some 3,500 NPC members and other delegations to tour the Gorges and 'inspect' the plans. Anyone with 'bourgeois liberal tendencies' was excluded from participation. 'Every political leader has his own pet project,' a well-placed journalist in Beijing explained to me in 1993. 'Deng Xiaoping has the Special Economic Zones. Party Secretary Jiang Zemin has Shanghai. Premier Li Peng has the Three Gorges. We all know how the system works.'

Heaven now came to the aid of the pro-dam forces. The catastrophic 1991 floods in central China – though devastating the lower rather than the middle basin of the Yangzi –

refocused attention on the threat of future disaster. More than 1.1 million families were made homeless in nine provinces: by October nearly half a million were still unhoused. In Hubei alone, 177 were killed and 8,000 injured in the first half of July, while 26 million people were affected in 67 of the province's counties and towns. The national death toll was officially 1,700 but probably much higher. The pro-dam lobby seized on the 1991 flood as a clinching argument even though it had been most severe on the Huai river and further downstream on the Yangzi in Anhui province. A new NPC investigation team concluded that 'indecision over the Three Gorges Project was holding back the region', and claimed that those on the ground hoped it would be started 'at an early date'. In March 1992 heavy pressure was put on the NPC to approve the project and opposing views were suppressed: the sound system was turned off to silence one critic. The final vote on 3 April was 1,767 in favour, 177 against, 644 abstaining and 25 who did not participate. The number of abstentions indicated the depth of concern, but at the 1993 and 1994 NPCs the Three Gorges Project was not even placed on the agenda.[16]

After four decades of debate, the arguments for and against the Three Gorges Dam have long become familiar to both sides. The project's advocates have always maintained that its sheer size is a positive virtue. It is a 'great project, capable of producing enormous economic results of a comprehensive nature, promoting flood control, the generation of hydro-electricity, and navigation . . .', Li Boning, deputy minister of Water Resources and in charge of population resettlement at the Three Gorges, has claimed. Li and other supporters also invoke the authority of the late Chairman, urging that 'This grand project should be carried out as soon as possible, so that [Chairman Mao's] dream of A Smooth Lake Over the High Gorges can be realised in our generation!'

Opponents have argued instead that the venture is simply too large, and that priority should be given to small-scale projects that 'produce quicker economic results and which can improve flood control, electricity generation, and navigation within this century.' Sun Yueqi, the veteran geologist who invited the American expert John Savage to survey the Three Gorges in 1944, opposed the scheme five decades later when Sun himself was in his late nineties. 'The Yangzi,' he warned, 'is the most important river course [in China] for navigation.' If a decision was taken on undemocratic and unscientific grounds, then 'the laws of nature will mercilessly punish us, and we will have to pay even more dearly!'

Rival views on flood control are also sharply opposed. Supporters of the project point to the vulnerable situation of the Yangzi middle reaches below the Gorges. They insist that China should guard against the one-in-thousand year flood which could devastate the whole Yangzi basin. Even the one-in-hundred year flood would be a disaster. They remind the sceptics that there has not been a big flood since 1954: meanwhile the retention pools have filled with people and crops, and the dykes cannot be raised in height indefinitely. Only a dam with the projected capacity (up to 22 billion cubic metres) of this one could save the middle and lower reaches.

Its critics claim instead that the causes of flooding are too diverse to be solved by a single dam. As much of the danger comes from below the dam as from above. Would not the enormous investment be better spent – as Li Rui has argued since the mid 1950s – on smaller flood prevention schemes on the tributary rivers? At best the dam will only protect the Jingjiang section, while it is quite possible that by altering the pattern of water flow in normal times it will actually weaken the existing dykes.

The problem of sedimentation is now much better understood than in the 1950s, with the cautionary experience of the Aswan and other big dams. But supporters still argue that the build-up of silt above the dam can be dealt with by 'storing clean water and flushing out the muddy'. This is already done on the Yellow River's Sanmenxia Dam, where the water is lowered in the flood season to flush out the silt, and raised in the dry season to store fresh water. They admit that silt may build up as far as the main river trough at Chongqing, more than six hundred kilometres above the dam, but claim that most of this too can be dealt with by dredging.

Mention of Sanmenxia is seized upon by critics. This Soviet-designed project was a total disaster: flushing out the silt was a desperate improvisation which reduced the dam's output of electric power to one-fifth of the original design. It also interfered with navigation and flood control. They also argue that calculations of the amount of silt are too conservative, failing to reckon with the growing effects of soil erosion and deforestation. If 'flushing out' is ineffective and the reservoir fills up with silt, the dam will then have to be raised even higher, thus flooding yet more land and creating an even greater hazard if it is breached.

Power generation is a strong component in the argument deployed by the dam's supporters. The dam when complete will generate 17.68 million kilowatts, serving a large area downstream of central and eastern China. This is a fast-growing area of economic growth with severe power shortages. The dam will help China reduce its reliance on poor quality coal whose transport clogs the railways while its combustion pollutes the atmosphere. But opponents argue that it will take twelve years for the dam to begin to generate power, and twenty years before full operation. Better results could be achieved sooner, they claim, by building smaller power stations on the tributaries.

Improvement in navigation is also cited as a positive benefit. The new reservoir will raise water levels sufficiently to eliminate rapids and shallows as far as Chongqing, allowing

10,000-tonne ships to navigate above Yichang. But critics argue that the locks in the dam which have to lift ships more than 100 metres will cause technical problems, and that the change in levels required in different seasons for flood control will also complicate navigation.

In 1969 Mao ruled out an immediate start to the project because he feared it could be the target of a Soviet attack. In a more peaceful world environment, say the supporters, this problem of safety no longer applies. If there were renewed international tension, they say, there would be ample time to lower the water to a safe level because signs of preparation for war would be obvious. (One local official with whom I spoke insisted that there would always be 'a week's warning of nuclear war'!). The critics reply that no one can forecast the future. The dam could be wrecked by a surprise attack, by an earthquake or landslides upstream. Such a large dam is a lethal water-bomb for the millions downstream. Mao himself, they say, once warned that 'Wuhan should not carry a basin of water on her head!'

Abroad, most critical attention has been paid to the problem of large-scale resettlement. Supporters argue that China's methods of handling resettlement in other large projects have been approved by the World Bank. The people of the Three Gorges are said to have waited in uncertainty long enough: it is claimed that they want to start relocating so that they can achieve prosperity. The cost of relocation will be reimbursed by a levy on the electric power produced (although these funds will only become available later on). Further delay, they also argue, will only increase the numbers to be moved.

Critics question China's previous record of resettlement, saying that since Beijing is the World Bank's largest customer, there was good reason to present its performance in the best possible light. They point to the admitted fact that of those moved to make way for the Sanmenxia Dam, 200,000 still lived in poverty 30 years later. Yes, the Three Gorges zone has been deliberately starved of investment for decades so that people will be desperate to move. But arable land will be severely reduced by the extent of the reservoir; new industry in this mountain area can never provide enough jobs. Tourism and the environment will also suffer.[16]

Finally, it is argued, the Chinese government simply cannot be relied on to provide objective information on such a contentious project, and it has a dreadful record of suppressing information on manmade disasters. In 1995 the Hong Kong-based organisation Human Rights Watch/Asia unearthed convincing evidence of two massive dam disasters in Henan province in 1975. The collapse of the Banqiao and Shimantan dams resulted in the loss, according to official figures in restricted publications, of at least thirty and perhaps as many as eighty-five thousand local people caught in the flood. Thousands more died later from epidemics and famine. Yet government arguments in favour of the Three Gorges dam have avoided even a passing reference to these catastrophes.[17]

The dam will dislodge at least 900,000 people now living on the side of the Gorges and further upstream. The numbers given by Beijing are imprecise: in 1994 the Chinese authorities were still quoting figures compiled in 1985. Then it was estimated that 725,500 would have to be moved, and that by the year 2008, when the dam was originally scheduled for completion, the total would have increased to 1.13 million. Delays in starting the project mean that these figures must be revised upwards: by 1994 the population had already risen to close to 902,000, so that the eventual total would approach 1.4 million. Defenders of the project argue that since 1949 more than ten million Chinese have been resettled in the building of over 8,000 dams, though they do not dispute that the dislocation caused by this project will be on a far larger scale. They also argue that about half the total to be relocated are peasants, scattered in small communities or individual farms on poor and marginal land. Those who cannot be moved 'up the hillside' (impossible in most cases for lack of cultivable soil at higher levels) will be found new employment in the towns, which themselves will in many cases be rebuilt on higher sites.

These advocates make light of rural traditions and affection for the land which, they say, have been much diminished in recent times. The result of resettlement, it is argued, will be to turn hundreds of thousands of peasants into urban wage-earners, which is exactly what most peasants want to do anyhow. Official advocates in Hubei province have produced a clinching argument for their own people. Because most of the resettlement will occur above the Second Gorge, this will affect Sichuan province far more than Hubei. Of the eventual 1.13 million to be moved (on the 1985 estimate), only 15.5 per cent – 175,000 – will belong to Hubei! This argument is not usually put forward in the presence of representatives from Sichuan.

In April 1993 a local government official in Wushan, the first town in Sichuan, gave me his much more sceptical view of the resettlement task ahead in carefully chosen but revealing words:

> Of course we have to do our job; we must carry out the instructions of the higher authorities. No one will have any objection if after resettlement they can receive a better house than before or a better job than before. If the plans are carried out as intended, then no one will complain. People are no longer so attached to their own piece of land as they used to be, and many of the younger people have moved to the towns looking for work anyhow. But it will be very difficult.
>
> This town has a population of 21,000. The plan is to expand it to 80,000 on a higher location: 800 million rmb have already been assigned. Part of the increased population will come from relocated peasants with

nowhere else to go, and the rest from mobile workers who will build the new town and then stay on. I already have 28 factories to relocate when the new Wushan is built. How shall we provide additional factories for the extra labour force? This whole region suffers from poor resources and communications. It is not clear how we shall attract enough investment.

If you move people up the slope when the water level rises, you cannot necessarily find any land for them.

If you move people into the towns, you cannot necessarily find any jobs for them.

We hope that the project will be successful, but we cannot necessarily exclude that we may have to make a sacrifice.

The official's three 'cannots' are echoed on the banks of the Gorges by ordinary residents with an air of resignation. The town of Zigui, 45 kilometres downstream in Hubei, is no longer the 'picturesque town' with fine gardens and lofty pagodas described by Isabella Bird and other 19th Century travellers, but it is still 'nobly situated' above the First Gorge. The temple of Qu Yuan (died c. 280 BC), the first Chinese poet to be identified by name, dominates the small town. Zigui will disappear entirely: the new water level will reach the temple steps. The town is to be moved 60 kilometres further downstream close to the site of the Three Gorges dam. It will be completely divorced from the temple which only moves 30 kilometres downstream to an isolated location, where it will exist solely as a tourist attraction.

Qu Yuan was the loyal minister of the State of Chu, falsely betrayed by enemies at court in league with the rival State of Qin. He committed suicide by drowning himself in protest. His death is the origin of the Dragon Boat Festival which, it is said, commemorates the search for his body by boat. Would he drown himself once more today in protest at the new dam? The local boatmen laugh when questioned.

'Qu Yuan couldn't do anything about it, neither can we,

so what's the point of protest? What they order above, we just have to carry out.'

Those with highest hopes of the Three Gorges Dam live below it in the Yangzi middle plain, particularly in the section known as the Jingjiang whose safety affects millions of lives in Hubei and Hunan. From Jicheng (where the Second North–South Trunk Line crosses the Yangzi) to Chenglingji, where the river touches Hunan and turns sharply north towards Wuhan, is 337 winding kilometres. The Jingjiang Great Dyke, first raised in the Ming dynasty, takes a straighter line over 182 kilometres. It directly protects 16,000 square kilometres of land on the north (left-hand) bank of the Yangzi and a population of eight million. On the south bank, opposite Shashi City, lies the great Jingjiang Flood Diversion Project completed on Mao's instructions in 1954. This vast hollow, scooped out and protected by dykes, into which flood waters can be diverted and stored, is in its way as impressive a monument to human endeavour as the Great Wall. But by the early 1990s doubts were growing as to whether the whole Jingjiang scheme could still withstand the now long overdue 'one-in-twenty-years' flood.

The Great Dyke was designed to cope with flows of up to 60,000 cubic metres a second while the Diversion Project could safely dispose of a further 20,000. Some of the water would also be led through other channels into the Dongting Lake across the Hunanese border. Over seven million people are protected by the south (right-hand) bank of the Jingjiang section of whom half a million actually live within the main diversion area and in several smaller ones. The Dongting Lake itself has always served as a vast natural retention basin for flood waters which enter every year by the main channel at Chenglingji, but its capacity has been steadily reduced by the deposit of silt which now reaches nearly 100 million cubic metres a year. The lake's water surface has shrunk by 40 per cent since 1949, creating new areas of reclaimed land which then also become vulnerable to flood. Another eight million people live in the Dongting area. Altogether 23 million (more than two per cent of the Chinese population) are therefore directly protected by the Jingjiang flood control scheme, without counting the inhabitants of Shashi, Wuhan and other vulnerable population centres further downstream.

The collective spirit which infused the heroic efforts of the 1950s has waned in more recent times, weakening the effectiveness of the existing flood prevention measures. The efforts of the flood-fighters in 1991 were officially described as 'a glorious chapter in the history of socialist water control', but the full story revealed a less glorious side. Throughout central China the floods had left 1.13 million homeless in nine provinces. By October nearly half a million were still unhoused; many more were living in what were described as 'makeshift shacks'.

Flood control had suffered in the more individualistic social climate of the Deng Xiaoping era. One official admitted that the 1991 floods were 'a man-made as well as a natural disaster ... The management of irrigation has been very much neglected over the years. The rivers have not been cleared of obstacles while flood control and prevention work has been less than vigorous'. The Hubei Party Secretary Guan Guangfu warned of 'slack attitudes' and said it was 'a political as well as an economic struggle'. The State Councillor Chen Junsheng listed Hubei's problems: 'food, shelter, disease prevention, medical care ... [and] to prevent people from dying from hunger, fleeing from famine, or begging for food and money in large numbers'. There were stories of looting, rape and armed fighting. Common adversity was no longer shared. The decline of collective agriculture meant that flood diversion helped the interests of some farmers while damaging those of others. In the single month of July 1991 the Hubei police stopped '176 fights with lethal weapons and mediated 399 disputes over flood water discharge'.

On a warm summer's day it is hard to imagine the threat posed by the Yangzi to the population on the banks of the middle plain. Buffaloes graze on the well-cropped sides of the broad dyke protecting the Jingjiang Diversion Basin. Wide enough for two cars to pass, its bends are protected by screes of massive stone. The basin is 90 kilometres in length with a circumference of 208 kilometres and an area of 921 square kilometres. On the river side, a considerable stretch of land has been reclaimed from silt deposited since the 1954 flood. A 1,000 metre long sluice at the north-western corner, never opened since 1954, is the key to the whole project. In 1988 it was discovered to be badly cracked and has since been reinforced, with new electric hoists to raise the 54 separate sluice gates. Inland the land is now densely inhabited – a further problem if it needs to be used for the diversion of flood water. The population has increased from 100,000 (a feasible number to move to special safety zones on the perimeter) to a much less tractable 400,000. 'Everyone has been issued with life jackets,' local officials say hopefully. 'Some of the houses have more than one storey, and some can even float!' Here and all along the Jingjiang section of the Yangzi, everyone looks forward eagerly to the construction of the Three Gorges Dam. When it is built, they confidently believe, the threat of a one-in-twenty-years flood will be reduced at last to that of one-in-hundred. The effects on those living upstream is not their concern, and arguments that new patterns of water flow will actually threaten the dykes which now protect them are dismissed.

No one can deny that China still faces a recurring threat of natural disaster which even in normal years still causes unacceptable death and damage. There was heavy flooding in the four years preceding the 1991 disaster. In 1988 the suffering in central China began with a severe drought which reduced the water flow by one-fifth and destroyed 30 million acres of crops. When the rain finally came, eleven inches fell daily for more than three weeks. More than 1,600 people died across China from flooding in that year; in 1989, nearly 3,000; in 1990, more than 2,000; in 1991, 6,600. Hubei was then hit by drought in 1992: 50 days without rain threatened half of its grain producing land. In 1993 more than a 1,000 people were killed nationally by summer floods. In 1994 the floods began early in June, devastating three southern provinces and killing several hundred before the summer was over.

Every new flood – or drought – strengthens opinion in favour of radical water conservancy projects such as the Three Gorges Dam. From pre-history to the present day, the integrity of the Chinese state has depended on the maintenance of effective irrigation. China's first water engineer was the Emperor Yu who has attracted more stories and legends than any other mythical figure. Yu, it was said, journeyed over fifty rivers and numerous mountains to tame the floods. He laboured so hard that for ten years he did not visit his home and no nails grew on his hands. The chronicles relate that 'Yu exhausted his strength in cutting dykes and ditches and in conducting the courses of rivers and levelling mounds'. In historical times the expansion of China southwards was dependent on the great water works of the seventh century AD which developed the Grand Canal and linked the Yellow River to the Yangzi. Historians have called China's system of government a hydraulic bureaucracy whose character was defined by the management and control of large-scale water works. Today the image of 'harnessing the waters' still has a powerful appeal.

Those most immediately affected are not so easily convinced. In summer 1994 townspeople in Wanxian (Sichuan), above the First Gorge, demonstrated against the diversion of resettlement funds by local bureaucrats, and security officials warned that more trouble should be expected:

> The difficulty in meeting [expectations] is spawning outrage among resettlers towards the government, resulting in resistance to resettlement and interference with the construction of the Three Gorges Project. In many cases, the dissatisfaction of resettlers combined with instigation by troublemakers will undoubtedly cause chaotic incidents such as sit-ins, demonstrations, petitions and even criminal acts including beating, smashing, looting, ransacking and kidnapping . . .[18]

This report from Wanxian's public security bureau forecasts growing tension between resettlers and local residents in mountainous terrain which is already overpopulated. Its only solution is to recommend a crack-down on organised crime and a 'swifter and heavier punishment policy, especially against any conspiracies aimed at disturbing the construction of the Three Gorges dam'. This is hardly the consultative approach which Beijing claims to have promoted. In reality, the big dam belongs to an age of revolutionary optimism and social discipline when grand schemes were more easily implemented either because they were genuinely accepted or because the Party could enforce its will. Today, in a less collectively minded society which still lacks the means to negotiate popular assent, opposition festers until it boils over. The Big Dam, in the next decade of construction, will certainly lead to much bigger problems.

V

A Tale of Two Cities

HUBEI

Since 1985, the environment in Chinese cities has been improved to some extent. However, urban residents still suffer from severe atmospheric, water, garbage and noise pollution. Infrastructure facilities, including coal and gas supplies, water supplies, drainage networks and waste treatment should be improved. Traffic conditions must be upgraded and green space enlarged. Communications between cities must also be improved.

(National Urban Environment Conference report, 1991)

It is still a novel experience to travel on a Chinese motorway. The government of Hubei, like that of every other self-respecting province, is intent on building a new network and in 1994 the first section of a new motorway was opened between Wuhan and Shashi, halving the journey time between these two cities on the Yangzi. Eventually the road will extend westwards through Yichang at the foot of The Three Gorges, and then cross the border to reach Chengdu, deep in western Sichuan. The Chinese for motorway is High Speed Road: soon after the opening there were already numerous burnt-out engines and collapsed axles where excited drivers had taken its meaning too literally. In one respect it is like all other Chinese roads. At five kilometre intervals a road sweeper steers the dust with his brushwood broom into the central reservation from which it billows back. His bike is parked hazardously on the hard shoulder, though he does wear a reflective yellow jacket.

Two lanes wide on each side, the motorway has been driven straight across the peasants' fields on a raised embankment safe from the Yangzi flood. Though compensation was paid, the larger part went not to the individual farmer who farmed the land but to the local People's Government responsible for its management. The county town where the motorway begins (it has not yet reached Shashi) has built a palace for its government headquarters, with six storeys, Chinese-tiled roofs and flanking pavilions – all no doubt with the proceeds of compensation. On either side of the motorway rice seedlings were being planted out as I headed towards Wuhan on a late spring morning in a new Japanese-made minibus. Water buffaloes turned the thick paddy with straining effort; peasants ran along the narrow dykes between, manure buckets on their carrying-poles, taking very short steps to avoid spillage. Sometimes they had to clamber across the motorway to reach land on the far side. Scenes such as these give ample reason to reflect on the widening gap between 'town and countryside'.

Arriving in Wuhan I bought that same evening a copy of the provincial *Hubei Daily*. In Zhijiang county (just north of Shashi), it reported, peasants had been forced to sell grain at a fixed price while the free market remained closed. They were caught in the classic 'scissors' as the costs of fertiliser and insecticide, essential for agriculture, rose faster than the price for their crops. They complained bitterly that they had been 'mahjonged' by inflation – referring to the end of the mahjong game when the winning hand is disclosed and everyone else loses.[1] Two weeks later the provincial government in Wuhan published a 47-article set of new regulations on 'lightening the peasants' burden'. The fact that these replaced similar regulations set eight years before could not have inspired much confidence among the peasants alongside the motorway. Dozens of illegal practices still being used by corrupt cadres to extort money were listed in the document. The following examples were given in just one paragraph of one of its clauses: 'Illegally extorting charges from, raising funds among, imposing fines on, confiscating goods from and apportioning expenses among peasants; forcing peasants to join insurance programmes, accept paid services, or buy valuable securities, materials, commodities, newspapers, periodicals or books'. Other reports have linked the peasants' plight to the problems of urban industry. Because of the recession in Hubei's textile mills, in 1992 the state was only able to pay cash for 30 per cent of the cotton which it purchased. Two years later there was a cotton shortage as the market picked up, too late for peasant producers who had shifted to crops they could sell privately.[2]

The 'triple city' of Wuhan, astride the Yangzi and the main north-south railway, has been on the map of modern China for the past century and a half. With a population today of eight and a half million, it is poised for further expansion yet burdened by loss-making industry, unemployment, over-crowding and chronic dilapidation. These problems are all typical of China's older urban fabric. A day's slow voyage up the Yangzi, the city of Shashi has a longer history. The walled town of Jingzhou, five kilometres inland from Shashi, dates back two millenia: Shashi, with a matching population now of 300,000, was once its riverside suburb. Nearly everyone who travels through central China has to pass through Wuhan, seeking to avoid stopping in the summer months when it is known as the 'furnace of China'. Everyone travelling on the Yangzi will pass by Shashi but often without being aware of it. Until recent modern construction, most of the town could hardly be seen behind and below its great river wall.

Hubei, with its rich agricultural resources and strategic location, has more towns (20 at the latest count) than any other province except Shandong and – across the Yangzi – Hunan. Both Shashi and Wuhan were chosen in the late 1980s as 'trail-blazers' for experiments in urban reform which sought to reduce political involvement in economic activity. In 1994 Wuhan became the third 'pioneer city', after Chengdu and Guangzhou, to attempt an even more radical reform: the slimming-down and transformation of state-owned industry. This means not just cutting losses but depriving people of their jobs, and it quickly led to serious industrial unrest.

Both cities are a magnet for migration from rural Hubei, and suck up investment funds of which the countryside is starved. It is urban Hubei which will benefit most from the new source of hydroelectric power when the Three Gorges Dam comes on stream. In 1990 Shashi was identified as one of only 36 Chinese towns with a 'medium' standard of living, together with two other towns in Hubei: these were Yichang at the mouth of the Three Gorges, which doubled in size while the Gezhouba Dam was being built, and Shiyan, a new town in the north-west built in the 1970s when industry was being relocated inland. Wuhan was also listed in 1990 as ranking eighth in the whole of China for its provision of urban infrastructural resources. The casual visitor to both towns would be surprised by these official claims: most of urban China makes a dusty and often dismal impression. But Shashi has a more dynamic atmosphere and is less burdened by past infrastructural neglect: it belongs to what is now called the 'second tier' of expanding urban China. China's urban future lies much more with these new, expanding medium-sized towns than with the vast dilapidated giants of Wuhan and similar provincial capitals.

*　　*　　*

The strategic location of the three cities of Wuhan (Hankou, Hanyang and Wuchang) was already evident during the Taiping Rebellion when they were taken and retaken six times in four years (1853–6). The western powers, anxious to move inland from the coastal ports to which they had been confined by the Treaty of Nanking (1842), demanded after the second Anglo-Chinese War (1858–61) that Hankou become a 'treaty port'. Britain, Russia, France, Germany and Japan secured concessions on the banks of the Yangzi where it joined by the Han river. The river embankment or 'Bund' with its foreign banks, businesses and warehouses, solidly built with porticoes and tiled roofs in the European style, extended nearly five miles by the early 20th Century, as famous in its time as the Bund of Shanghai. Large steamers reached Hankou from April to November when the river was at its highest. Tea was at first the staple export, shipped directly to the tea markets of London and Odessa. Other products of the rich central plains – hides, wood and vegetable oils, seeds, cotton, tobacco, bean-cake and more exotic items such as musk and fungus – generated total exports of nearly £10 million in 1907. As central China's greatest trading centre, Hankou was called the 'Chicago of the East', though its appeal was marred by temperatures reaching over 40 degrees centigrade in the summer heat.[3]

Wuhan's governor-general, Zhang Zhidong, one of the new generation of provincial officials in the late 19th Century who sought to counter Western aggression by modernising China, established the country's first steel-making plant in 1890. Zhang also established a naval force on the Yangzi and built China's first steamers. Wuhan soon acquired an arsenal, cotton mills, and other modern industries. The railway north to Peking was opened in 1906; work on the extension south to Canton began six years later. Largely funded by Chinese capital, Wuhan seemed destined to rival Western-dominated Shanghai and Japan-dominated

Manchuria as a future industrial heartland. The Chinese revolutionaries seeking to overthrow the Manchu dynasty, after years of frustrated efforts in the south, also chose the Yangzi valley as a more promising centre. Their underground work within the province-based 'new armies' succeeded in the Wuchang Uprising of 10 October 1911. Changsha, capital of Hunan, was the first to follow in declaring independence. Wuchang experienced some of the worst fighting in the last struggle of the Manchus which followed: it might otherwise have become the first capital of the new Republic. Nanjing, capital of Jiangsu province on the lower Yangzi, was chosen instead.

Wuhan's strategic position became a liability rather than an asset as post-imperial China succumbed to three decades of internal warlord fighting and war with Japan. Hubei fell very early on into the hands of Wang Zhanyuan, an incompetent leader even by warlord standards who was intensely hated by the people. A movement in the early 1920s for provincial self-government led instead to intervention by the rival Anhui and Zhili warlord cliques. In 1927 the success of the Nationalist revolutionary army in liberating Wuhan from warlord rule was the turning-point in its drive to unify China. This time Wuhan did become briefly the new revolutionary capital, seat of a new government seeking to maintain the 'united front' between Communists and Nationalists. But Chiang Kai-shek secured his road to personal power by a bloody purge of the left in Shanghai, ignoring the Wuhan government which eventually submitted to the right-wing Nationalists and conducted its own anti-left purge. Once again the new capital was established in Nanjing. Wuhan's industrial dreams also evaporated. The Hanyeping iron and steel complex collapsed in 1925, after ceasing to make steel at all and only managing to produce one-third of its previous iron output.

Wuhan's third brief chance to occupy a central political

position came in the winter of 1937–38, but only because the Nationalist government was in retreat from Japan. Once more the effort was bold but brief-lived, with the Communists and Nationalists again making common cause. Looking back on this period after the second 'united front' had broken down, two US journalists wrote of Hankou in the winter of 1937–38 as a 'miracle in China':

> The seat of government was transferred to the upriver port of Hankow, 800 miles from the sea, and the most complete unity of spirit and motive that China had ever known existed there for a few months. The Hankow spirit could never be quite precisely defined by those who experienced it there and then. All China was on the move – drifting back from the coast into the interior and swirling in confusion about the temporary capital ... In Hankow the government and the Communists sat in common council, made common plans for the prosecution of the war ...
>
> The élite of China's writers, engineers, and journalists converged on Hankow to sew together the frayed strands of resistance. By spring of 1938, when the Japanese resumed the campaign, with Hankow as their ultimate objective, the new armies and the new spirit had crystallised.[4]

W. H. Auden and Christopher Isherwood, the left-wing English poet and writer team, caught the 'Hankow spirit' while it lasted in 1938 in their *Journey to a War*. 'This is the real capital of war-time China,' wrote Isherwood, observing that everyone was in town, from missionaries to spies, from Chiang Kai-shek to Zhou Enlai. 'Hidden here are all the clues which would enable an expert, if he could only find them, to predict the events of the next 50 years. History, grown weary of Shanghai, bored with Barcelona, has refixed her capricious interest upon Hankow. But where is she staying?' It was a prescient question – who would win eventually, the

Nationalists, or Japan, or the Communists? – but without an answer. On surer ground, Auden in his sonnet 'A Major Port' caught the misery, the uncertainty and the fragile hope of Hankou as it existed then.

> No guidance can be found in ancient lore:
> Banks jostle in the sun for domination,
> Behind them stretch like sorry vegetation
> The low recessive houses of the poor.
>
> We have no destiny assigned us,
> No data but our bodies: we plan
> To better ourselves; bleak hospitals alone remind us
> Of the equality of man.
>
> Children are really loved here, even by police:
> They speak of years before the big were lonely.
> Here will be no recurrence.
>
> Only
> The brass-bands throbbing in the parks foretell
> Some future reign of happiness and peace.
> We learn to pity and rebel.[5]

The Japanese entered Hankou on 25 October 1938. Two days before, the 18-ton turbine of the Hankou power plant had been inched on board a steamer and transported west towards Sichuan where whatever could be salvaged from Wuhan's industrial base had already been sent. At Yichang the turbine was offloaded onto pontoons, which were then lashed to pairs of steamers and painfully carried through the rapids of the Three Gorges. A textile mill from Shanghai, taking the same route, was packaged onto no less than 380 native junks. Though 120 of them sank in the Gorges, the junkmen raised all but 21 and eventually reached Chongqing.[6]

By 1949, Wuhan had still not recovered from the loss of most of its industry: what survived was mostly small-scale and inefficient. In machine and ship building, there were more than 140 firms sharing a labour force of only 11,000. The province as a whole had suffered badly from war and flooding. Eighty per cent of all Hubei industry was located in Wuhan, and 90 per cent of this was in textiles and light industry.[7]

The communist planners now revived the half-century old vision of Wuhan as an industrial centre to rival Shanghai and Manchuria. It was chosen from 22 alternative proposed sites in central-south China. By the late 1950s three massive projects had been completed in the new industrial suburb of Qingshan with Soviet aid: the Wuhan Iron and Steel Company (Wugang), the Qingshan Thermoelectric Plant, and the Wuhan Heavy Machine Tool Factory. The first bridge anywhere along the Yangzi was completed in 1958. To visitors like the veteran US journalist Edgar Snow, who remembered Wuhan's squalor and exploitation of the 1930s, a new socialist paradise seemed to be taking shape. Nothing was 'more pleasing to an Old China Hand', wrote Snow, than the new rail-road bridge across the Han and Yangzi rivers. At the iron and steel plant, he admired the 'large blocks of well-spaced three-storey apartments', the schools, sports facilities, lake-side rest-homes and the 'graceful ultramodern structures' of Wuhan's two main hospitals. The celebrated Chinese opera singer Mei Lanfang had even performed in the workers' club![8]

The Wugang complex, with seven main and six auxiliary plants built with Soviet aid and engineers, was China's biggest post-Liberation project, designed to shift the industrial balance inland and revitalise the central region. By the late 1950s one in five of Wuhan's growing population were building workers and their family members who had migrated from elsewhere.[9] But the focus of economic investment shifted in the 1960s and 1970s further inland to the north and north-west of the province, as national strategic thinking favoured the relocation of industry in more remote areas. Shiyan in north-west Hubei, on the newly completed railway line to Sichuan, was designated in 1969 to become home to the Second Automobile Works, China's largest truck manufacturer. The first workers had to live with peasant families while new homes were being built in the rice paddy fields. By 1990, Shiyan had become a city of 378,000 people producing 135,000 trucks yearly, one quarter of the national output, but it still had the feeling of a frontier town. A visiting US journalist reported on the contrast between urban and rural life:

> The city has shown off its affluence by building an 800,000 renminbi (US$170,000) musically synchronised fountain that provides residents with a colourful water symphony every weekend . . .
>
> But poverty still clings tenaciously to the mountainsides of Shiyan. Beyond the drab, functional apartments for factory workers, farmers hack away at tiny vegetable patches next to their crumbling brick and mud one-room homes . . .
>
> Mule- and man-pulled carts carry produce and supplies, and the few traffic lights in the self-designated Motor City of China are turned off.
>
> Street lights on one main avenue are also blacked out, and couples stroll down the middle of the moonlit street. Outside the city limits, the road quickly deteriorates into potholes and construction sites where young boys chip away at mountainsides with pick-axes.[10]

Wuhan's early advantage as an industrial centre had turned against it in the 1960s and 1970s: new investment went elsewhere while its own infrastructure declined. Many of Wuhan's more than four thousand industries became heavily polluted and uneconomic. Though Wuhan was chosen by Beijing in the 1980s to be a pioneer of the new reforms, the impetus soon petered out. Wuhan officials called this 'getting up early but going to bed late'.[11] Wuhan was quickly outstripped by the coastal cities and Special Economic Zones. By the end of the decade its foreign trade volume was only one-quarter of one per cent of the national total.[12] Until 1984, Wuhan was also inhibited by having to defer to the provincial Hubei government on many important decisions. It then acquired more freedom through the 'single planning city system' which made the city directly responsible to Beijing – though the province protested against its loss of control. At issue was a serious question of policy: how far should the provincial metropolis, recipient of many past advantages from the state and indirectly from the fruits of peasant labour, contribute to the development of the province as a whole? An official of the Wuhan Municipal Planning Committee explained the problem (from the city's point of view):

> Before 1984 the provincial government put a heavy financial burden on us; our targets for budgetary income were hard to meet, so we always had a deficit, e.g. in 1984, we had a budget deficit of 80 million renminbi; e.g. the monthly transportation fees for vehicles went to the province and the provincial government never invested a cent in the building of roads etc. We called this *shoufei bushou* [draw out our fat, add to our thinness], a kind of egalitarianism since they used these funds to build up the whole province. Of course, the provincial government thought this was reasonable, and we went along (we did not give any income directly to the centre [Beijing]; the province was responsible for this). Before 1984, Wuhan provided about 80 per cent of the total budgetary income of the province.[13]

Once it acquired independence from the province, Wuhan also acquired a direct tax burden towards the central government, second in quantity only to that of Shanghai. In 1992, Wuhan paid the equivalent of over half a billion US dollars in taxes to Beijing. But the relationship with

Beijing eventually paid off with renewed encouragement to 'open up' Wuhán's economy. Deng Xiaoping's policy of the 'Three Alongs' (developing economic hubs along China's borders, along the coast and along the Yangzi River), gave Wuhan its chance. When the city finally got the go-ahead for expansion in 1992, this was closely linked to Beijing's adoption of the Three Gorges Project. The project, if and when successful, would also favour the city more than the province. Wuhan's industry would benefit most of all from the cheap power and the improved river transportation. The province would also enjoy these benefits but to a lesser degree, while it would have to fund its other flood prevention works without central financing.

Was Wuhan finally, in the early 1990s, about to recapture the role it had enjoyed nearly a century ago as one of China's principal ports open to the outside world? Zhao Baojiang, who became the city's planning director in 1980 and mayor in 1987, certainly believed so. He even revived the old treaty port comparison: Wuhan, he said, would once again become 'the Chicago of China'. He hoped to tempt foreign investors with two powerful arguments. First, coastal China was becoming both too crowded and too expensive. Wuhan could offer wages at one third the rate in the Shenzhen Special Economic Zone. Second, by developing industry in Wuhan, the foreign investor would leap-frog into central China, 1,200 kilometres inland from the coast and with potential new markets not only in Hubei but in the adjacent provinces.[14]

In a China where no new economic policy could be judged successful unless it attracted support from Hong Kong, two of the territory's tycoons quickly obliged. The more flamboyant of the two was Peter Woo, chairman of Wharf Holdings, son-in-law and successor to the late shipping magnate Y. K. Pao. The official Chinese news agency quoted his declaration that 'Whoever grasps Wuhan controls an important chain in the economy of central China and all China'. Mr Woo spread the message at business seminars in Asia, Europe and the US. Wuhan was on the way to becoming not just the Chicago of China but the Dallas as well![15]

> The key commercial, industrial and educational centre of Wuhan forms the third leg of the Economic Tripod [with Hong Kong and Shanghai]. Traditionally the 'crossroads to nine provinces', Wuhan lies on China's economic axes, with major rail systems running north and south, and transport along the Yangzi to the east and the west ... This is China's future transportation hub, and relying on Wharf's infrastructural strength, we are developing a major inland port driven by a mega-containerisation centre. Containers will take the vast industrial output of Wuhan by rail shuttle to the port of Hong Kong, and along the river to the east coast ports. We are upgrading Wuhan's light rail passenger system, and seizing property development opportunities ...[16]

Wharf's proposed container port was located at Yangluo below Wuhan, where it also planned to invest in a new power plant. The port was linked to a grand design for freight traffic along the entire navigable length of the Yangzi. Motorised barges would move goods from Chongqing downstream to this 'mega-containerisation centre' at Wuhan, for transshipment to a fleet of river freighters which would shuttle down the river to the coast and then to the port of Ningbo (home-place of Y. K. Pao). Plans for this Yangzi River Shipping Link did not mention the Three Gorges Project but depended on the improved navigation it was supposed to provide upstream.

The planned light railway in Hankou arose from a smart piece of personal observation by Mr Woo. The old railway line through the city was only used for freight traffic after a splendid new station had been built with a separate rail link. Wharf now proposed to take over the virtually disused line, construct a badly needed overhead light railway – and exploit the property potential beneath the tracks along its entire 9.2 kilometre length. Mayor Zhao was delighted: Peter Woo was 'a visionary', he enthused – before adding defensively 'If Wharf had not come along, we would have gone ahead with the same plan, only more slowly'.[17]

Within a year, another Hong Kong conglomerate claimed to have discovered Wuhan's potential. Cheng Yu-tong, chairman of the New World Development Company, announced his intention of investing more than five billion US dollars over the next five years. Mr Cheng, who made his fortune in the diamond and jewellery business before moving into Hong Kong real estate, was ranked among the five richest men in Hong Kong. 'I feel very honoured to have the opportunity to develop the country,' he explained. Most of the money would go into infrastructural development, particularly in transport, including money for the new airport, an expressway to it, no less than three bridges across the Yangzi, and an 86 kilometre ring-road. Just how New World would get an adequate return on these investments, if they ever came to fruition, was not explained.[18]

Ambitious schemes of this kind for investment in China tend to become more modest as the practical difficulties emerge. A Wharf real estate project went ahead: Wuhan Times Square, with its 'four office and residential towers on a four storey retail podium' was a self-contained site project in the highly visible Hong Kong style much favoured by Chinese city governments. But by 1994 projected costs of the light railway project had risen dramatically, while the ability of Wuhan city to find its own share of the funding was in question. 'The problem is not with their sincerity in wanting to go ahead,' explained a Wharf official, 'it is with their cash ability.' Its viability now depended entirely on whether the associated property development would pay. A second difficulty, particularly affecting the harbour and the Yangzi navigation project, was the multitude of Chinese authorities whose approval was first required. River transport and ports came under the Ministry of Communications, but approval was also needed from the authorities of the four provinces, plus Shanghai, through which the river flowed from Chongqing to the sea. In addition, the project would have to go for final approval to the State Planning Commission and the Premier's office.[19] Mr Woo admitted that 'the question is where the capital is coming from'. By the end of 1994, Wharf was said to have 'quietly backed away' from most of its infrastructure projects in Wuhan, while its main China investment was now concentrated in the safer coastal cities of Shanghai and Guangzhou. Talk of Wuhan as the Chicago of the East provoked more laughter than admiration.[20]

Wuhan's Great Leap onto the multi-coloured pages of brochures of Hong Kong conglomerates has left the grey reality of everyday city life far behind. These grandiose plans, adopted piecemeal by the Wuhan authorities, have done little to tackle the sheer decrepitude of the urban infrastructure, the overcrowding made worse by peasant immigration, and rising unemployment as the massive state industries set up in the 1950s now seek to survive. Along the Bund in Hankou, plans are now being made to follow Shanghai's example and seek foreign buyers for the magnificent, but dilapidated, mansions from the treaty port era. (Though overseas interest is discouraged by the unrealistically high prices being asked. Wuhan, after all, is *not* Shanghai.) Behind the Bund in the old streets of Hankou, lighting at night still consists of a few lonely low wattage bulbs at irregular intervals, while missing manhole covers present a constant hazard for the pedestrian or cyclist. Traffic pollution and noise are among the worst in China.

Life is only slightly more tolerable in Wuchang on the

peninsular land between the Han and Yangzi rivers. Here at least the inhabitants can climb Pagoda Hill beneath the vast TV tower (adorned with an advertisement for Kent cigarettes) to catch a breeze in the furnace heat of the summer. Hanyang on the right bank of the Yangzi has become the most crowded of the three towns. At weekends the pavements are so tightly thronged that young women, out for the afternoon, sit on the curbstones to avoid the crush. A visiting Western journalist has described Wuhan in these terms:

> The city's factories are mostly crumbling, many of them dating before the 1911 fall of the Qing dynasty. Some 800,000 itinerant workers live in makeshift cardboard-and-tin sheds along alleys and railroad tracks. The sun is rarely visible through the city's polluted air. The city's streets are coated with decades of accumulated grime that rain transforms into a greasy slime that sends bicyclists tumbling to the pavements.[21]

Wuhan's other massive problem in the mid-1990s is unemployment as its loss-making state industries are forced in the new economic climate to reduce welfare benefits to employees and dependents and to cut jobs. 'The amount of losses is increasing,' Governor Jia Zhijie stated bluntly at a city conference on social stability in May 1994, 'and the numbers of enterprises completely or partly suspending production is expanding constantly.' In the previous two years the Wuhan Iron and Steel company had reduced its directly-employed workforce from 120,000 to 50,000. Most of the 70,000 made redundant were not sacked outright but relocated in new companies: yet the 'iron rice bowl' of guaranteed work for life had been smashed, for after a period of subsidy these companies had to pay their way or collapse. 'We are helping the workers mount a horse and leading it a short distance in the hope that it will gallop!' Wuhan Steel's president explained optimistically.[22] Wuhan's biggest success story in this period was the No. 2 Printing and Dyeing Factory, in which the Hong Kong-based Hongtex bought a majority share. It became the first joint-venture in Wuhan to be controlled by foreign interests. The new arrangement was praised for turning the balance sheet from red to black. But it was only achieved by laying off 70 per cent of the plant's 2,400 workers and stripping the labour union of its powers.[23]

The social costs of re-structuring industry soon began to be felt, and urban inflation in 1993–94 of more than 20 per cent added to the pain. At a provincial meeting in May 1994, senior Hubei and Wuhan officials discussed the 'urgent task' of maintaining social stability. The reforms, they admitted, had caused 'temporary difficulties in economic life and destabilising factors in social life'. No doubt they were referring to such events as a demonstration by a group of pensioners who had blocked the bridge over the Han River, in protest at the erosion of their pensions by rising prices. The city and provincial governments sent 'inspection teams' seeking to enforce restrictions on essential items but prices continued to rise. Meanwhile official corruption was on the increase in Wuhan, as elsewhere in China. In June the city authorities announced they had disciplined almost a thousand cadres though punishment was light. They also revealed that more than 350 city cadres were holding down posts in industry and business as well as their official jobs. Party officials controlling the output of state industries and stockpiles of agricultural products (purchased compulsorily from the peasants) had to be bribed to release supplies. Hubei's textile mills were crippled by a shortage of cotton which had been held back by corrupt officials. (This raw material became so valuable that waggon-loads of it were hijacked by organised gangs on the railways.) One despairing factory manager in Wuhan spoke out: 'Everyone knows – even the mayor knows,' he said. 'These people are so powerful now that we have to beg them constantly for cotton. We give them free gifts of cotton cloth, cigarettes, liquor; we even write cheques to them.'[24]

Wuhan is an old, exhausted city trying to renovate itself. Shashi is only slightly younger; hungry foreign eyes were also cast upon it in the late 19th Century. Further upstream, it only developed slowly: this now gives it a considerable advantage. Here in the middle-sized towns of Middle China, life is changing explosively with positive benefits for those able to take advantage of it, although many others are left out of the economic boom.

Japan acquired the rights to a concession in Shashi through the Treaty of Shimonoseki, imposed after defeating China in the 1894–5 war. The concession was never developed: the treaty port at Yichang, opened earlier to foreign trade in 1887, was a more attractive location. If Wuhan was Chicago, then Shashi was the 'Manchester of China', dealing in local raw cotton which was woven and exported all over China. But foreign goods from abroad, particularly from Japan, including cotton manufactures were already widely sold in Shashi's shops when Isabella Bird visited the town in 1896:

> Foreign articles, few of which find any place in the customs returns, are to be bought in the shops. Very many of them are Japanese, owing to the energy or, as our merchants call it, the peddling and huckstering instincts of the Japanese traders, who through their trained Chinese-speaking agents find out what the people want and supply it to them. The cotton gins largely used in the neighbourhood are of Japanese make, and cheap clocks, kerosene lamps, towels, handkerchiefs, cotton umbrellas, cheap hardware, soaps, fancy articles of all descriptions, and cotton goods are poured into Sha-shih (Shashi) by that alert empire. Among English goods are rugs, blankets, and preserves and tinned milk and fruits. Most of the dealers in 'assorted notions' are Cantonese.[25]

Shashi had the reputation of being exceptionally anti-foreign: tourists who went ashore were likely to be pelted with mud. The influx of foreign goods which weakened domestic industry may have inflamed local feeling as it did elsewhere in China. Later the town suffered from the same combination of civil war and flood followed by Japanese aggression which held back Wuhan in the 1920s and 1930s. It continued to have a poor reputation. Visitors commented on the fine stone embankment guarding Shashi – and on the filth which overflowed into the river from the town behind. Shashi and the neighbouring city of Jingzhou only began to revive after 1949. While ancient Jingzhou became the administrative centre for the extensive flood prevention works of the 1950s, its former suburb Shashi grew into a substantial centre for light industry. Towards the end of the decade several large cotton and silk factories were moved from Shanghai upriver to Shashi as part of Mao's policy of regional diversification. The older city of Jingzhou was rebuilt and its gardens and mansions were turned into factories and workers' dormitories: as a result the current attraction to tourism of its well-preserved city walls is now much diminished. Three decades later Shashi entered a third phase of development and from 1988 onwards it was allowed to seek direct foreign investment. A rail link was built to join the Second Trunk Line where it crosses the Yangzi, though in 1994 the track had not yet completely settled in the marshy land on which it was constructed. An airport was also under construction.

The visitor to Shashi can easily explore, on foot or by pedicab, these successive layers of post-war urban expansion. First, a high embankment – 50 steps up – protects Shashi from the Yangzi floods. The old part of town lies squeezed against it. Wooden houses with cracked shutters line the narrow lanes. Small stalls sell small items, from bars of soap to bundles of paper money to burn at funerals. Private restaurants serve the boatmen: a single open room with wooden stools and a stove heated by cakes of coal dust. Under neon lights, women work long hours on sewing machines; men play mahjong with clacking tiles. It is a rough but villagey atmosphere which would still be recognised by pre-1949 visitors. Water is just a tap at the corner, sanitation a communal bath and lavatory.

Through this old part of town runs a more modern main street, built in the 1930s and 1940s under Nationalist rule. Houses are brick or stone with two or three stories and balconies. The hotel, cinema and other public buildings date from the 1950s. They look shabby, damp and have not seen a paintbrush in 40 years. Here the most common form of transport is still the three-wheeled pedicab. Large characters are painted on their wooden sides, saying 'Civilised and Law-abiding'.

The neglected shelves in the New China Bookstore, once a focal point of Shashi's cultural life, reveal the shift away to more modern entertainments. There are few new titles in the bookshop's dusty stock. In April 1994 these included: *My Father Deng Xiaoping* by the veteran leader's daughter Deng Rong; some computer manuals; a series of *The World's Most Famous . . .* (sportspeople, women, scientists, disasters); a few lurid crime stories; a book of '7,000 advertising slogans' for the aspiring entrepreneur; *Anna Karenina* in translation; and – in a locked cupboard – a Chinese version of the *Kinsey Report*. The English textbooks for high-school students are still written in the didactic style of the 1970s. One volume for 15 year-olds teaches them how to say 'The Communist Party leads us from victory to victory', and 'Switzerland was once ruled over by the Austrians'.

From this main street, a steep lane leads down to what used to be wasteland, now occupied by a bus station and open-air market. Every patch of pavement is covered with stalls or goods laid out on a cloth. Schoolchildren buy chunks of pineapple or sugar cane on their way home.

There are Hong Kong-style clothes, tapes and CDs, film and romance magazines, as well as vegetables and fruit. Beyond this area lies an ornamental lake with public gardens, a newer hotel and guesthouse for visiting officials. From here to the walled city of Jingzhou the road used to run through empty paddy fields. In the last twenty years it has been completely built up, at first with small industry and workers' dormitories, and more recently with the shops and homes of a new generation of entrepreneurs. There are glass shop façades and modern apartment blocks. Large gold characters proclaim the names of new banks and businesses. Here too are the hairdressers, flower shops, and small restaurants with karaoke bars attached beside the lake. Young men in leather jackets spend their trading profits ostentatiously, a mobile phone on the table.

New Shashi has its seamy side. In April 1994 the *Shashi Daily* featured, on successive days, police sweeps against prostitution in beauty parlours and against thieves on the public highway. There were no less than 138 beauty parlours in Shashi, of which 82 had no licence to operate. The 'highway robbers' were not petty thieves either: many had stolen at knife-point, boldly assaulting passengers on the local buses to Jingzhou. Two such robbers were executed after being paraded through the streets.

On the edge of New Shashi are grouped the wholesale shops buying grain and cotton from the farmers, or selling fertiliser, cement and other industrial products to them. Outside, men in tattered clothes wait with miserable, boney horses, hoping for a customer in need of transport. There are hand-drawn wooden barrows too, pulled by young men, desperate for work. They sleep on their carts, a dozen or more outside each warehouse, waiting for the occasional fare.

Shashi's rapid development is paralleled by that of several other medium-sized towns in the central plain of Hubei. Already centres of commerce before the revolution, they acquired some industry after 1949 but stagnated in the 1960s and 1970s. They too benefit from favourable locations on the Yangzi or one of its tributaries and from the construction of new highways and bridges. As in the past, they continue to rely on cheap peasant labour and the supply of raw materials from the countryside, including pigs, flax, cocoons, hides and other farmland produce as well as grain and cotton. Unlike Wuhan, these fast-growing towns are less burdened with tracts of run-down housing. Their population is younger and more manageable: Shashi has less than 300,000 compared with Wuhan's four million. Yet there is still high (though often concealed) unemployment. The beauty parlours, the street stalls and the sleeping carters all bear witness to the social problems of rural immigration and youth unemployment concealed by the new dynamism of medium-sized urban development.

These new 'contradictions' puzzle and confuse older Party members in Middle China, but local government is now dominated by a new generation which itself is full of entrepreneurial energy. Until the 1990s, Party propaganda still celebrated the selfless exploits of model workers, peasants and officials who laboured for the public good. The new urban model is that of the small-time entrepreneur who makes good for himself or herself. Party and government headquarters in one Yangzi city launched a campaign to 'speed up prosperity', handing out awards to those who had become 'Model Soldiers of Wealth Acquisition'. The local paper published their profiles with full details of their capital investment, number of employees, and profits. 'Emulate the model soldiers,' townspeople were urged, 'and plunge into the competition for wealth!'[26]

Shashi continues to expand. In November 1994, it was formally merged with neighbouring Jingzhou and four surrounding rural counties to form the new city of 'Jing-Sha' with a combined population of more than a million. Plans were also announced to build a new rail link from Wuhan directly to the Three Gorges via Jingsha and Yichang. The new city is in a particularly favoured position, and its chances are better than those of many other medium-sized towns bidding for expansion. The whole middle plain below the Three Gorges will clearly benefit from the enormous infrastructural investment poured into the project for the next decade and more.

The Yangzi cities of Hubei also feature in the even more ambitious plans announced in 1992 to develop the Yangzi River Valley into a single economic region. As officially defined, the area covers 330,000 square kilometres – from the coast inland through the seven provinces of Zhejiang, Jiangsu, Anhui, Jiangxi, Hubei, Hunan and Sichuan – with a population of 168 million or nearly 15 per cent of China's entire population. The area's gross domestic product (GDP) accounts for one-fifth of the national total and per capita GDP is twice the national average. Shashi is one of 28 cities 'opened to the world' and allowed to seek foreign investment directly. For all these reasons central Hubei enjoys special advantages. The new Jingsha can be expected to grow rapidly, following the example of Xiangfan 200 kilometres to the north which was listed in 1992 with Wuhan among China's top 54 cities (all had GDP exceeding ten billion renminbi annually). Xiangfan, a long-established marketing town on the Han river, benefited earlier from the construction of the Danjiangkou reservoir in north-west Hubei. The city of Huangshi, 70 kilometres east of Wuhan, where the first iron and steel works were established by the late 19th Century modernisers, is also expanding fast. It is already linked to Wuhan by a new motorway. But like Wuhan it has the uphill task of seeking to modernise a large and outdated industrial base.[27]

Yet the Yangzi Valley plan may mean less in reality than

on paper. As with other regional plans, it is to a large extent a restatement of existing projects, with little in the way of new funds attached to it. The inland cities also have to contend with the dominance of Shanghai. While the Yangzi river is compared with a dragon, snaking inland for thousands of kilometres, Shanghai is hailed as the new 'dragon's head'. For all the talk of cooperation, Wuhan and Shanghai remain competitors, while the new Jingsha and other medium-sized cities will seek to challenge the dominance of the giants. They will compete among themselves too: each seeks to become a 'hot-spot of development for the 21st Century'. After the boom subsides, how many will actually make it?

VI

The Legacy of Mao

HUNAN

Shaoshan Revisited

Like a dim dream recalled, I curse the long-fled past —
My native soil two and thirty years gone by.
The red flags roused the serf, halberd in hand,
While the despot's black talons held the whip aloft.
Bitter sacrifice strengthens bold resolve
Which dares to make sun and moon shine in new skies.
Happy I see wave upon wave of paddy and corn,
And all around, heroes homeward bound in the evening mist.

(Mao Zedong, on 25 June
1959 after an absence of 32 years)

I arrived by bus at a dusty crossroads outside Shaoshan, birthplace of Mao Zedong, in a fine mist which stippled the dark water of the paddy fields. An out-of-work student with a motorbike for hire drove me to the Shaoshan Guesthouse. It was damp and empty except for a group of civil servants from some other town in Hunan province making a desultory visit at official expense. They sat in their rooms smoking, eating tangerines, and playing cards while it rained outside.

The choice at the Guesthouse was between a tourist room with three single beds and dirty sheets, or Mao Zedong's old suite, with a wooden canopied double bed and a bath almost as large, at five times the price. I chose the suite, less for the clean sheets than for the opportunity to sit at his desk, listen to the wind in the bamboos outside, study the ink spots on the worn leather, and think about the Chairman.

Chairman Mao . . . The Red Sun in our Hearts . . . Sailing the Seas Depends on the Helmsman . . . Making the Revolution Depends on Mao Zedong Thought . . . I first came to China in 1971 when the air stewardesses still sang Mao-songs in the aisle, and people waved goodbye at railway stations with Little Red Books held carefully aloft. Over the years after his death, the Cultural Revolution was repudiated and nearly all the policies associated with Mao were abandoned. Yet his own reputation was protected – on Deng Xiaoping's personal orders – with the judgement that though Mao had 'made mistakes' in later years, his 'achievements were primary'. Time passed: Mao memorabilia from the Cultural Revolution such as badges and Red Books became saleable items on street pedlars' stalls. There was a 'Mao craze' among younger people; older people remembered in silence. By 1993, 17 years after this death, the Deng-approved formula still inhibited serious appraisal of Mao. A nation embracing new economic systems and ideas was still psychologically unable to deal with the dominant political figure of its recent past. In Beijing, people either could not or would not talk. So I headed for Mao's birthplace to seek deeper insight.

Shaoshan is a small village in a hillside valley 100 kilometres from Changsha. It takes four hours to reach it by a very slow train, designated Train No. 1 – first in the entire Chinese railway system – in honour of Mao Zedong. Or it takes four hours by a lopsided bus with grinding gears and a talisman portrait of Mao hanging from the windscreen. But without the Mao connection, there would be no railway and perhaps still only a dirt road for the last 20 kilometres. This is archetypal rural Middle China. Water buffaloes turn the dark chocolate earth of the paddy fields, guided by barefoot farmers with the flick of a bamboo wand. Villages are half concealed behind a thicket of trees. The L-shaped peasant houses have overhanging eaves supported by pillars to provide shelter from the heavy spring rain, and decorated roof tiles to ward off evil spirits. Nearer Changsha the hills have been denuded but around Shaoshan there is still reasonable tree cover with a splash of bright maple in the autumn. Mao's Old Home is in a small side valley just below the village square. The sign-board giving its name over the doorway, before which every single visitor poses for a picture, is written in Deng Xiaoping's calligraphy (replacing a previous inscription written by the late Guo Moruo, distinguished scholar but also a literary hatchetman who sided with Mao in the Cultural Revolution). It is a more substantial house than the others, with three sides and a small internal courtyard. Mao's family was better off, lent money and rented out land. Restored in the 1950s, its authenticity was approved by Mao himself, but the statue of the God of Wealth and the Mao family ancestral tablets disappeared in the Cultural Revolution and have not been replaced.

The pond into which Mao plunged during an argument with his father still lies outside. Above a viewpoint on its far side stands the Mao Family Restaurant whose owner, the enterprising Mrs Tang, is interviewed by every visiting journalist to Shaoshan – she opened a branch in Beijing in time for the centenary. A small path winds up one side of this miniature valley and down the other, passing several more houses. One, also a small restaurant, is owned by Mao Xiasheng who is related to Mao and was once photographed in a famous picture sitting and smoking with him. He complains that Mrs Tang has no business to appropriate the family name. In a house at the top of the valley, an old toothless peasant watches his son in the field below and claims that he too met Mao. His floor is still made of tamped earth with chickens running around. The mudbrick walls are bare except for a calendar, an enormous rattan sieve and a few other farm tools.

During the Cultural Revolution (1966–76), Shaoshan became the most sacred place of pilgrimage for millions of Chinese and many thousands of foreign visitors. In the peak year of 1966 when the Red Guards roamed China, there were nearly three million pilgrims. With an average of almost ten thousand daily (40,000 on one memorable day), a one-way system on foot had to be devised around the village, tunnelling at one point through the hill behind Mao's old house. The memorial museum on the main square was doubled in size with a duplicate exhibition so that twice as many visitors could pass through simultaneously. That was when the spur railway line was built to Shaoshan town five kilometres down the road past the Youth Reservoir. The station waiting room with its polished floor of coloured marble can seat 500 passengers at a time and still displays two massive paintings of Mao in the revolutionary romantic style. The numbers of visitors fell off sharply after Mao's death in 1976, dropping to 210,000 in 1980. The direct rail link was suspended and the service cut altogether in 1985 but it was restored two years later as numbers rose again. In the 'Mao fever' of the late 1980s visitors increased sharply from 650,000 in 1989 to 910,000 a year later and peaked at over a million in 1991.[1]

In June of that year Shaoshan town was elevated to city status. Its deputy mayor travelled to Hong Kong to seek foreign investment for a holiday resort with 'hotels, playgrounds, shopping arcades, a cultural village and a sanatorium'. In China's new entrepreneurial atmosphere, the people of Shaoshan knew that they too would have to provide new attractions to maintain the visitors' interest. Mayor Mao

Shiwen, a distant junior relative of Mao, attended the 1992 Communist Party congress in Beijing in a three-piece suit and silk tie. 'In establishing a socialist market,' he said, 'we people in Shaoshan will go for it with a free hand and do honour to Chairman Mao ... If Chairman Mao knew we were better off, he would surely be happy about it'. By 1993 more than two thousand shops and open-air stalls had been licensed throughout Shaoshan County. A new open-air market was also built in the village square in front of a new bronze statue of Mao.

Some 30 million visitors have come to Shaoshan since 1950, including 150,000 foreigners. The business and Mao fevers which swept China in the early 1990s became tightly interwoven in Shaoshan as it sought to become the country's first revolutionary theme park. Yet there is still much to be learnt about Mao there, from talking to those who met him and by reading the abundant literature on sale locally. Understanding begins with the simple but revealing fact that *in Shaoshan, Mao was a visitor too*, returning to his birthplace only twice after the victory of 1949. This was not a matter of being too busy. Returning to one's native roots is an intensely significant and emotional experience in China. The occasions when Mao returned, in 1959 and 1966, came at two of the most critical moments in his – and the nation's – political life. What was he seeking on those occasions, and did he find it?

Mao had last visited Shaoshan in 1927 when the first 'united front' between Communist and Nationalists was about to fracture and lead to two decades dominated by civil war. He left hurriedly with Chiang Kai-shek's police in search of him, saying that he would not return until the revolution was successful 'even if it takes 30 years'. Several years passed after victory in 1949 before he announced his intention of visiting in 1957 – which would have been exactly 30 years on. After some delay, he finally came in June 1959 when China was engaged in another revolution. The Great Leap Forward, launched the previous summer, was intended to mobilise popular energies and enthusiasm on an accelerated road towards communism. In the countryside the new People's Communes would provide the organisation for collective efforts on a far larger scale than the more modest agricultural cooperatives set up in the mid-1950s. New rural industries were to be set up: the aim was to 'catch up' with the capitalist world and enormous efforts were made to rival Western production of steel by setting up local 'backyard furnaces' in almost every village. Communal dining halls would establish a new socialist togetherness and save the time usually spent by individual families in preparing food.

The Great Leap was a period of immense officially-inspired optimism, which at first many peasants shared. 'If the sky had a handle to hold it by', went a Hunanese peasant poem, 'we would lift it up with ease. We could pick up the earth if only it had a ring to seize. Whatever the task Chairman Mao gives us to do, we shall victoriously carry it through'. But by mid-1959 there was mounting concern, even on Mao's part, that the Leap had stumbled badly. Local cadres set unrealistic targets and then reported inflated figures. When more food was produced it was badly stored or consumed wastefully. Some crops failed because of untried farming techniques such as planting seedlings too close together. The dining halls were unpopular and the backyard steel mostly too poor to use. Mao had already sent members of his entourage to study the situation in other rural areas: other leaders including Peng Dehuai, Minister of Defence and also from Hunan, had made personal inspection tours. Mao knew the Hunanese countryside well from his student days: on more than one occasion he and a friend travelled without money, staying with the peasants or sleeping out in the open. Later he conducted surveys into relations between landlords and peasants and rural support for the revolution.

Mao's 1959 visit to Shaoshan was, in very abbreviated form, another such 'rural investigation'. He could no longer simply set off with umbrella, towel, notebook and a bundle of clothes. From 1957 onwards the Minister of Public Security Lo Ruiqing made several advance visits to check on the arrangements in Shaoshan. The Chairman's safety was a serious business, yet Mao still hoped to avoid too much formality. He instructed Lo that no army or police should be sent to Shaoshan while he was there, that he should be able to go wherever he chose, and that he should have free access to the local people.

Mao arrived in the early evening of 25 June 1959. Mao was accustomed to work by night and sleep in the morning but the next morning he was up before 5 am. He headed out of the guesthouse with officials scampering to keep up. 'First,' he said, 'we shall visit my parent's tomb.' They struggled up the wooded slope. There was no paved path then and the site was overgrown because Mao had not announced his intention in advance. Hastily some villagers made a wreath out of pine branches and wild azaleas, knotted together with long grass. Mao bowed deeply as the sun rose through the trees. 'Life was hard for our parents. It will be happy for our children,' he told the local people.

Mao's filial visit would later bring great misfortune during the Cultural Revolution to the Hunanese writer Zhou Libo. Zhou is best known for his novel *Great Changes in a Mountain Village* which describes with sympathy and humour the rural cooperatives campaign of the late 1950s. (It even has a rare love scene, modest but tender, between two young people in the open air.) In 1965 Zhou had written a rather pedestrian and in places inaccurate account of Mao's 1959 visit to Shaoshan for a provincial newspaper, including a one-line reference to Mao's parental tomb. A year later the article was denounced by the national secret police chief Kang Sheng as a 'Great Poisonous Weed which Slandered the Brilliant Image of our Great Proletarian Leader'. Zhou defended himself calmly: 'Don't communists have parents too?' he asked his Red Guard persecutors. But he was beaten for daring to reveal that Mao had indulged in this 'feudal' custom.

Mao's return to his old home was more than a family pilgrimage. The really interesting question, never properly answered until now, concerns the investigative purpose of his visit. Did Mao learn the real truth about the failure of his Great Leap policies from his fellow-villagers, and if so did he admit it to himself? Most Western writers have concluded that the peasants told Mao what he wanted to hear – that everything was fine. In fact local eye-witnesses and publications reveal that Mao asked some critical questions and got some devastatingly honest replies in return.

Mao descended from the hillside into the narrow valley of his family home, stopping to chat with the peasants working there. One young man, Mao Xiasheng, ran barefoot from the fields to be photographed with the smiling Mao. Many millions of copies were later printed of this picture to show the Chairman 'at ease with the masses'. One copy is displayed outside the small restaurant where his daughter serves meals, halfway down the valley. It is called, simply the Mao Xiasheng Restaurant. When he is not watching his neighbours play mahjong, Xiasheng sells postcards to the diners. Once a sale has been made, he will answer questions about the past. In conversation with Mao, he had at first given him a wildly inflated figure for grain yields on the paddy fields. But when Mao queried the figures he revealed that they had been supplied by the local cadres and seized the chance to say more.

'Chairman, please tell our cadres not to oppress the common people, not to beat us. My auntie was denounced in public last year because she told the truth. These days those who speak honestly come to grief; those who tell lies get promoted. I'm afraid what I say won't please the leaders.' Mao assured him that he would be safe. He had to repeat the assurance that same evening.[2]

Mao had planned a dinner with relatives, army veterans, village cadres and elders to be the highpoint of his return. He met them in the guesthouse with some courteous words before the meal. 'I've been away for more than 30 years,' he said. 'Please let me know what you think about life today, about the government and even about me!' After some polite muttering that everything was fine, the complaints spilled over so fast that the old men interrupted one another. 'Chairman, did you really order that we should plant our crops so close together that they died?' 'Chairman, did you really say that women and men should eat separately in public canteens?' Mao answered defensively: policies which were not suitable should be changed. He would make sure of that. 'Chairman,' said one old man, puffing furiously on a long-stemmed pipe, 'they call us "Old Conservatives" when we say these things.' 'Chairman, if you had not come to Shaoshan,' said another, 'we would all be dying soon of hunger!'

Mao wound up the session with some reassuring words. Their criticisms showed how much they supported the government and the Party. They should go on uttering them. When he got back to Beijing he would personally issue a document to settle the question of public canteens. If there were problems, he was responsible. He finished with some advice for the local cadres. They should make sure that life went well for the people of Shaoshan because foreign guests came there. If they noticed things were wrong, that could affect China's socialist reputation! It was time to eat.

Mao was an affable host and toasted the village elders over their protests that they should be toasting him. But he could not help noticing how some of the guests fell upon their food so ravenously that they choked. He himself drank and ate very little before leaving the table. He put on a smile to pose for photographs, then went back to his room. Late at night he was still walking up and down and only slept when it was dawn.

If during those sleepless hours Mao acknowledged the truth, he also found a way to rationalise it, writing a poem (quoted at the beginning of this chapter) to commemorate the return to his native home. In it he defiantly celebrated the spirit of the Great Leap Forward as it should have been, not as it had just been revealed. The sun and moon shone in new skies, the paddy and corn filled the fields, and all around he saw 'heroes homeward bound in the evening mist'. These were the images of the propaganda poster, not of the reality in his own village.[3]

The next day Mao left the guesthouse in a hurry without going down to the village or meeting anyone else. Two weeks later at the Lushan Party Plenum, he turned savagely on the critics of the Great Leap, forcing the resignation of fellow-Hunanese defence minister Peng Dehuai. Peng was replaced by Lin Biao, later to become Mao's 'chosen successor', playing a malign role in the Cultural Revolution where he led the chorus of praise for the Thought of Mao Zedong (until he died fleeing from China, exposed as a plotter against the state). Mao's colleagues were shocked and disoriented by his assault upon the Lushan critics, which made serious argument within the Party impossible from then onwards. But his rejection of unwelcome criticism began in Shaoshan on his way to the Plenum. The peasants had spoken and Mao had listened but, in the end, he refused to hear.

Mao's second and last post-Liberation visit to Shaoshan was of a very different order. In 1959 he had suggested to the provincial party boss, Zhou Xiaozhou, that they should build 'a simple retreat' in the hills where meetings could be held and officials could relax. 'When I'm old, I'll come back and live there!' he added. The result was the secret guesthouse at Dishuidong, invisible from the road below and guarded by the army.

Mao arrived on 18 June 1966 in three cars with his bodyguards from the élite 8341 Unit. They were disguised in plain clothes. (A popular magazine in the centenary year claimed that they carried accordion cases in which their weapons were concealed.) Mao looked at the wooded slopes. 'This is a nice place,' he commented. 'When I was young I used to herd buffaloes here, cut firewood and grass, and sometimes fight with the other kids.' On this occasion a young girl was gathering fuel on the hillside. Seeing the activity in the guesthouse below she ran home to tell her father that Chairman Mao had returned. The story spread quickly through the village: security guards soon arrived to warn that she had been 'mistaken'. Hearing the story, Mao's surviving brother-in-law went up to the gate but was turned away by the guards. During ten days at Dishuidong Mao never left the compound. He only surveyed the peasants' fields – badly hit by drought that year – from a viewpoint high above the valley. He was dissuaded from visiting his grandparents' tomb on the hillside with the argument that there was no convenient path. This time he would not push through the undergrowth.

By now Mao was engaged in his final and most destructive political struggle: the Great Proletarian Cultural Revolution. He had deliberately stayed away from Beijing since November 1965 while ultra-left supporters led by his wife Jiang Qing and Minister of Defence Lin Biao maneouvred against the Head of State Liu Shaoqi and other old colleagues. They claimed to be struggling against 'those who take the capitalist road'. On 1 June, Mao had approved the text of the first 'big-character poster' attacking the academic staff at Beijing University (China's leading academic institution where the Cultural

Revolution was launched). On the 13th exams were cancelled throughout China as the educational system became the first battlefield and the Red Guards began to emerge. Mao worked late at night in Dishuidong, receiving piles of documents daily by plane from Beijing. His return to Shaoshan was both symbolic and subtle. He had returned 'to the mountains' (as he previously threatened to do when facing criticism) to bring to its climax a classic guerrilla operation against his former colleagues. No one knew where Mao was, nor where he would move next. Unaware that the Red Guards had been encouraged by Mao and his ultra-left supporters, the unsuspecting Liu Shaoqi, Party general secretary Deng Xiaoping, and other national leaders took an equivocal attitude towards the popular student movement. The 'mistakes' which they made in handling it then provided Mao with political ammunition against them when he finally returned to Beijing and showed his hand.

Chinese accounts of this ten-day visit to Shaoshan are thin by comparison with those of Mao's two days in 1959. Since Mao never met the local peasants they have nothing to recall. The guesthouse staff recall Mao's allegedly simple tastes in food and clothing – a familiar theme in the official hagiography. There was no air conditioning against the humid summer heat, only a home-made system: giant blocks of ice (brought daily by truck from Changsha) were placed in a wooden tub with a fan behind to cool the air).[4]

On the 24th, Mao went swimming in Shaoshan reservoir, now part of the grounds of Dishuidong, where he had swum on his previous visit. The author of the popular book *Mao Zedong and Shaoshan*, on sale in every souvenir shop, is driven to make a rare editorial comment contrasting the two occasions:

We may remember that when Mao went swimming in 1959, a sea of spectators covered the hills in a great hubbub of welcoming cries, refusing to go even when it was dusk, so that Mao could appreciate the affection of his fellow-villagers. This time the hillside was covered by security guards, Mao was only accompanied by a few attendants and lifeguards, and the atmosphere was cold and cheerless. We may wonder what Mao's feelings really were on this occasion.[5]

One of Mao's bodyguards recalls that he seemed to chafe at his isolation, and yet it was self-imposed. A group of provincial officials, meeting in the village guesthouse where Mao had previously stayed, was invited up to Dishuidong and sworn to secrecy. Mao listened to their reports, gave them 'important instructions' and was photographed stiffly among them. In a letter to Jiang Qing written a few days after his departure from Dishuidong, Mao referred to his sojourn 'in a western cave' as if he had been in hiding. Mao told Jiang that he spent every day reading documents and offered this reflection: 'Chaos on earth gives way to order but in seven or eight years chaos returns and evil spirits spring up again. This is determined by their class nature from which they cannot escape.'[6]

It was just seven years since Mao's last visit to Shaoshan and the Lushan meeting immediately afterwards when Mao had been assailed by the 'evil spirits' of those criticising the Great Leap Forward. Brooding in his western cave, Mao again sought comfort from the familiar surroundings of his childhood as he faced a new political crisis of his own making. This time he did not even consult the peasants on whether or not to precipitate more 'chaos': there was no advice for him to reject.

Three weeks after leaving Shaoshan Mao completed the disorientation of the Party hierarchy by returning to Beijing to inform them they had made serious mistakes in handling the student revolution. Within a month Liu Shaoqi had been demoted and a purge of the leadership began. But first

Mao insisted again on swimming the Yangzi at Wuhan. He performed this *coup de théâtre* on 16 July, the day before he arrived in the capital. The news that he had swum ten miles was published a week later in triumphant demonstration that the Chairman was in control of 'all beneath the sky'. There were photographs to prove it. Some accounts now allege that the famous close-up of Mao in his swimming robe, published in the People's Daily on 25 July, was not taken in the Yangzi but at the pool in Dishuidong. If this proof of this celebrated swim was doctored, could the others have been too?

Mao never returned again to Shaoshan. In the early 1970s the guesthouse at Dishuidong was improved under the supervision of Mao's security chief Wang Dongxing. This is when air conditioning was added, and the bathroom embellished with an immensely tall stand-up urinal which now excites the attention of visitors always on the alert for personal details. The air-raid shelter was also added at the back: visitors now walk through it on their way to a souvenir shop. One account published locally claims that in his last year of life, Mao sought several times to return to Shaoshan. The staff at Dishuidong were alerted but he never arrived. In August 1976, we are told, he expressed the wish again but 'the Party Politburo would not give its consent'. If true, this might be because of fears that if Mao were removed to the countryside, he could be manipulated by those close to him. The same account alleges that Mao's wish was finally granted but too late: Mao died in Beijing on 9 September. (Others argue that Mao's wishes could not have been opposed in this way).[7]

It is also possible that Mao wished to be buried in Shaoshan: the decision to construct his mausoleum in Tiananmen Square was only taken after his death. There he still lay embalmed in the centenary year of 1993, remote from his native home. It was after all an appropriate end, for the story of his later life was one of a growing remoteness from the people, not only in Shaoshan but the rest of China as well.

For a number of years after Mao's death Shaoshan disappeared from the political map. On an earlier visit in 1985, I found Mao's old home was almost deserted and the whole town had a sleepy air. The duplicate section of the memorial museum was closed and the concrete paths of the one-way system along which the Red Guards used to file were overgrown. The Shaoshan Management Office which ran the public buildings had a staff of 300 and appeared distinctly underemployed. The first sprouts of private enterprise were emerging with a dozen or so souvenir stalls near the old home. They stocked a modest assortment of wooden badges, canvas bags, and handkerchiefs with pictures of Mao or Shaoshan. I was surprised to be asked by one if I could 'change money': outside Beijing, such requests were still rare. But it was a scene of tranquillity compared to the frenetic commercialism I would find in 1993. There were as yet no restaurants, hotel touts or mini-buses competing for passengers to the station or Dishuidong.

In Beijing politics, Mao's reputation became entangled in the leadership struggle which followed his death. His immediate successor Hua Guofeng relied on the claim that Mao had personally endorsed him. Hua was even said to have altered his hairstyle to look more like Mao and posters of the two leaders were displayed side by side. Deng contested Hua's claim that Mao's policies should be followed in all particulars, arguing that no one could be infallible. But Deng took care to protect Mao's reputation in the official Party resolution adopted in June 1981 when Hua Guofeng was finally replaced as Chairman. Though Mao had committed 'gross mistakes' in his later years, it was mandatory to assert that 'his merits were primary and his errors were secondary'. Efforts by independent-minded scholars to conduct a more open debate on Mao's legacy were stifled from the start. The Thought of Mao was bypassed, not rejected as China under Deng abolished the People's Communes, rehabilitated the victims of the Great Leap and subsequent campaigns, and opened the door to foreign investment. The general public simply lost interest in Mao. Students, no longer obliged to study his works, sought inspiration in a wide range of translated works from Plato to Dale Carnegie. Waves of enthusiasm swept the colleges as new ideas were found. There was a Sartre Fever, followed by a Freud Fever and even a Nietzsche Fever.

Yet Mao remained a central part of China's official political culture while his myth was deeply embedded in popular memory, unresolved and unsettling. Some of his most spectacular statues survived, including one in front of Shaoshan railway station and another in Changsha, because no one would take the responsibility for removing them – so did his portrait over the main gate in Tiananmen Square. In May 1989, at the height of the student democracy movement, it was the scene of a dramatic episode in the run-up to the Beijing Massacre. Those involved, like Mao, were Hunanese.

Yu Zhijian, Yu Dongyue and Lu Decheng were from Hunan's Liuyang County, birthplace of the reform-minded Communist Party leader Hu Yaobang whose recent death had triggered off the student protest in Beijing. They were ordinary young men, a teacher, a journalist and bus company employee, all in their late twenties. They had arrived in Beijing on 19 May 1989 on a train packed with provincial students eager to join the demonstration. They marched up from the station to Changan Avenue where, guided by friendly local bystanders, they turned left for Tiananmen Square. For the next three days they joined processions and heard speeches calling for democracy, science and an end to corruption. At night they slept on the hard marble, huddled together for warmth and at some point – perhaps in a wakeful early dawn – they conceived their plan. On the morning of the 23rd they bought ink and oil paints in the main shopping street of Wangfujing, and on the way back begged some empty egg shells from a street stall selling pancakes. They then filled the egg shells separately with black ink and white, red and yellow oil paint. Squatting on the hot pavement, they wrote out two posters with the slogan:

> *End 5,000 years of feudal rule;*
> *End decades of the cult of personality*

At just before three o'clock, the three young men walked quickly up to the gate to the Forbidden City and pasted the posters in the entrance. Then, stepping outside again, they hurled their eggs at the portrait of Chairman Mao which watches over the Square. They were immediately seized by university students who suspected they might be saboteurs sent by the police to provoke an incident. The students then put up a banner in English and Chinese: 'This is not done by the people and students'. The portrait was quickly covered with green canvas and before evening a new portrait, kept in reserve for the purpose, had been hoisted by a fork-lift truck. The three young men from Hunan were handed over, after some heated debate among the students, to the police.

The students' suspicions had tragic consequences for the three who were genuine protesters against the dictatorial rule of the Communist Party from Hu Yaobang's native town. In September they were sentenced respectively to life, 20 years' and 16 years' imprisonment on the charge of 'counter-revolutionary sabotage'. Transferred back to Hunan they were later reported to be enduring solitary confinement in damp dark cells under a 'strict regime'. In 1992 the US human rights organisation AsiaWatch published an account of conditions in the solitary cells of Lingling prison where they were held.

The solitary confinement cells at Lingling Prison are just over two square metres each in area. They have no ventilation or heating, which makes them freezing cold in winter and unbearably hot in summer, and they are almost pitch-dark. In addition, the cells are damp and sanitation is extremely deficient. Prisoners are only allowed to leave their cells for brief, thrice-daily meal periods during which they must eat their food while walking around in a tiny exercise yard.[8]

The portrait incident took place on the day of Beijing's biggest pro-democracy protest and was regarded by the leadership around Deng Xiaoping as a significant 'counter-revolutionary act' which strengthened the case for strong action against the students. One hundred thousand people had marched triumphantly with slogans denouncing martial law and calling for the dismissal of Premier Li Peng, the man who had brought in the troops. The march was returning to the square under a bright cloudless sky just as Mao's portrait was defaced. Then, within half an hour, it rained in a furious downpour. Some marchers flattened themselves against the walls of the Forbidden City to gain the barest shelter, but most simply got drenched. Later when the news spread of the portrait incident, some marchers believed it was more than a coincidence. Had not the Chairman shown his displeasure at the insult to his image by calling a storm out of the clear sky?

After the Beijing Massacre a new Mao Fever spread to everyone's surprise among the students, although they were suppressed by a regime still acting in his name. A few posters had been carried in Tiananmen Square with Mao's picture by demonstrators making the point that the Communist Party had been less corrupt when he was alive. The motives for the Mao Fever were more complicated. Some students wore his badge and quoted his slogans at the political meetings they were obliged to attend merely to tease the authorities. 'The Party know that this is a form of political satire,' one student explained, 'but it has to pretend that we are sincere.' Others found a more genuine appeal in Mao's emphasis on the Party's need to 'listen to the masses' and avoid autocratic behaviour. His injunction to the Red Guards in the Cultural Revolution that it was 'right to rebel' also struck a chord with the class of 1989. Most had only been infants at the start of the Cultural Revolution and knew nothing of the disillusionment with Mao which had converted some Red Guards into critics and opponents of his rule.

The Party authorities sought to gain the best advantage from the Mao Fever even though some aspects of it might have disturbed them. In February 1990 twelve universities in the capital convened a seminar with the title 'the quest for Mao Zedong', where it was claimed that the students had found the 'historical answer to the salvation of China in Chairman Mao'. Over ten years from the Sartre to the Mao Fever, explained the *People's Daily*, young Chinese intellectuals had come to realise that western prescription could not cure China's problems. They had learnt from Mao's Thought how to 'stand on the yellow ground of China'. Senior leaders remained wary of commenting on this ambiguous phenomenon, except for the leftist ideologue Deng Liqun who had led an earlier campaign against 'spiritual pollution' from the West. He now claimed that the Mao Fever was a healthy phenomenon which promoted 'unity and stability' after the troubles of 1989. Unlike previous crazes, it would become 'an eternal subject'. It proved that China could escape the crisis of communist confidence in Eastern Europe and the Soviet Union.

Outside the student world, Mao Fever took on the appearance of a popular cult in the early 1990s as the centenary of his birth approached. Laminated plastic cards with loops of ribbon bearing his picture were sold alongside similar portraits of the Guanyin goddess, famous temples and other tourist attractions. Thousands were hung from taxi and bus windscreens to 'ward off evil' though this had no noticeable effect on the standard of driving. Tales of the Chairman were sometimes treated on the same footing as stories of the supernatural. One popular broadsheet which I bought from a street-seller in Changsha in the centenary year told the tale of how, in a certain Fujian village, an 'evil spirit in fox's disguise' had been frightened off by a portrait of Mao on the wall. Many private entrepreneurs hung Mao's picture behind shop counters to bring good luck to their business.

For young people who had been children in the Cultural Revolution, the songs and souvenirs of that period were now simple curiosities and an amusing change from Hong Kong popular culture. 'I get a special, fresh feeling,' a young purchaser said, 'whenever I listen to cheerful and lively songs of this kind.' For older people it recalled memories of a more ordered time when the state, acting in the name of Chairman Mao, took care of everything. In Shanghai an enterprising branch of the China Record Company brought out a tape of 30 old songs in praise of Mao, set to a disco beat. 'Red Sun' sold over three million copies and the company was sued for royalties by the composer of some of the original songs. The *Wen Hui Bao* newspaper in Shanghai organised a solemn seminar to discuss the phenomenon. Some speakers warned that the popularity of the tape showed how people still failed to appreciate the damage done by the Cultural Revolution. Others argued that on the contrary it demonstrated a new spirit of tolerance and light-hearted humour about politics. Signs of official concern, published in an internal Party bulletin, only encouraged more publicity. A second tape was rushed out and a special version for use by karaoke singers was produced in the Zhuhai Special Economic Zone.[9]

> The sun is reddest, Chairman Mao is dearest
> Your brilliant Thought illuminates my heart.

The spring wind is softest, Chairman Mao is dearest,
Your revolutionary Line guides my voyage.
Your exploits are higher than heaven,
Your thinking deeper than the sea,
The sun in my heart will never set,
Ah, you will always be the heart in our hearts.

These and similar verses, sung mirthfully in the karaoke bars of Shanghai, were given a more solemn rendering in Beijing where a minority of older cadres and Party workers retained a deeper loyalty to Mao. In the run-up to the centenary, I attended a remarkable concert staged by a group of ageing enthusiasts from the Ministry of Culture, the first in a series of music and poetry concerts to celebrate the Chairman. These were held, rather incongruously, in an Art Salon on the first floor of the Holiday Inn Hotel in central Beijing. The performers were splendidly dressed: dark suits for the men, evening dresses adorned with lamé or sequins for the women. Yet the audience was addressed as 'comrades' and the songs were delivered with shining-eye fervour.

Genuine loyalty to Mao also endured among some older peasants and workers who had followed him in the revolution. Grannie Li, whom we have already met in Henan province, had this to say about Deng Xiaoping's rejection of Mao's policies in the countryside:

Deng Xiaoping just ordered the communes to be abolished. There was no mass movement. What has been achieved since then is based on Mao's great contribution, not Deng's. Mao did not make the masses pay for the government deficit and prices were stable. There was no foreign debt and no internal debt either. Now we eat more but we owe more. As they say around here, 'we have meat in our mouths but curses in our hearts!'

Deng has ruined Mao's organisation. He doesn't ask us first, he just doesn't care. We don't want to restore the collective land, but all this privateering [Grannie Li can't get her tongue around 'privatising'] just means higher prices. What about Deng's cat theory [it doesn't matter whether the cat is black or white as long as it catches the mice]? It means that as long as you get rich it is OK to rob and kill. Whatever method is used doesn't matter. That was never Chairman Mao's way!

Many middle-ranking cadres in the provinces still talk with an anachronistic *naïveté* about Mao, retailing anecdotes about his modest living habits and long hours of work. In Changsha the head of the Cultural Bureau, an essayist with some reputation, has compiled a collection of such anecdotes for children to coincide with the centenary – though his purpose is also to make money from the sales. These simple parables are repeated in popular magazines: they tell of how Mao insisted on the holes in his underwear being repatched repeatedly, how he preferred a bed with a wooden board for a mattress, how his favourite foods were 'coarse grain and vegetables'. He is portrayed as a man of 'superhuman energy: no one could keep a record of how many hours he worked in a day'. He is said to have cried with grief when he was shown the mouldy bread eaten by peasants in the Great Leap. These examples are all taken from a book by his bodyguard Quan Yanchi, which has been widely serialised and quoted.[10] But other reminiscences, published in the more sensational Chinese magazines which now operate on the margin of legality, hint at a very different picture of the Chairman's lifestyle.

In the old clan temple where his family used to worship their ancestors, opposite the new bronze statue in Shaoshan, a magazine on sale at the time of his centenary offers to reveal 'the tragedy of Mao Zedong's last years'. The cover carries a clumsy montage of a Mao look-alike with an attractive woman in a white blouse at his side. The contents page promises a sensational revelation about Mao's return to his native village in 1966. He was, it claims, under the thumb of a beautiful girl and had been driven into hiding by his jealous wife Jiang Qing. Who was the girl? 'A certain Ms Zhang from north-east China'. The article retells the story of Dishuidong which I have narrated above, but adds a significant tit-bit. When Mao took his swim in the reservoir, it claims, he was accompanied by a certain 'female comrade'. Crudely parodying the style of classical Chinese novels when they describe female beauty, the article continues that: 'She was well-developed in physique with a graceful carriage, agile in her movements . . . sporting in the water around the Chairman like a lovable mermaid'. Her name was Zhang Yufeng and one of her most important qualifications, the magazine adds slyly, was that 'she could swim and dance'.[11]

Confidential information about Mao's alleged relationships had already been leaked to a Hong Kong magazine in 1992. This claimed that Mao's personal file as a Communist Party member was still extant in the Party's personnel department. It was supposed to show that 'from 1951 to 1974 Chairman Mao had 29 female secretaries, attendants or nurses, of whom 21 were assaulted or incorrectly treated'. Mao was said to have had 'five marriages or cohabitations, and nine irregular affairs'. He had also been criticised at least five times between 1953 and 1965 by his colleagues, 'in the spirit of inner-party democracy', for his personal behaviour.[12]

It seems likely that this information, whatever its factual basis, was passed to Hong Kong by reformers in the Beijing leadership seeking to weaken the position of the 'leftists' who still claimed allegiance to Mao. They in turn sought to defend his reputation, denying that he behaved like an 'emperor'. The most prominent of the 'leftists', the ideologue, Deng Liqun, argued that though Mao was devoted to the revolutionary cause and possessed outstanding wisdom, he was also 'an ordinary person with flesh, blood and human feelings'.[13]

In China as in the Soviet Union, there has long existed a tension between two different versions of revolutionary morality, one which insists on permanent partnership and the other which rejects conventional – bourgeois or Confucian – restraints. Mao was not the only leader to have affairs or change partners during the Yanan years (1937–45) when he divorced his second wife (the first had been killed by the Guomindang) for Jiang Qing. Zhou Enlai's faithfulness to his wife was much commented on as the exception proving the opposite rule. From Yanan onwards, gossip about sexual affairs within the leadership was surprisingly widespread though much of it was unreliable. Chinese political culture had encouraged relationships between young women (or men) and senior leaders which could be quasi-parental and entirely non-sexual. Dancing parties were regularly held in Yanan, observed by those foreigners who visited the revolutionary base, without a hint of sexual misbehaviour. The practice continued after 1949 in the Zhongnanhai – the lakeside area in central Beijing reserved for top leaders – but (if the stories are true) with less innocent intentions.

These innuendoes about Mao were published in English for the first time by the veteran American journalist Harrison Salisbury, who had unusual access to the Chinese leadership, in his book *The New Emperors*. Citing sources in Beijing, Salisbury wrote of the 'hundreds (more likely thousands) of erotic books' collected for Mao by his secret police chief Kang Sheng, and claimed that 'couplets, triplets, or even greater numbers' of women were supplied for the Chairman's bed. He also described Mao's alleged new taste for 'water sports' in the Cultural Revolution, during which he filled his heated swimming pool with 'bevies of unclad young women . . . The new emperor's water sports had all the subtlety of a rutting walrus'. *The New Emperors* was published in 1992, intriguingly without a word of public protest from Beijing.[14]

In December 1993, on the eve of Mao's centenary, a still more explicit version of the story was broadcast by BBC Television in London. Its documentary 'Chairman Mao: The Last Emperor' portrayed Mao as a tyrant with a voracious appetite for young girls. It relied heavily on the account supplied by Li Zhisui, a former doctor in Mao's entourage by now living in Canada and shortly to publish his own memoirs under the title *The Private Life of Chairman Mao*. The Chinese Embassy in London unsuccessfully urged the British government to prevent the film from being shown and accused the BBC of ulterior political motives. Bejing's protests had the unintended effect of appearing to reinforce the film's credibility although its case rested mainly on the strength of one man's recollections. The result was that the Western press focused almost entirely on Mao's alleged sex life during the centenary. (In an ironical sequel, a later BBC programme in 1994 – commemorating Deng Xiaoping's 90th birthday – suggested that the sex stories had been given publicity by Deng's own supporters to settle scores with the dead Chairman!)[15]

During the anniversary year, I had the opportunity to meet one member of Mao's entourage in the last years of his life, together with one of his more distant relations. Both were now living quietly in Beijing. Like all of those involved, they refused to discuss personal relationships or Dr Li's allegations, but they were more than willing to reflect in critical terms on the anniversary celebrations. I had wondered what Mao would think if he returned to China now. Indeed they had wondered too! Neither had any intention of attending any of the events: it would be too distressing. The authorities were only staging them because 'it would look bad if foreigners paid more attention to the anniversary than the Chinese government'. Those who would take a prominent role were not those who really felt for the Chairman. Those who were loyal to Mao had least to say.

Those who wrote most about Mao understood him least. Those who were really close would never write their memoirs – or be allowed to do so. Who knows, in the end, what kindnesses may have been bestowed on Mao by his young, attractive, admiring nurses and attendants? But as for most of the allegations, I was reminded, 'it is always the evil who make the first complaint'.

Nearly two decades after Mao's death, it is still impossible for Chinese to form a coherent view of the most powerful figure of their modern history. While innuendo and gossip circulate, with a strong suspicion that it is in some degree officially encouraged, serious criticism has been virtually banned since Deng Xiaoping first prohibited it in 1980. Only a few Chinese scholars, taking advantage of political relaxation towards the end of that decade, have tried to offer an alternative view. One of the most outspoken has been Mao's former secretary Li Rui (the vocal opponent of the Three Gorges Dam).

Li had joined the revolution in Changsha in 1936 and returned there in 1949 to become editor of the official party paper *New Hunan Daily*. He also researched the material for a book on Mao's early career which is still a valuable source. Forty years later, on the eve of the 1989 democracy movement, he published a book on Mao's last years. 'Should we not feel ashamed' he asked, that China 'lags behind foreigners in research on this great figure'? Though Mao embodied the 'dangers, hopes and fears of the Chinese people', he had committed 'very big mistakes indeed in his later years, bringing serious disasters to the country and people and creating an historical tragedy for himself'. If China was to genuinely reform itself, he continued, it would be 'ridiculous' if Chinese scholars did not study the persistent influence of Mao upon contemporary politics. No other scholar had gone so far in print though many discuss Mao privately in far more outspoken terms. Li was dismissed from the Party after the Beijing Massacre. In 1993 he returned to the subject of 'Mao's last years' in an issue of the magazine *Bridge* which was promptly banned.[16]

The anniversary on 26 December 1993, passed without a breath of independent or intelligent comment anywhere in China on the legacy of Chairman Mao. The formal ceremonies were of the type described by Chinese as 'empty words'. In Shaoshan's village square, a six-metre high bronze statue now stands, measuring exactly 10.1 metres from the base of its plinth to the top of Mao's head – a symbolic reference to 1 October 1949 when Mao proclaimed the establishment of the People's Republic of China. Behind the paddy fields rises Mount Shao, the hill which gives the village its name. A forest of stones, inscribed with Mao's poems, has been erected on its peak. A Buddhist temple has also been restored there: new and old religions co-exist side by side. In front of the statue, the square is lined with rows of new souvenir stalls selling busts, badges, medallions, portraits, lockets and other mementoes of Mao. Here, culled during my visit, is a brief selection:

1. Heart-shaped locket, with an inner heart which revolves showing the young and old Mao on opposite sides.

2. Medallion with laser-image of Mao surrounded by sun-rays.

3. New Year portrait with *fu* [good fortune] character suspended below.

4. Cassette tape of songs: 'Chairman Mao, we cherish your memory'.

5. Fountain pen, 'Forever' make, inscribed with Mao's poem on Shaoshan.

6. Tieclip with Mao's head in profile.

7. Small plaque with slogan in Mao's hand-writing: 'Learn from [model soldier] Lei Feng!'

8.   Antimacassar for armchair, with picture of Mao's birthplace.

9.   Shoulder bag with map of Shaoshan.

10.   Jumbo badge showing Mao's head over Tiananmen Square.

All the national leaders in Beijing have over the years made their pilgrimage to Shaoshan, taking care to leave inscriptions or poems in praise of the great leader. Some of these are engraved in stone and displayed on the road to Dishuidong. In December 1993, none of the leaders went to the Shaoshan ceremony, attending instead a memorial meeting in Beijing's Great Hall of the People. A large portrait of Mao was flanked by huge red flags and the figures '1893' and '1993' in gold, and most of the Party's ruling Politburo and its elders were on the stage. The proceedings were unemotional, consisting solely of a lengthy speech by the Party's Secretary-General Jiang Zemin. Jiang called Mao 'a great leader who grew out of the masses. He always belongs to the people', but repeated the standard formula coined in 1981 that Mao had made mistakes in his later years, though 'his achievements are primary'. At least half of Jiang's speech eulogised the policies of Mao's successor Deng Xiaoping.

After the centenary, interest in Mao quickly subsided in Beijing but in Shaoshan a new cult has developed. Visitors burn incense and paper money and set off fire-crackers before the statue. Some kowtow to Mao as if he were a god who could grant good fortune. The souvenir stalls have seized the opportunity to sell incense sticks and other items of worship. Holy earth from Shaoshan, holy water, and holy stones with a magical curing power are also on sale. Other places in China have also sought to capitalise on associations with Mao – or simply invent them. In Hainan island a natural rock formation has been identified, one kilometre in length, which is said to resemble Mao's features. The promoters of this new tourist attraction have even secured the personal approval of Mao's daughter, Li Na.

Mao and his real role in history are obscured from the Chinese people by a mountain of propaganda, ritual, myth – and increasingly now by sheer indifference. What incentive do Chinese youth, born when Mao was dying or afterwards, have to ask serious questions about the past? A year after the 50th anniversary, a survey showed that two-thirds of a sample of primary school pupils in Beijing had not even heard of Mao (and only one could recite the national anthem). But all of the children, reported the *China Labour Daily*, 'knew about Hong Kong pop singer Andy Lau, including his birthday and the names of the movies he has starred in'.[17]

VII

The Silent Writer

What I wrote or failed to write reflect the serious injuries I suffered both physically and mentally, which could not be remedied despite all my efforts. I have now been nearly 60 years in Beijing and my life is nearing its end, yet my feelings remain those of a child. Though I took a serious attitude towards writing, I still lack the understanding I should have regarding my successes and failures. Perhaps [my old friend] Professor Zhu Guangqian was right when he concluded that although warm-hearted and fond of friends, at heart I am lonely. This may explain why all my writings have so little in common with the achievements of other contemporary writers.

(Shen Congwen, Beijing, September 1981)[1]

In the last chapter we travelled into rural Hunan looking for clues to the real Mao Zedong. Now we travel much deeper into western Hunan to rediscover another remarkable Hunanese who is hardly known today, the writer and poet Shen Congwen (1902–1988). Both Mao and Shen began life when the emperor was still on the throne and grew up in a China which was searching, amid endemic violence and under enormous foreign pressures, for a new national identity. For both, 1949 marked a new stage in their careers, which raised Mao to ultimately tragic heights of leadership while Shen was consigned to an equally tragic obscurity. Both were typically Hunanese – and Middle Chinese – in their attachment to their native origins. They left the countryside as young men and made their reputation outside the province, yet at critical moments in their later lives both sought reassurance by returning to their native homes. Having followed Mao's footsteps back to Shaoshan we now trace those of Shen after 1949 (as infrequent as Mao's) back to the hills of western Hunan.

Both Shen and Mao come from a province which has contributed much more than its share to Chinese history. Hunan has long been renowned for its lakes and mountains, its red-hot chillies (Mao used to chew them raw) which inflame the local cuisine – and for its many famous sons and daughters. In the mid-19th Century Hunan was the scene of the fiercest battles between the Taiping revolutionaries and the local forces raised by one of the earliest 'modernisers' of the Qing dynasty, Zeng Guofan. Zeng's 'Hunan braves' checked the Taiping advance and were the forerunners of the modern Chinese army. Hunan was the province most affected by the 1898 Reform Movement in which the young Guangxu Emperor sought unsuccessfully to modernise his court and shake off the grip of the Empress Dowager. Tan Sitong, the first person to sacrifice his life for political reform, came from Liuling in Hunan. The province supplied many figures in Sun Yat-sen's revolutionary movement which, collaborating with the new army, overthrew the Qing empire in 1911. They included Song Jiaoren whose assassination two years later led to the usurpation of power by the Chinese warlords. The Hunanese Xiong Xiling became for a while premier and president, seeking unsuccessfully to defend the constitution against them. Sun's widow, Soong Qingling (1890–1981), was born near the provincial capital of Changsha. Qi Baishi (1863–1957), long-lived, artful painter of simple shrimps, flowers, birds and blossoms, was also from Hunan. The playwright Tian Han (1903–) who became one of the first targets of the Cultural Revolution was a Hunanese. Hunan supplied many famous names among the new generation of communist revolutionaries in the 1920s. They included Peng Dehuai, Liu Shaoqi, He Long, Wang Zhen, all leading figures in the Chinese government after 1949. A younger generation of Hunanese communists who would become prominent in the 1970s included Hua Guofeng (temporary successor to Mao Zedong in 1976–80) and Hu Yaobang (whose death precipitated the 1989 student movement and Beijing Massacre).

Fenghuang, where Shen Congwen was born in 1902, was a garrison town deep in the mountains close to the border with Sichuan province. It had been established in the Qing dynasty to subdue the Miao tribespeople who rebelled at intervals against tyrannical Manchu rule. Five hundred forts were needed to keep five hundred villages in check. Shen's fathers and uncles were all army officers although there was Miao blood on his mother's side. During his schooldays in Fenghuang he often played truant, exploring the streets, the river banks and the hillsides and asking questions of everyone. At twelve he went to a military training school and at 14 followed the regiment a hundred kilometres to Huaihua. There in the space of 16 months, Shen would recall, 'I saw 700 executions by decapitation. I learned how torture was employed, how men behave before execution, and I saw so much stupidity that even now I have no idea how these things can be told'.

Fenghuang is still as difficult to visit, compared to most other destinations in China, as it was in the early 1920s. Then, the young Shen, sick of recording daily executions as an army clerk, walked two days and rode by boat for three more to escape these remote hills. (Yet this would be his most quarried material for the next 30 years of writing.) In a faster age, it is still a slow route from the provincial capital Changsha, a full day's journey by juddering bus or even slower train to Jishou, district capital of the Tujia and Miao minority peoples.

The road to western Hunan passes south of the Dongting Lake, through Yiyang and into more hilly country. Here the Hunanese novelist Zhou Libo, who was censured for mentioning Mao's family tomb, gathered material for his brilliant novel on land reform in the mid-1950s, *Great Changes in a Mountain Village*. There have been great changes since then too. The road has been widened; there are modern filling stations and dense traffic. But in the fields, peasants are still mobilised in large groups to clean out irrigation ditches. A slogan makes the point: 'The countryside belongs to the collective; only its use is private'. The county towns bustle with commercial activity. Carts of limestone and coal stand ready for sale. So are bamboo beds, cupboards and chairs, chickens, vegetables, and fish piled high on the hard surface of the road.

Further west the road crosses the Yuan river, once the principal thoroughfare from western Hunan to the river plain. In 1932 when Shen went home, the roads were cut by warlords and it took him over three weeks sailing slowly upstream. The road passes Taoyuan where Shen boarded his boat. Here the poet Tao Yuanming (AD 365–427) set his utopian poem the 'Peach-blossom Spring', which describes how a wandering fisherman explored a rocky cleft and discovered an idyllic world on the other side. After returning home, he could never find the entrance again. Today's travellers can drink tea in the very same teahouse where (it is said) Tao watched 'the brilliant peach petals' of his poem falling to the grass.

The road then climbs into the Wuling Mountains where

the skyline is broken by more peaks than can be counted. Here rural Hunan seems less changed. The views are as sharply drawn as a Chinese woodcut. Farmhouses with black tiled roofs sit comfortably on ground levelled out of the hillside. They are built of wood with eaves supported on pillars and overhanging the tamped-earth verandah, where piles of firewood are stored. Haystacks are built around tall poles or living trees in the small, hilly fields. There is a gleam of sun upon sickle; brightly coloured clothes are spread out on grassy banks. Water is ladled from the irrigation ditches by hand. An old man with fur cap and apron leads his buffalo home.

The Second North–South Trunk Line now cuts through the Wuling mountains, having crossed the Yangzi river from Hubei province to curve south-west towards Guangxi. It has opened up this remote area where four provincial boundaries (Hubei, Hunan, Sichuan and Guizhou) meet in the space of less than 100 kilometres. Jishou is the capital of western Hunan, designated an 'autonomous prefecture' of the Tujia and Miao minorities. New industry has arrived with the railway; tourism is expanding in two new national parks in the Wuling mountains. Other new arrivals in the late 1980s included more than ten thousand Han Chinese seeking to escape from the restrictions of national family planning policy. The minority areas have been exempted from the 'one-child-family' requirement.

Fenghuang lies another short stage west of Jishou into the highlands, past hill forts of the Miao people which held out against the communists until well after the 1949 Liberation. Their walls have come down but the Miao still have a fierce reputation if crossed. 'They are friendly as long as you don't cheat them', say local Han Chinese. There is also a little rhyme: 'Good water in the mountains, fine flowers in the plains, beautiful maidens in Miao forts'. Some of the old courtship customs have survived, and were recently observed by the scholar Jerome Ch'en in his pioneering study *The Highlanders of Central China*. At the market town of Ala, 28 kilometres from Fenghuang, young people sing love songs in duet on the *malangpo* or village green. 'Before the day ends, the young man and woman have already made many promises to each other'. The love songs of the Miao were noted for their frank joy in simple sexual pleasure. Shen Congwen quoted one of the milder examples in one of his short stories:

> In the skies, clouds are upon clouds;
> On the ground, graves are upon graves;
> In the kitchen, plates are upon plates;
> On your bed, a man is upon a woman.[2]

A new bridge spans the tributary of the Yuan river on which Fenghuang town lies, with a view of maple leaves, black-tiled roofs, and wooded hills upstream. Old Fenghuang is still a town of flagstoned paths, curved eaves (in appropriate phoenix-shape), crowing cockerels, barking dogs, Miao women with heavy silver ornaments and brocade tunics, and small babies in woven baskets. Shen is now the town's most distinguished name and his family home has become a museum. The second famous name is his nephew, the painter-cartoonist Huang Yongyu, even though he exiled himself to Hong Kong after the Beijing Massacre. There are still stepping stones across the river where Shen used to play truant. Sometimes he would watch an ox being slaughtered by the waterside. Upstream on the way to Shen's grave, there survives a range of old buildings on stilts over the water, known locally as 'hanging foot houses', and a pagoda — restored with money from Huang Yongyu in Hong Kong.

In his gently but perfectly shaped short stories, Shen Congwen conveyed the ineradicable beauty of his native western Hunan and of its people in the midst of life which was often brutal and short. He wrote of golden rivers and lakes, of chrysanthemum-covered hills, of prostitutes and their lovers, of foresters and ferrymen, garrison soldiers and the wild tribesmen of the hills, of bandits and executions. His only aim, he told his readers, was that they should 'try to understand the momentary sorrows and joys of the people, a glimpse, nothing more'.[3] The wartime journalist and poet Robert Payne wrote of Shen:

> In twilight or under moonlight, on the rivers and hills of his native place, this contemplative scholar finds his continual sustenance. His career is unique. With no axe to grind, writing a prose which is often as intricate as poetry, he has come into the forefront of Chinese writers. He is like a mirror, reflecting the earth and skies of Hunan . . . He has been criticised because he has insisted on the beauty of the Hunanese, both the men and the women; but those who have been in Hunan can testify that they are as beautiful as he has described.[4]

Shen Congwen is compared by his admirers to Thomas Hardy and is regarded as China's most brilliant 'nativist' writer. Shen himself sought to emulate Dickens whose novels he revered. 'He tells me everything I want to know – he makes no attempt to explain – he only records'. In fact Shen never moralises like Dickens and wrote nothing longer than a 100-page novella, *The Border Town*. He was closer to his rural subject-matter than Hardy, and wrote without feeling the need to disguise the force of sexual attraction and physical love. He began to write after moving to Beijing at the age of 20 where he came under the influence of the modern literary movement. He wrote as he studied, driving himself hard and producing 40 books between 1924 and 1932. In 1933 he returned to Fenghuang to visit his sick mother: his letters home were then published as a travel volume. He continued to draw on his early life, blending autobiography and fiction, in *West Hunan* (1937) and other reminiscences which appeared in 1947 but were then forgotten until after the Cultural Revolution. His essays and poems were also much admired in the 1930s and 1940s though only his short stories are known today.

All the stories are beautifully structured and narrated and – in spite of Shen's declared refusal to moralise – convey a strong sense of humanism and sympathy for misfortune. One of the most perfect examples, less than ten pages in translation, is *Dawang* [*The Great Lord*], the story of a former bandit chief who joins the local army. He falls for a woman prisoner who is executed – to punish him – the night after he sleeps with her. He then threatens to return to the hills and is himself executed. Shen's artfully simple narration captures in a few pages the reader's sympathy – not just for one particular brigand but for life and love against brutality and death.

Suddenly the commander came out into the hall. He looked very self-possessed, he held an ivory pipe in his hand and stood under the eaves, graceful and smiling, looking up at the officers who gazed down from the galleries.

'Commander,' [cried the bandit chief] 'have mercy on me, do me a favour, don't kill me!'

Then the commander replied:

'None of this nonsense! You are disgracing yourself! A man should die bravely when he has done wrong and deserved his death. That is the custom in our army. We are guests here, yet you violated a woman prisoner at night in gaol ... No more nonsense! I'll look after your wife and children! As for yourself, be brave and be a man!'

Hearing this, the Dawang did not cry out any more, but smiled at the people in the galleries and appeared to be at ease.

'Good, my commander,' he answered. 'Commander, thank you for your kindness through the years. Good-bye, brothers, good-bye brother.' ...

There is little more to relate. General Chang, our

commander, was killed by machine-gun fire three years later together with his bodyguard and four sedan-chair bearers as he entered the inner gate of the old examination hall at Chenchow, while trumpets were sounding a welcome. He had been invited by a junior brigadier of his to dinner. A year later, at exactly the same place, this brigadier was murdered by someone sent by the general of another army.[5]

'In Uncle Congwen's works,' wrote his nephew Huang Yongyu, 'you never find a superfluity of epithets such as: Beautiful! Heroic! Magnificent! Elegant! Tragic! But you sense the presence, very aptly conveyed, of these qualities'.[6] Shen's novella *The Border Town*, written in 1934, is generally regarded as his masterpiece. Like so many of his stories it is inspired by the lives of the riverside dwellers of western Hunan, telling of an old ferryman, his granddaughter Green Jade, and two brothers who want to marry her. One brother dies in a whirlpool, the other goes downstream, the ferryman dies of old age, and Green Jade keeps the ferry and continues to wait. The gentle inconclusiveness of this ending does not diminish the story's charm and sadness, with the character of Green Jade just as appealing as that of Black Jade, heroine of the famous classical novel *The Dream of the Red Chamber*.

> Because their home was among bamboos and hills of a glorious emerald green, the old boatman gave the poor mite the name Green Jade.
>
> Wind and sun have tanned the growing girl's skin, her eyes resting on green hills are as clear as crystal. Nature is her mother and teacher, making her innocent, lively and untamed as some small wild creature. She has the gentleness of a fawn and seems not to know the meaning of cruelty, anxiety or anger. Should a stranger on the ferry stare at her, she fixes her brilliant eyes on him as if ready to fly any instant to the mountains, but once she knows no harm is meant, she finishes her task calmly.[7]

Shen had written so many stories by the time he was 40 that, in the words of one critic, 'piled up, they measure twice his height'. After 1949 he wrote no more. The entire sum of his published creative writing until his death another 40 years later was a few essays and a handful of poems. There were at first rumours that he had been arrested or even executed: foreign admirers of his work claimed that he had been 'silenced by communism'. The truth was more complicated. Shen was already writing less in the 1940s and there was an unexplained attempt at suicide in 1947. Yet in the same year he was also denounced by the Communist scholar Guo Moruo, the brilliant but venomous intellectual who was close to Mao. Guo accused Shen of clothing his works in 'peach-blossom pink' to condone the evils of the old society. Personal and political pressures combined to make him psychologically ready to accept the self-censorship imposed by the new society after 1949.

After Liberation Shen spent half a year in the company of other intellectuals at a Revolutionary College attached to Beijing University, engaging in self-criticism and learning about the new politics. He and his colleagues were then assigned to the Beijing Palace Museum. Before long they were all offered the chance to transfer to another institution. Shen could have taught – and written in plentiful spare time – at the Beijing Teachers' College or People's University. Instead he, alone out of all the group, preferred to stay at the museum and label antiquities. Over the years he had become a passionate collector of ancient mirrors, glass, jade, lacquerware, brocades, furniture, old paper . . . Now, he later explained, he was delighted to have access to a collection of a million items.

Shen's course was the reverse from that of Lu Xun (1881–1936), the other great modern Chinese writer by whose side Shen should be ranked. Lu Xun took refuge in archaeological studies in the confused years of the first republic after 1912, but emerged to lead the left-wing movement for a new culture and was sympathetic to the early communist cause. Lu Xun became, safely dead, a heroic symbol of commitment to progressive ideas. Shen instead turned from writing to archaeology when the revolution succeeded, and declared he had nothing more to say. My purpose in visiting Fenghuang, 30 years later, was to find out why. The only explanation I had so far found was in quietly ironical comment by Shen's nephew Huang Yongyu:

> So many things were new to this old writer, he shied at them in dismay. It must have been most painful for him to give up his customary way of life. But he loved the new society. He predicted, correctly, that we should see a tremendous, unprecedented breakthrough in our culture. That would suit him down to the ground. He loved the soil of China and her people; but how could this new society with its new outlook understand him? That would have required a detailed analysis, and who had time to spare for the feelings of such an insignificant fellow? In that great age, so many important tasks needed to be done.[8]

In 1953 Shen's path crossed directly with Mao, the ultimate arbiter of all cultural matters. Shen was allowed to attend the second All-China Cultural Congress – though he was admitted as a museum employee rather than as a writer. When Shen was introduced to him at a reception, Mao enquired after his work and state of health, then pronounced casually: 'Why don't you write some stories?' Shen gave a slight smile but no reply. He had just received a letter from his publishers in Shanghai informing him that all copies of his works, including unbound sheets and matrices, had been incinerated. The reason given was that they were *guo shi* or 'out of date'. This, in the view of his only Chinese biographer, was the moment when Shen's surviving spark of creativity was finally extinguished. Shen now immersed himself in his museum work, waiting outside the Tiananmen Square entrance early each morning for the gates to open. When his former student Wu Han, now a deputy mayor of Beijing (and playwright) visited the museum, Shen refused to meet him fearing to cause embarrassment.[9]

When the first political thaw arrived in the Hundred Flowers movement of 1956–57, the People's Literature Press quickly brought out a collection of Shen's short stories. In an introduction, Shen expressed rare optimism, saying that he now hoped to write 'something quite good and quite new'. Early in 1957 he returned to Fenghuang among a group of journalists, artists and other intellectuals, seeking new inspiration in familiar territory. But early on in the journey, a chance encounter at a ferry crossing made him painfully aware how much life had already changed and how little he now understood it.

At Fort Zhangbai in Luxi County Shen had deliberately chosen to cross on an old-fashioned boat instead of using a new motorised ferry: the ferry girl tugged on a bamboo rope strung from bank to bank to propel the boat across. With a cliff on one side dark green with clinging creepers, and a rocky beach on the other covered with old trees, it seemed for a moment as if nothing had changed. Yet the scene, he reflected, was strange as well as familiar. Just upstream a new-style ferry was loading up with the raucous traffic of the new China including his own tour bus. Shen recalled how in this very place some years before seven local officials had been killed in a wild shoot-out. Such an incident today was inconceivable.

The ferry girl with her twin plaits and cheerful face at first reminded him of Green Jade in *The Border Town* but her conversation belonged to the new age. She had been to primary school and was now teaching the little children herself. She talked of the advanced cooperative to which her village belonged, of floating timber down the river so that they could build factories in the towns, of 'working for socialism'. It turned out too that her elder brother was working on the new railway bridge across the Yangzi at Wuhan. The village had watched a film about it. Had Shen, asked the passengers with awe, actually seen the great bridge for himself?

Travelling on to Fenghuang, Shen found new industries – a phosphate mine which produced twenty thousand tons a year – and a new attitude to work even among the old and the blind. He was genuinely impressed by the social transformation of the 1950s (now regarded by many Chinese as a golden period of Communist Party rule after 1949). He contrasted it with the western Hunan of his last visit in 1934 when warlords vied for control of the local opium poppy industry. All this should have provided him with abundant material for new creative writing on the New China. Most of his literary colleagues, whether dutifully or out of real enthusiasm, took it readily enough as their theme. Yet instead of being inspired by the rural cooperatives and factories in the towns, Shen's imagination seems to have been paralysed, and his most vivid memory was of the ferryboat crossing and the young girl. The visit only produced a couple of essays. In one, he reflected that he used to regard himself as a local man, but in the 'clear unblemished eyes' of this real country girl, he was a townsman who enjoyed the luxury of eating white rice! Everything he knew about the countryside belonged to the remote past. How could he possibly understand how the peasants of China had become 'masters of their own land'? And how (his readers might infer) could he possibly write about it?[10]

Shen kept silent during the Hundred Flowers movement when intellectuals were briefly encouraged to criticise the Party, refusing to utter a word of complaint about his previous treatment. When the political backlash came and those who had spoken out were labelled as 'rightists' and 'sent down' to the countryside (or in some cases to labour camp), he remained untouched. After the purge, he was even invited to become chairman of the Beijing Cultural Association. Again he refused, no doubt realising it was almost as dangerous to take sides with officialdom as against it. (Those with jobs in the world of literature and arts would become prime targets in the Cultural Revolution.) Three years later at the end of 1961, during another political lull, Shen was invited to join a small group of writers visiting the revolutionary base of Jinggangshan where Mao and Zhu De had established the Red Army in 1927. The project was supposed to inspire a new crop of socialist literature. This time Shen agreed, planning to write a novel based on the story of a 'revolutionary hero' in his wife's family. He soon gave up; so did the other writers. The peasants of Jinggangshan either could not remember the old days or spoke about them in unrevealing set phrases, regarding their visitors with suspicion as 'city folk from above'. The other writers played cards and danced. Shen wrote poems instead, and recalled again the lesson he had learnt from the ferry-girl at Fort Zhangbai. The original intention was to stay in Jinggangshan for two years. Shen left after two weeks – the others gave up even earlier.

By now Shen had acquired a new reputation as an anti-quarian through his diligent research at the Palace Museum. In 1963 Premier Zhou Enlai observed to Qi Yanming, deputy minister of culture, that China lacked a museum of costume such as he had seen in other countries. He also suggested the need for a volume on the subject which could be given as a gift to official visitors to China. Qi interrupted the Premier: 'Shen Congwen could do that!' 'Good, let's give it to him!' Zhou replied and the matter was settled. Delighted at Zhou's patronage, Shen plunged into this new work with a team of researchers and it was completed in little more than a year. It was still too late. By now the political mood was shifting as Mao prepared to launch the Cultural Revolution. The publishers were wary of a work which might be accused of 'celebrating feudal tradition and neglecting the class struggle': publication of the book was postponed.

Two years later, Shen's *Study of Chinese Costume and Adornment in Ancient Times* formed part of the dossier against him for 'prettifying the past' and engaging in 'reactionary scholarship'. His rooms were 'searched' eight times until there was nothing left to steal or smash. He was 'struggled against' in public meetings, arms pulled back and shoulders forced forward in the 'airplane position', but not actually beaten. As other intellectuals were tortured, crippled or committed suicide, Shen counted himself to be 'fortunate among the unfortunate'. He spent a year cleaning the toilets in the north-east corner of Tiananmen Square before being 'sent down to the countryside' in Hubei. Conditions were hard but he still managed to admire the beauties of Danjiangkou Dam at sunset and the 'splendid lotuses' outside one peasant house where he was lodging. During 1970–71 he was moved six times, and fell seriously ill three times, before being allowed to return to Beijing. Finally rehabilitated in 1978, he was at last able to complete the study of Chinese costume: even in the countryside he had continued to work on it from memory.[11]

In June 1982 Shen returned home to Fenghuang for what was only his second visit since 1949. After decades of neglect he was now acknowledged to be a celebrated local figure. His short stories had at last been reprinted: a newly published history of Chinese literature had declared him to be no longer a 'reactionary writer'. For what would be the last time, Shen retraced the steps of his youth in a thoughtful, sometimes melancholy, mood. In the town theatre – a rare survival of the old courtyard stage – he shed tears as he watched a local play. At a river crossing near Jishou which reminded him of the ferry in *The Border Town* he sat and stared for so long that he had to be led away. He was courteous, self-deprecating, polite about the Party – and left after two weeks instead of the month he had planned. Did Fenghuang remind him too much of what he had written, what he had failed to write, what others had stopped him from writing? Or was he just tired?

Shen's happiest time was spent visiting the newly opened canyons of the Zhangjiajie national park. Here he could be a simple tourist: enjoy the virgin forest with its 500 species of trees including redwood, gingko, tung oil and tulip; watch out for golden monkeys, musk deer and flying squirrels; and listen indulgently to the fanciful names invented to describe the 'strange rocks and weird stones' of the area. At the Golden Whip Brook he posed for a photograph, squatting on a pile of boulders while his wife embraced him round the neck. It was a rare scene of pleasure for both, and Shen was smiling as happily as . . . a small boy.

Local biographer Liu Yiyou of Jishou University recalls how Shen became briefly more animated at an old-fashioned ferry crossing in the town. He watched a small boy who had taken off all his clothes, bundled them on his head and was swimming across the stream – just the kind of foolish enterprise which Shen himself might have undertaken when playing truant from school to visit a local fair. Suddenly Shen said to his companion with a flash of enthusiasm: 'I could write a journal about my travels in new Hunan'.

The inspiration passed and he wrote nothing about his second visit. If he had really intended to, he would soon have been deterred by the campaign which broke out in 1983 against 'spiritual pollution'. In this counter-attack by ultra-left dogmatists and literary hacks, Shen was frequently cited. He was accused of 'yellow (obscene) writings', of overlooking the black side of the old society in works such as *The Border Town*, and of representing the 'bourgeois tendency' in literature. Reprints of Shen's works were delayed or published in small runs which would attract less attention. The first edition of his cherished *Study of Chinese Costume and Adornments in Ancient Times* was mostly bought up by Japanese collectors. No one thought of reprinting it for the domestic market. By the time that the campaign against 'spiritual pollution' had run out of political steam in early 1984, Shen had fallen ill. Liu Yiyou recalls how Shen's wife commented, with a sigh:

> 'How lucky he managed to go back to western Hunan the year before last. Otherwise, he wouldn't be able to manage it in his present state'. I [Liu] thought to myself, even if he were not ill he could not easily have gone back last year. The political climate would have been enough to give him a fever.[12]

Shen died in 1988 still insisting that none of his work before 1949 was useful. 'I am a fake intellectual,' he had told a meeting at Jishou University on his last visit to Fenghuang. 'My stuff belongs to another generation.' His writings, he said, described a society which no longer existed and should be regarded as 'negative material'. There was no point in researching his works because they all belonged to the past. He had simply 'muddled along for 60 years with an undeserved reputation'. What happened after 1949 was his fault, he told the university in the same speech. He had never understood abstract concepts and so he easily made mistakes. Researchers who sought him out in Beijing were strongly advised to choose another subject. This insistence on belittling his own talents went well beyond the formal requirements of Chinese literary self-deprecation. No wonder that in Fenghuang the memorial stone to him, on a hillside overlooking the river he loved, records that 'throughout his life, he treated his reputation like water'.

Yet it was also in Fenghuang that I finally found more revealing evidence of what Shen really thought about the blighting of his literary career. His family home is now a museum, though in 1992 the elderly wife of his younger brother still lived in one of the rooms. Another room contains Shen's bed, decorated with painted flowers and wooden carving. There is a solid wooden desk with a stone top on which he wrote *The Border Town* and his chair, smashed the Cultural Revolution and since restored. It is a solid house with dark wooden beams and supporting pillars on two floors around a small courtyard. At the entrance, tickets are sold and a few publications. In one of these I found what I had been hoping for.

A small volume in the series 'Materials on the Literary History of Fenghuang' was published locally after Shen's death and devoted to reminiscences of him. It was prefaced with a chronology compiled by his wife and two letters from Shen himself written in October 1979 soon after he had emerged from more than a decade of darkness. Fortunately I had purchased two copies of the same volume. In one, the letters had been cut out and their titles blocked out from the contents page. In the other, they had escaped the scissors. The first letter, dated 17 October 1979, is in reply to a Hunanese journalist who had asked for his help in getting his work published. Perhaps because it came so soon after Shen's rehabilitation, the request stung Shen to some uncharacteristically sharp observations. First he recalls how in 1953 not only did the publishers burn all his books, bound, unbound and matrix copies, but the public libraries 'unanimously cooperated' – Shen underlines the words. He muses on the 'weird situation' which this created: in Beijing his writings were banned as 'out of date' while in Taiwan they were prohibited as 'immature'. So, Shen continues wryly, he preferred to settle down at the Palace Museum and do some 'odds and ends' (underlined again) for 30 years. His days were quiet but, he notes, relatively peaceful. Though his house was searched eight times in the Cultural Revolution, there was not enough left to justify him becoming a real target of the Little Generals (Red Guards).

Behind the wry humour of this reply lies sadness and a measure of self-disgust. He probably saved his life by accepting the Party's verdict and not writing seriously – even during the short periods of political relaxation. Over the past three decades, he notes, his days have passed more peacefully than those of most his old colleagues. Should not that be reckoned a piece of good fortune? Later in this letter there is a spark of anger too as Shen brushes aside recent attempts by well-wishers to restore his reputation. Why should they bother? he asks. The order of literary precedence has already been laid down. Lu Xun, of course, is 'in the first class' (underlined). Then come Guo Moruo (who attacked him before 1949), Lao She (author of *Rickshaw Boy*), Ba Jin (author of the *Family* trilogy) and other great names. Then there is a whole set of new Little Generals who have occupied the first rank under the Party's tutelage. 'Their merits are evident before history,' he concludes with a sort of humble irony. 'There's no space left for me.'

In the second letter to the same correspondent, Shen explains how his pre-Liberation writings have been overtaken by the speed of social transformation in China. As for the past 30 years, he repeats that his changes of profession have allowed him to pass his days in comparative peace. Is that not a blessing? As for writing in those years, since he had no right of speech, how could he have the right to write?[13]

These letters reveal a very different emotion from the complaisant acceptance of political tyranny over the arts which Shen normally professed. They reflect such deep bitterness that, as I discovered in Fenghuang, they still had to be censored after his death. Their self-mocking anger is shared by other intellectuals of the pre-war generation who chose to 'serve the people' and suffered so much for it. Most of the time it is well concealed even from the victim him or herself, for the act of self-censorship is psychologically very complex. But Shen seems to have carried it to greater lengths than almost anyone else.

Self-preservation must have been a strong motive in Shen's behaviour, and in his last years he was accused of ignoring old friends who were out of favour with the Party. But one researcher who knew Shen well has no doubt that he chose silence for another reason. Shen, he says, was 'of all Chinese writers most firm in not being influenced by politics'. He believed that politics twisted people's hearts and was against human nature, that 'Communism was disgusting and Marxism did not suit China'. In Changsha in 1992 these explanations, delivered over a fiery lunch of eggplant and peppers, still have to remain anonymous. So does the same researcher's final verdict: 'Shen Congwen never hurt anyone in his life, but he was hurt by others all his life'.

After political rehabilitation in 1978 Shen was generally ignored in the official record of modern Chinese literature. In a rare tribute the *Guangming Daily* (19 December 1985) observed that Shen's literary career had been cut off in mid-course because of the 'misunderstanding of history'. After returning from the countryside after the Cultural Revolution, Shen and his wife were forced to live apart, only being given a four-room apartment in 1980. Less than two years before he died, Shen was finally rewarded by Hu Yaobang, the liberal-minded (and fellow-Hunanese) Party Secretary-General, with a more spacious apartment on the scale reserved for deputy ministers. (According to one story, Shen was angry with the friend who had interceded on his behalf to gain this concession.) Yet Shen's death was only briefly noted by the official English-language New China News Agency, and virtually ignored by the domestic press.

When I visited Changsha four years later, the 90th anniversary of his birth, there was not a single copy of anything written by Shen to be found in the city's biggest state bookshop. A young assistant explained patiently: 'We've got plenty of Lu Xun because Chairman Mao approved of him. But Shen was criticised, wasn't he?' Shen's anniversary passed without a single line beng published or any commemorative meeting in his home province. A few months later the 95th birthday of the Hunanese playwright Tian Han, a loyal leftist writer who was also attacked in the Cultural Revolution, was celebrated in Changsha with a front page story in the *Hunan Daily*. The Party remembers its own, while Shen remains a victim of 'historical misunderstanding'.

VIII

From Cannibalism to Karaoke

GUANGXI

I felt so tense when we said goodbye,
Exchanging numbers, but not a word,
It is you I can't forget;
I want to whisper that I love you.
I hope you'll say you love me too.
This morning I dreamt of that night,
My heart leapt in the honey-sweet moon,
Yet I don't know how to make another date,
Should I phone or should I not?
You are the one of whom I dare not dream.
I want to whisper that I love you.

(Karaoke song heard in Wuxuan Town, Guangxi)

Wuxuan County with its population of 300,000 is tucked into the western folds of the grey and misty Great Yao Mountains in central Guangxi. It grows rice, rapeseed, tobacco and sugar cane. Yields and incomes are much lower than the provincial average and rural industry employs less than two per cent of the working population. Wuxuan has always been 'backward' in Chinese terms, and is only just beginning to be touched by Deng Xiaoping's consumer revolution. I arrived by boat from the lively port of Guiping, in a five-hour journey which only passed one or two small villages. The scenery, almost as beautiful as that of the famous Li River near Guilin, is unknown to foreign or even Chinese tourism. It was the evening of National Day (1 October) 1993 – the main holiday of the year after the Spring Festival (Chinese New Year), but Wuxuan was quiet. There were no street lights in Wuxuan's main square: a couple of food stalls served oily noodles in the dark, and I heard before I saw the large sow rooting through piles of rubbish in the gutter. Rats ran down the outer wall of a cinema showing an old Kung Fu film. I bought a stale moon cake and some ancient chocolate in the dingy department store before it closed its shutters. I soon abandoned them to the pigs.

In Guiping there were shops with neon signs selling video recorders, stylish lights and furniture. Cheerful street stalls offered bright displays of fresh fruit, and in the evening the teenagers paraded in Hong Kong-style clothes. Wuxuan seemed like the China I knew from ten years before. Most of its people were plainly dressed in tunics and trousers. The two main stores were dusty, ill-lit, with empty shelves. The only bright display of goods was outside a shop selling plastic buckets and household goods. Piles of rubbish had been left in the street, and the pavements were muddy and broken.

Yet a few splashes of consumerist light in Wuxuan's darkness are beginning to appear. At the new end of town, along the modern highway past Party headquarters, cultural palace and government guesthouse, the first scouts of Deng Xiaoping's revolution have arrived – the hairdressers and karaoke bar operators (often using the same premises). A young entrepreneur from the city of Liuzhou, newly established in Wuxuan, asked me to approve his window display of fashion posters and cut-out Chinese characters. He was struggling to make a start, but complained of high rent (500 rmb or £50 a month) and the business. Too many people still have their hair cut in the old market, sitting on a broken barber's chair with a mirror hung against the wall.

The karaoke bars are simple affairs without giant screens or strobe lighting – just a few tables crammed into a small shop serving beer and peanuts, the screen an ordinary TV set. But they are crowded with young people with nowhere else to go. I joined one group, discussed English football which is shown regularly on Chinese TV, and watched a well-shaped young lady in two-piece bathing suit floating on a surfboard somewhere in the South China Sea. The lyrics could have been heard anywhere in East Asia.

I registered at the government guesthouse, telling the startled staff that I was on my way to Liuzhou and had stopped off to see Wuxuan's 'cultural relics'. Wuxuan is one of 16 counties in Guangxi which still possesses a *wenmiao* – a Temple of Culture dedicated to Confucius. Successful candidates in the imperial examinations would bring fame and patronage to the county of their birth: education then, as now, was the means of escape and elevation. A temple to Confucius, it was believed, would increase the chances of a local boy winning first place in the results, gaining the prestigious title of *zhuangyuan*. First built in the Ming dynasty in 1431, Wuxuan's temple was in modern times the largest in size of those surviving. It covered an area of nearly 5,000 square metres with five halls, entrance gate and 'moon pool' with its '*zhuangyuan* bridge' over which only the successful scholar could walk.

Today the main hall with its 15-metre high wooden columns is derelict and the caretaker's chickens scrabble on the ground. The other buildings have been taken over by the town police station, only their yellow-green glazed tiles visible from the street. The temple's status as a 'Wuxuan Protected Cultural Unit' has evidently not protected it. I had guessed as much before I arrived. My real reason for being in Wuxuan was not to inspect its condition, but to seek the answer to a very different question.

Did they really eat people in China during the Cultural Revolution? Many people interested in China asked me this question after a dissident writer from Beijing had made the claim, a quarter of a century after the events were alleged to have taken place. Former 'friends of China' in the West were particularly upset. So many of their illusions about the Mao era had already been shattered: could this possibly be true as well? The writer Zheng Yi had brought out some convincing documentary evidence but there was only one way to be absolutely sure. That was to visit the town of Wuxuan where the most horrific and widespread cases were claimed to have occurred.

On the second morning I walked a few hundred metres from the guesthouse towards the old part of town. Beneath the covered market in Wuxuan's main square, sacks of rice and bundles of tobacco were being traded in an early morning grey mist. Peasant women from the Yi minority in broad-brimmed straw hats sat outside, with stacked tomatoes, piles of garlic, bundles of greens and a few eggs laid out on a cloth before them. In spite of the occasion, there was none of the variety of goods found in most Chinese markets these days: just a few piles of rubber sandals and some cheap clothes. Outside the department store a huckster from out of town selling sets of shoddy stereo speakers had attracted a crowd of poorly dressed young men.

The subject of cannibalism is not an easy one to raise, even at such a distance from the alleged events. But within half an hour, I had secured an unambiguous answer. Mr Li, a friendly middle-aged government clerk, was surprised I had heard the story but eager to confirm it. (Li is not his real name, although he wrote it down readily enough – and his address – in my notebook.) 'Yes, it was really bad in Wuxuan,' he told me. 'Just over there' – he pointed towards the main street of the old town stretching behind the market – 'I saw them. There was a big explosion next to the market and bodies everywhere.' But were people really eaten as well, I asked? 'Of course they were; it's true, not false at all! In Wuxuan,' Mr Li added with a touch of pride, 'we ate more people than anywhere else in China!'

Suddenly everything around me began to make sense, as I recognised the actual locations described in the documents and eye-witness reports brought back by Zheng Yi. Old Wuxuan has hardly changed in the last quarter of a century, and its walls still carry the faded slogans of the Cultural Revolution. The market square lies on the eastern side, the broad Qian River to the west. The main street – less than five minute's walk from end to end – runs between the two, descending to the water's edge in a long flight of well-worn flagstone stairs. Most of the killings in May–June 1968 followed the logic of this simple geography. The market was where the victims were put on show while the river was the scene of the worst butchery. On the main street in between, these 'class enemies' were paraded before the horrified (or simply curious) population, their hands and feet lashed with electric wire, forced to kneel and 'confess their crimes'. They were then dragged down the steps to the riverside. Some large flattish black rocks near the water's edge became Wuxuan's killing stones. They made a convenient butcher's table and the unwanted bits could be disposed of in the river.

The fast-flowing Qian river rises near the Vietnam border, loops through Guangxi province and eventually – 500 kilometres downstream from Wuxuan – debouches not far from Hong Kong. These days it carries little smoky freighters, small river-steamers with narrow bunks for human sardines, and tiny barges towing enormous rafts of timber. At the height of the Cultural Revolution, it carried bodies. The Hong Kong police fished dozens of corpses out of the harbour in the summer of 1968. Reports of fearsome fighting between Red

Guard factions in Guangxi had reached the outside world, and even Mao Zedong was known to have expressed alarm. Fighting had been intense at the river port of Wuzhou near the border with Guangdong province where the Qian joins other tributaries to become the West River, but Wuxuan was too distant for its worse horrors to become known. Within China, rumours of cannibalism in Guangxi were already circulating in the early 1970s, but hard evidence was only provided in the secret Party documents obtained by Zheng Yi in the late 1980s. Here, summarised from a report compiled by Wuxuan's county government in 1987, are two examples.

(1)   Zhou Shian was dragged to the town crossroads by a barber called Niu Huoshou and forced to kneel down. Beaten half to death, he was then pulled down the long flight of stone steps to the riverside. Wang Chunrong then used a five-inch knife to cut Zhou open and extract his heart and liver. Others joined in and soon stripped him to the bone. Then they used a wooden boat to dump his remains in the river.

(2)   A raiding party from across the river seized three brothers from the Li family, and dragged them to the vegetable market where they were knifed to death. Their bodies were then carried down to the river where the gang removed their livers and cut off their penises. The bodies were thrown into the river. That night they raped one of the widows, killed her pig and held a feast to celebrate the 'great victory of the people's proletarian dictatorship'.[1]

This secret report, compiled with bureaucratic thoroughness by local investigators, listed the 'different forms of eating human flesh'. These included 'killing and then having a feast, cutting up together but eating separately, baking human liver to make medicine, etc.' It also catalogued the 'eleven different ways in which people were killed'. These were 'beating to death, drowning, shooting, stabbing, chopping to death, dragging to death, cutting up alive, squashing to death, forcing someone to hang himself, killing the parent and raping the daughter, raiding to kill'. These investigations were carried out as part of a nationwide internal Party enquiry into the excesses and crimes of the Cultural Revolution, after being delayed and obstructed by Guangxi leaders fearful for their reputation.

'Those who participated in eating human flesh were, when all is said and done, a small number,' the report calmly concluded. 'But it has still blackened the reputation of the people of Wuxuan and inscribed an inglorious page in their history'. It then proceeded to list by name 27 local officials (*ganbu* or cadres) who had been removed from the Party's register or expelled 'because they had eaten human flesh'. Fifty-nine peasant Party members had been similarly penalised. Another 17 non-Party cadres had lost their jobs (though some were allowed to continue work while no longer formally employed) or had demerits entered on their records. Twenty-six workers, also guilty of cannibalism, had lost their jobs or had their salaries reduced. More severe punishment – jail sentences of between one and 14 years – was reserved for the worst cases of murder in the factional fighting of this period, whether or not the bodies were subsequently eaten. The total of Party and non-Party individuals involved in murder was 137, not all of whom were jailed. No one was sent to jail for cannibalism alone. Altogether 526 persons in Wuxuan Town and the surrounding County were killed at the height of the Cultural Revolution, in summer 1968. In 75 of these cases, the victims' livers were then extracted and eaten.

It is clear from this report that many of the killers and flesh-eaters remained at large, some still working in local government offices. When Zheng Yi visited Wuxuan (and four other Guangxi counties where cannibalism had occurred on a lesser scale) in 1986 and 1988, he was warned not to go out at night. Some of the killers had powerful local connections. This lenient treatment stemmed both from the Party's instinct to protect its own and from its concern to keep the affair from being known abroad. At one stage an internal bulletin issued by the provincial Party authorities calling for action against those found guilty of cannibalism was withdrawn for fear a copy might reach the Hong Kong press.

Zheng Yi managed to interview a few officials dissatisfied with the cover-up, a number of witnesses and family survivors, and even one or two of the butchers. After the Beijing massacre Zheng and his wife, Bei Ming, went into hiding. In 1992 they escaped via Hong Kong to the US where Zheng joined Princeton University's China Project. Determined to the point of obsession to make the tale known, Zheng published several articles in the Hong Kong press and produced a full-length book *Red Monument* to document his claims.[2] A report published in the *New York Times* was reproduced in several Western papers, and the well-known dissident journalist Liu Binyan wrote a powerful article in the *New York Review of Books* summarising the story.[3] But further reaction was muted. Foreigners – including most China specialists – found the whole affair inexplicable, part of an episode in modern Chinese history which had already been written off as a personal aberration of Mao Zedong. Overseas Chinese and other exiled dissidents also recoiled from the story, fearing it would reflect badly on China as a whole.

Even for those willing to face the story, it is hard to believe and harder still to comprehend why it happened. Yet such events, in a 'backward' area such as Wuxuan, appear less extraordinary in the context of the near-total breakdown of state authority and social discipline during the Cultural Revolution. By spring 1968 the whole of Guangxi province had been torn by political struggle for over a year between rival Red Guard factions, each claiming to 'defend Chairman

Mao to the death'. These were manipulated by political cliques in the provincial capital of Nanning, and through them from Beijing. After a lull early in 1968, the more radical grouping – known as the April 22 Group or 'Small Faction' because of its numerical weakness – was roused by signals from the 'ultra-left' (Madame Mao and her 'gang' in Beijing) to a last-ditch struggle. The dominant United Headquarters grouping, known as the 'Big Faction', controlled by Guangxi governor and army boss Wei Guoqing, moved in literally for the kill. All Party officials, right down to the village level, were ordered to 'wage a Force 12 typhoon against the class enemy' and to carry out 'merciless class struggle'. The official (and minimum) estimate is that 90,000 throughout Guangxi died in what are now termed 'unnatural deaths'.

Wuxuan's savagery stemmed from this wider politically sanctioned conflict. In less than two months 87 people were killed in large-scale clashes in Wuxuan town and surrounding county, and a much larger total of 439 in local incidents. Scores were settled not just with the Small Faction but with others who had previously been in political trouble. They included former landlords, rich peasants, 'right-ists' denounced ten years before, 'bad elements' and some with families overseas. Proceedings started with a 'struggle meeting' and usually ended in death. What made Wuxuan exceptional (though not unique) was that one out of seven cases led to dismemberment and eating.

On 4 May 1968, the Small Faction in Wuxuan seized the river harbour office and requisitioned its funds. In confused skirmishes, a Big Faction leader was shot dead. His colleagues then called for reinforcements from two neighbouring coun-ties and on the night of 12 May captured the Small Faction's base. The survivors, mostly teenagers, fled to a rocky outcrop in the harbour at the foot of the old steps where they were rounded up early the next morning. According to the official account, at least 30 were killed on the spot. Altogether it records 95 deaths over a period of 40 hours of fighting at this time. At a memorial meeting for the dead of the Big Faction, two prisoners (both students) were hung on trees as a 'sacrifice'. (It is not clear whether they were already dead or still alive.) Witnesses told Zheng Yi that they were then butchered, and that their hearts and liver were removed, cooked with pork and consumed communally. If this is true, they were the first to be eaten. At the same time, the head and feet of the Small Faction's leader, Zhou Weian, were put on display in the market place. Witnesses say that his wife was forced to come and 'identify' them. Zhou Shian, whose slaughter by the town barber is described in the extract summarised above, was singled out because he was Weian's older brother.

I shall only quote sparingly from the official account of cannibalism in Wuxuan and from the supporting evidence gathered by Zheng Yi from eye-witnesses, officials, family members of some victims, and even a few participants. In a typical example, the official dossier lists the following episode under the heading 'Human flesh dinner parties':

> 10 July 1968: The police picket from Dongxiang District, on the pretext of 'suppressing bandits', shot dead Xi Qiye on Mount Jiama [the surname Xi indicates that the victim belonged to the Yao minority]. Luo Xianquan used a five-inch knife to cut out Xi's heart and liver. These were carried back to the police office in a bamboo basket by picket member Huang Tingjie. Some was given to the District Organisation Committee member Tan Rongguang. That evening the team gathered around the pot in the police station kitchen to consume it. In addition, the militiaman Huang Wenliu took two pieces of flesh home for his mother (Huang was later promoted to deputy head of the County Revolutionary Committee).

Such episodes, the dossier comments with formal disapproval, 'had a very bad influence on the masses'. Even worse, it also notes, were those instances when there was no liver or flesh left to eat, 'and people were not content but even wanted to take the left-over bones and intestines'.

Zheng Yi records that many school teachers were killed and at least two were eaten by their students. The head of Tongling Middle School, he was told, was the object of many struggle sessions. Although a guerrilla during the revolution, he had come from a landlord family. One night the students got tired of guarding him and killed him instead. The first person to eat his flesh was the girlfriend of his eldest son who had broken off the relationship. Many years later the family re-buried his bones for fear that some of the students (who were now government cadres) might dig them up to dispose of the evidence.[4]

There was an element of bravado in some of the acts of slaughter and cannibalism. A victim might be paraded and abused for some time before one or two bolder individuals 'dared' to kill him, watched with horrified fascination by the 'masses' – and by local officials who feared for their own lives. At first the victims were dragged to a secluded place before dismemberment, but within a month they were being openly butchered on the main street. The official record frequently notes in a chilling phrase that other people then 'swarmed around to remove the flesh'. The most active killers were young men in their teens and twenties, including former members of the defeated Small Faction who sought to prove their new loyalty.

The taboo on eating human flesh was eroded by degrees. Zheng Yi suggests the following sequence: (1) furtive eating by night, by individuals or families; (2) human and animal flesh are mixed together – those eating can delude themselves that they are 'only eating pork'; (3) as the blood craze spreads, eating becomes a vogue. Different parts of the body are prized for their therapeutic value and cooked in a variety of ways. At the peak of the movement, human flesh is served at banquets with wine and loudly shouted guessing games.[5]

By July 1968 the violence in Guangxi had reached such dimensions as to alarm Mao Zedong and the Cultural Revolution leadership in Beijing. Though still insisting that some social disorder was a 'minimum price to pay' for routing out the 'capitalist-roaders', they knew it had to be stopped. 'A thousand houses have been burnt in Guangxi,' the army chief Lin Biao told Mao, 'and no one was allowed to put out the flames.' The conflagration from the wild south-west could not be allowed to spread. The army was finally given clear orders to move in all over China, evict the Red Guard factions from their bases and send them 'down to the countryside'.[6]

The special horrors of Wuxuan only became known in Beijing as the result of a remarkable act of courage which must have saved many lives. Wang Zujian was an honest ex-official, sent to a state farm in Wuxuan for criticising Party policies which had led to starvation in the Great Leap Forward. Released from the farm, he was now working quietly in the town's cultural office, hoping to keep out of trouble. Every day as he walked to work he was confronted by the slaughter on the streets. His wife, pregnant at the time, had arranged an abortion at the local hospital. She was so terrified that after two attempts to reach it she gave up. Wang resolved to denounce the cannibalism to the authorities, knowing that if his letter were intercepted he would probably get eaten too. An envelope addressed directly to Beijing would have aroused suspicion. He sent it to a relative, asking him to forward it to an old friend from the revolution, who in turn sent it to the capital. The ruse succeeded with dramatic results.

One morning early in July the rumour spread that a 'big chief' was arriving to inspect Wuxuan. Soon a long convoy arrived at the river port. Soldiers quickly fanned out to cover their commander as he entered the town. He was Ou Zhifu, commanding officer of the Guangxi Military District.

Striding through the carnage, he confronted Wen Longsi, the head of Wuxuan's ruling 'revolutionary committee' and went straight to the point.

'How many people have you eaten here? Complaints have been made to Beijing! Why didn't you stop it? Why didn't you report it?' Pointing directly at Wen, he thumped the table. 'Wen Longsi, from tomorrow, if one more person is eaten I'll make you pay. I'll blow your head off!'

The killing stopped immediately. Wen wished to save his head: so too did the Guangxi commander whose career would be blighted if Beijing blamed him for the consequences of the 'Force 12 typhoon'. The heroic Wang was identified after a friend revealed his name under torture. Wang was sent back to labour camp but left alive. The town leaders feared subsequent investigation if they killed him too. His wife had the baby – their fourth child.[7]

After being released again from labour camp following Mao's death, Wang Zujian continued to lobby the Party leadership in Beijing for an inquest into the Wuxuan affair. A second letter sent by him in 1978, at a time when material which discredited the Cultural Revolution suited the purposes of the Deng Xiaoping faction in Beijing, was actually published in a high-level internal news bulletin circulated by the *People's Daily*. Yet more than a quarter of a century later these grisly events remain an obscure footnote to the Cultural Revolution, and the Chinese government still officially denies that they ever took place. Without the efforts of Wang and later of Zheng Yi, the victims of Wuxuan would be totally forgotten, except by their surviving families forced to mourn in silence. That remains the fate of other victims in counties which have not shared Wuxuan's notoriety.

The 1987 report detailing Wuxuan's outbreak of cannibalism was printed in a limited edition of 39 copies. Of these, 30 went to party offices in Liuzhou city and the regional capital of

Nanning and nine remained in Wuxuan County where they were kept secure in the party headquarters. Such secrecy applies to much less sensitive aspects of local history all over China, contributing to a general ignorance about the past. Wuxuan's bookshop, when visited in October 1993, did not contain a single publication on local affairs. The main bookshop in Guilin City only offered, apart from simple map-guides to the region, one volume on 'famous historical figures of Guangxi'. Yet almost every county in China possesses an archive and a team of local historians who, since the Cultural Revolution, have resumed their work of collecting material and producing local gazetteers, *difangzhi*. These are a direct successor to the *fangzhi* compiled in imperial times from the Song dynasty (960–1279) onwards. Only a small number were produced in the 1950s before a succession of political campaigns brought historical work to a halt. Though revived in the early 1980s, the compilation of county histories still poses enormous political problems. Only a minority of Guangxi counties have produced new county histories, *xianzhi*: Wuxuan, whose last *xianzhi* was published in 1936, is not among them.

China's local historians have to contend with the dilemma of how fully or accurately to report the 'irregular deaths' from malnutrition and disease of the Great Leap Forward, and the factional fighting and resulting deaths of the Cultural Revolution in 1968. Some also face the opposite dilemma of how to handle statistics showing that agricultural production actually did quite well during the Cultural Revolution, even though it was supposed to be 'ten years of chaos'! Though secret reports similar to that on Wuxuan's cannibalism were compiled in each county, they could not be quoted in the county histories. National policy, laid down in a decision of April 1985, is that 'it is better to write sketchily than in great detail'. All entries on politically sensitive matters have to be referred to higher authorities for approval.[8]

A survey which I have made of six Guangxi county histories (Gongcheng, Hengxian, Binyang, Yangshuo, Fusui and Shanglin) shows how patchily these difficult areas are reported. Three of the six give precise information on the number of 'irregular deaths' during the Great Leap Forward. In Gongcheng County, we are told that eight per cent of the population died in 1960. Hengxian reports that there were 21,000 cases of oedema of whom 1,480 died. Shanglin gives exact statistics for deaths from oedema, rickets, prolapse of uterus and malnutrition. The other three counties are much more circumspect.

The violence of the Cultural Revolution is also unevenly reported. Yangshuo only records one death in the county, though offering a vivid description of the street corner shrines to Mao before which the people sang 'The East is Red' in the morning and performed the Loyalty Dance. Fusui County reports with unusual candour 'more than 500 deaths' from fighting in 1968 (a similar figure to that given in Wuxuan's secret report), while Hengxian reveals that 144 died in the 'worst case' of the period. Binyang County's publicly available county history notes 36 deaths in June 1968, and an unspecified number in the following month. Yet Zheng Yi claims that Binyang's secret report on the Cultural Revolution, acquired by him during his investigations, records a total of 3,681 who were killed or 'driven to death' in July, including 51 cadres and no less than 87 teachers. Shanglin's county history merely records that the fighting in July 1968 led to 'serious cases of killing'. Zheng Yi has seen documents showing that 1,100 were killed in July and August, including 72 slaughtered at a memorial meeting for the death of a Big Faction leader. These also reveal more than 70 cases of cannibalism in Shanglin, although it is explained – as if by way of extenuation – that the people there 'only ate the liver'! Whatever the real truth may be, it is not publicly available.

The Party's investigation in the early 1980s which led to

the disciplining or imprisonment – however inadequate – of some of those responsible was also kept secret. Only very rarely did any cases appear in the press. On 10 September 1984 the *People's Daily* carried an exceptional front page report. A Guangxi official who 'plotted and directed mass slaughter', it said, had been unmasked in his native province of Sichuan whither he had fled 'on the pretext of returning home to look after his parents'. Xu Mingde was a 'rebel' leader in Lingui County (near Guilin) during the Cultural Revolution and a member of the county's 'revolutionary committee'. The paper reported that from June to September 1968, Xu had 'personally plotted and directed the mass slaughter of a large number of Party and government cadres and innocent masses, including the county deputy Party secretary, the deputy county head and 17 other county or district officials'. Xu was also accused of having 'personally killed people using extremely cruel methods' (perhaps a veiled reference to cannibalism).

Xu was described as a plausible fellow who was skilled at ingratiating himself. The Chongqing officials had been shocked when police from Guangxi arrived to arrest him: 'No one could understand how such a well-behaved person could have committed such heinous crimes', the report concluded. This story probably emerged because Xu was exposed in another province which had no reason to cover up his crimes. It also gave the *People's Daily* – then the most radical voice among Beijing newspapers – the opportunity to publish an editorial comment arguing that criminals from the Cultural Revolution who had slipped back into respectability should be exposed. 'Their speeches in public are very pleasant to the ear,' it warned, '. . . and their records are "very clean". But they are the most dangerous people.'[9]

Such revelations of everyday cruelty during the Cultural Revolution are rare: only the sufferings of famous leading officials such as Liu Shaoqi and Peng Dehuai (former Head of

State and former Minister of Defence respectively) have been given prominence. Even in the laxer climate of the 1990s, the popular tabloid weekly papers focus on such well-known cases while avoiding the topic of mass violence. Ordinary Chinese people continue to be kept in the dark about the past even in their own localities. The same applies, with rare exceptions, to contemporary events such as the peasant riots discussed in chapter II. As Zheng Yi's close friend Liu Binyan has observed, the ordinary Chinese citizen knows only 'the tiny part that he or she [has] experienced personally', resulting in a collective historical blindness which is one of the society's greatest weaknesses today.[10]

Even with more information, the tragic events of Wuxuan are not easy to understand. For the dissident researcher Zheng Yi, passionately anti-communist in the Solzhenitsyn mode, the answer may seem very simple. The Communist Party and Mao Zedong, he maintains, are more savage, more inhuman, than Chiang Kai-shek or even Hitler and there is no necessity for further explanation. The only need is to expose what has been covered up by timid or complicit Party officials for the past 25 years. Guangxi's cannibalism in this view was just another crime in the sequence which includes the persecution of hundreds of thousands of intellectuals in the 1950s, the millions of famine deaths in the Great Leap Forward, the murders and forced suicides of the Cultural Revolution, and the Beijing Massacre. Within China, among those who are dimly aware of such events as the cannibalism of 1968, the answer is rather different. What happened in Wuxuan was an extreme act of madness during ten years of madness and, if further explanation is needed, it occurred in a 'minority' region of China where only half of the population is Han Chinese. Besides (as I was told by several people in neighbouring counties to Wuxuan, anxious to excuse the blot on Guangxi) 'only a few got eaten'! Another explanation points to episodes of cannibalism in the past during floods or famines: 'It happens everywhere from time to time'.

Our own enquiry should range more widely and delve more deeply. The eating of human flesh in Wuxuan and elsewhere in Guangxi in 1968 has nothing to do with the 'famine cannibalism' recorded in China whenever millions starve through war or natural disaster. (Some cases were recorded during the Great Leap Forward – although these are also officially denied.[11]) It was 'revenge cannibalism' in which the victor demonstrates extreme contempt for the defeated foe by consuming parts of his body after (or sometimes before) death. The philosopher Mengzi (Mencius, 374–289 BC) observed long ago that 'when men depart from righteousness and benevolence, they become like animals, even devouring their fellows'. Chinese dynastic history has recorded a large number of such cases over several thousands of years. Though many may be apocryphal, the practice is not unknown in more recent times and has been recorded in many other societies.[12]

Revenge cannibalism in China is also related to a belief in the therapeutic value of consuming certain parts of the human body. The notion of *yi nao bu nao, yi xin bu xin* (nourish the brain by eating brain, and nourish the heart by eating heart) can be extended from animal brains and hearts to those of human beings. Bread soaked in the blood of an executed criminal was popularly thought to have powerful medicinal properties. (One of Lu Xun's short stories, 'Medicine', was based on this theme.) Eating the gall or liver of a defeated enemy was believed to impart to the consumer some of the courage of the victim. At the same time, it was a way of expressing contempt and punishing the offender most severely by consuming the body's most vital organs.

At this point we have to consider the contrary view of some anthropologists that cannibalism is a powerful myth which has no evidential basis (except in rare cases of famine cannibalism). Ever since the Conquistadores first traduced the Aztecs, Professor P. Arens has written in *The Man-eating Myth*, Western societies have used the slur of cannibalism to de-humanise those whom they conquer, especially in the so-called Dark Continent. Though Livingstone found no evidence of cannibalism, Stanley saw it everywhere.[13] Is cannibalism in China anything more than a powerful metaphor for the most destructive forces in human society? Lu Xun's most famous short story, 'A Madman's Diary', describing the patient's delusion that 'now they are eating children' in the streets outside, was a powerful allegory for the heartless conduct of the rulers of warlord China after the failure of the 1911 revolution. The contemporary writer Wen Yuhong in her story 'Mad City' has described an atmosphere of mounting blood lust in which an entire community progresses from killing dogs to butchering human beings. The violence of the Cultural Revolution, though often very severe, was also subject to exaggeration. Red Guard documents at the time routinely spoke of 'sanguinary atrocities' and 'bloody battles' even in the case of minor incidents. Is it possible that the entire Wuxuan episode of cannibalism is a myth generated by the community at a time of extreme tension and conflict, which has been reinforced by years of second-hand rumour and repetition?[14]

Though this interpretation has to be considered seriously, it does not stand up against the sheer volume and circumstantial detail both of the Party documents and of Zheng Yi's investigations. The locating in Guangxi in general, and Wuxuan in particular, of stories about cannibalism during the Cultural Revolution is also suggestive. It is very hard to read through all the material without concluding that, though some episodes may have been embellished in the retelling (whether to the Party investigators or to Zheng Yi), the picture of a wave of cannibalism over a limited period of time is substantially correct.

Why Guangxi alone? The anthropologist Wolfram Eberhard has listed six types of cannibalism in historical China which, he observes, has been treated insufficiently in general studies of the subject. These are cannibalism out of 'perverse passion', out of real need (famine), as a test of courage or an ordeal, for medical reasons, for ritual purposes, and finally 'cannibalism as revenge'. The majority of examples which he has found were located in southern China among minority ethnic groups including the Liao, Miao and Yao.[15]

Though this correlation may partly explain the strength of the tradition of cannibalism in the area, as an explanation for the events of 1968 it is not borne out by Wuxuan's current racial composition. The Yao Nationality Autonomous County lies in the Great Yao Mountains immediately to the east of Wuxuan. But the only Yao involved by name in the 1968 episodes were victims and not aggressors. About 60 per cent of the population of Wuxuan County is composed of the Zhuang minority who give their name to the Guangxi Zhuang Autonomous Region. Yet the Zhuang have long been sinified by Chinese culture through inter-marriage and education. Many no longer speak the Zhuang language and cannot be easily distinguished from Han Chinese.

It is however true that the people in this part of central Guangxi, of whatever race, have long had a reputation for unusually fierce behaviour. In neighbouring Guiping County, just across the boundary from Wuxuan, the great Taiping Rebellion which rolled up half of China in 1951–64 was first launched from the foothills of Mount Thistle. One of its leaders, the 'Western King' Xiao Chaogui, came from a Wuxuan peasant family. The Taipings' very first military foray was actually launched into Wuxuan. In later years, the Taiping soldiers were alleged to indulge in the practice of eating the hearts of their prisoners to make themselves braver in combat.

Certainly, the area from which they originated was known

to be particularly impoverished. 'The poverty of the inhabitants was a powerful auxiliary,' a contemporary French writer noted, 'and an army of adventurers could easily recruit among a population living in a sort of destitution'.[16]

Guangxi's soldiery earned a reputation for fierce combat in the Sino-French War (1884–85) and during the 1920s Guangxi was virtually independent under the warlord rule of the Guangxi Clique. 'The sense of provincial identity within Guangxi was very strong,' one study concludes, 'created by the isolation of Guangxi, by its sense of being disparaged by other provinces, and by its history of rebellion against central authority.'[17] In 1933 Wuxuan was visited by the Chinese traveller Tian Shulan, a perceptive geographer and anthropologist from Hunan who had decided to study his native land by personal observation, beginning his journeys in Guangxi. Wuxuan's inhabitants, he wrote, were 'simple in their habits, accustomed to bitterly hard work, martial in spirit, ferocious in fighting, practical-minded and not concerned with the outside world'. He also observed that:

> The people of Wuxuan were directly influenced by the Taiping Army, which instilled a revolutionary mood among them. There was a time when they joined the army in large numbers, becoming adept in the martial arts; they were brave in combat, forming military bands which terrified people everywhere. They had a deep sense of clan loyalty, and whenever there was some dispute over poorly marked land boundaries, they would fight with weapons in groups, sacrificing their lives and sparing nothing. The current county head Mr Zhu has strictly ordered them to desist. They have responded to his injunction and this habit is gradually dying away.[18]

It did not die away completely. The Wuxuan Party's own secret report in 1987 offers some more recent historical evidence. It notes that 'during the anti-Japanese war, there were cases when soldiers from the aggressors' army – who had raped, burnt and slaughtered the local people – were captured. Due to the popular wrath, a small number of Japanese puppets were cut up and eaten after they had been killed'. Then, it continues, during the Cultural Revolution, a few individuals 'fell into the same habit'. Some were forced to eat human flesh, but others were influenced by 'the ignorant story ... that cooked human liver or flesh could cure numerous ailments'. Yet how could this happen, the report concludes plaintively, in the modern age when the people of Wuxuan had already reached 'a high level materially and culturally'?

That is indeed a very good question, to which the most probable answer in that Wuxuan was *not* (and still is not) at a high material and cultural level. In Wuxuan as in the rest of China, a desperately poor community, with little more than a veneer of socialism over its traditional outlook, was expected to act out a political drama which it barely understood. Conflicting signals from Beijing destroyed the authority of those Party officials who still believed in 'serving the people'. *If* the people of Wuxuan had been as politically mature as Beijing propaganda pretended, and *if* they had enjoyed a reasonable standard of living and education, it might have been different. Rather, control was seized by the ignorant, the insecure, the power-hungry and the pathologically violent. A primitive kind of class struggle did take place in which those with more education and slightly better jobs (particularly teachers) were vulnerable targets. The result was tyranny by a few, terror for the majority, and a growing mob hysteria in which this traditional form of revenge-taking, established with particular strength in this area of Guangxi, was dreadfully revived.

Guangxi remains heavily disadvantaged to this day. The region was trebly isolated for three decades by geography, strategy and politics. Its geographical remoteness made it a weak contender for central funds: in the first Five-Year Plan it only won two per cent of state investment, falling to less than one and a half per cent in the next two plans. On the map, Guangxi's situation should have been eased by the 1,600 kilometres of coastline which opened the door to trade across the South China Sea. But Guangxi's strategic significance, in the years of Western embargo (and later of the Vietnam War), kept that frontier closed or undeveloped. In these circumstances Guangxi's political life tended to reflect in an intensified form the more extreme, 'leftist' features of national politics. In a deprived society, grand solutions seem more tempting. In the Great Leap Forward the so-called 'wind of communism' was particularly intense in Guangxi with catastrophic results. In 1961 the value of agricultural output had fallen by one-third compared to the last pre-Leap year of 1957, that of industry by over one-half. In the Cultural Revolution, leftist leaders proclaimed the unrealistic goal 'of catching up with national advanced levels in industry and agriculture by 1975'. A massive hydroelectric project at Xiaqiao produced less than one-twelfth of its planned output. A campaign to build a nitrogenous fertiliser plant in each county collapsed without a single plant going on stream. Ten years after the end of the Cultural Revolution, Guangxi reformers still warned that the 'rigid and ossified ways of leftist thinking' had not been properly eradicated. Guangxi, said the chairman of its provincial government in 1987, was 'several years late in . . . bringing order out of chaos'.[19]

National Chinese leaders recognise that Guangxi poses a particular challenge to their policies of economic development and in 1988–93 it was visited in turn by each of them. They were also concerned by rapid population increase: in 1981–85 growth was an average of 670,000 people annually, reaching a total of over 40 million by 1987. Because of flooding, output of grain actually decreased by over twelve per cent in 1988. Retail prices went up by over

20 per cent in the same year – as is often the case, the poorest regions suffer from the worst inflation (Guangxi had the fourth highest inflation rate in the 1980s). In 1990 Guangxi had the second lowest gross national product (GNP) of any Chinese province, and the fourth lowest educational provision. Per capita GNP in 1992 was 668 renminbi lower than the national average, yet inflation in the following year was the third highest in the country. Bank interest rates shot up from eight to as high as 25 per cent. In 1993 the national propaganda chief Li Ruihuan reported, after touring Guangxi, that there were 'still several million people who have not resolved the problem of adequate food and clothing'. Average incomes had barely increased while the gap between towns and villages widened, indicating that rural incomes had actually declined.

Zhao Fulin, an energetic official from Hubei province, was brought in to run the Guangxi Communist Party in 1990. He was joined by Lei Yu, an entrepreneurial official from free-wheeling Hainan, as deputy-governor. In September 1993, Zhao gave an unusually frank interview to the provincial broadcasting station:

> Even to this day, in the myriad mountains of western and northern Guangxi, there are still over five million people of different ethnic origins who do not have adequate food or clothing. Whenever I come face to face with the people there, I cannot help sighing and grieving. Forty years have passed, yet Guangxi's economy is still so backward and the people are still so poor. As a Communist Party member, how uneasy I feel! Comrade Deng Xiaoping's remarks in southern China were a great catalyst. Guangxi can no longer remain in a state of inertia. We must do all we can to catch up to the pace of national progress . . .

It has now been decided to make Guangxi the 'gateway to the sea' for the landlocked provinces of south-west China, investing new funds in road, river and rail transport. Zhao outlined the new plan with a numerical formula of the kind always popular among Chinese political leaders. 'One river' will be developed – to improve navigation on the West River below Nanning for freighters above 1,000 tons. 'Two railways' will be constructed, Nanning-Kunming and Yulin-Wuzhou, the first of which creates a new rail link with Yunnan province. 'Three airports' will be built or improved, for Guilin, Wuzhou and Liuzhou. 'Four seaports' will be expanded (Fangcheng, Beihai, Qinzhou and Maoershan). And 'five highways' will be built, establishing new trunk roads from Nanning to most parts of the region.[20]

Opening up Guangxi in this way, if enough funds can be found for infrastructural investment, will go some way towards correcting the region's historical disadvantages. But will it help Wuxuan and the other 'backward' counties of Guangxi, or will the gap between rich and poor, town and country, only widen further?

The difficulties of 'opening up' Guangxi are illustrated by its tourist industry, which is almost entirely focused on one attraction, matched elsewhere in China only by the Great Wall and the Yangzi Gorges. Over half a million tourists from abroad now visit Guangxi yearly, nearly three times as many as in the early 1980s. Ninety-five per cent of them head for Guilin to view the rounded peaks of the limestone karst hills on either side of the Li River flowing south to Yangshuo. The Li River first attracted tourism in the Tang dynasty when the poet Han Yu wrote that 'The river winds like a blue silk ribbon, while the hills stand up like green jade hairpins'. In the language of classical guidebooks still quoted today, the 83-kilometre journey by boat to Yangshuo sails between 'green hills, clear waters, fantastic caves and peculiar rocks', passing through 'deep pools, dangerous shoals, cliffside springs and splashing waterfalls'. Every other peak has been given its own fanciful identity: there is the Elephant Hill and its Water-moon Grotto, the Fighting-Cock Hills, the Horses Galloping on a Fresco, the Green Lotus Peak, the Monkey Holding a Watermelon, the Black Bear Looking up to the Sky, the Lion Riding on a Carp, and many more.[21]

Most of this tourist traffic flies in and out of Guilin without venturing elsewhere in Guangxi. A small number reaches the Li River by land or boat directly via Wuzhou, near the Guangdong border, from Guangzhou or Hong Kong. The cities of Nanning, Liuzhou, Beihai and Wuzhou attract most of the remaining five per cent of visitors. Guiping County, where the famous Taiping Rebellion was launched in 1850, receives less than a hundred foreign visitors in the year, most of them Overseas Chinese. Tourist revenue is largely confined to the Guilin region which earned 64 million US dollars in 1990. Poor communications, lack of hotels and bureaucratic obstacles still prevent other parts of Guangxi from developing access to natural sights as beautiful as anything which Guilin can offer. Guilin was officially 'opened' (*kaifang*) to foreign tourism in 1973. Twenty years later, many potential tourist attractions within a few hours' bus ride from Guilin were still 'closed'. Temples and other historical buildings which were neglected after 1949 or severely damaged in the Cultural Revolution are now being restored in a few counties. Wuxuan is not one of them.

Beyond the Great Yao Mountains to the east lies Gongcheng, a far more accessible county in the Guilin region which enjoys many advantages compared to Wuxuan. Gongcheng's *wenmiao* or Temple of Culture, originally smaller than Wuxuan's, now claims to be the largest in Guangxi. During the Cultural Revolution it was unintentionally 'protected' by becoming the headquarters of the Big Faction. Rows of large wooden placards bearing Mao-slogans were placed along the main roof, preserving its fine decoration in glazed tiles of serpents and mythical beasts. A miniature version of the buildings at Confucius's birthplace in Qufu (Shandong province), the Gongcheng temple is now a rare place of tranquillity: in the summer months, large black butterflies hover with drooping wings over flowering azaleas and the curved eaves cast cool shadows. Gongcheng lies less than one hour's bus ride from the tourist centre of Yangshuo where the menus of all the street restaurants are written in English. In 1993 it was still officially 'closed' to foreigners, and a bus ticket could only be purchased in Guilin after a phone call to the Public Security Bureau. Other buildings including a fine *wumiao* or Martial Temple next to that of Confucius are finally being restored by the province. It will have taken Gongcheng nearly two decades since the Cultural Revolution to inscribe itself on any map known to the outside world.[22]

Wuxuan's attractions will remain hidden for much longer. The town lies four hours upstream from Guiping on the isolated Qian River as it skirts the Great Yao Mountains. The river, never less than 100 metres wide, runs swiftly between misty peaks with trees marching up their sides. The Flying Leap, an elderly steamer from Guangzhou, offers third class accommodation in rows of unpartitioned bunks ranged from bow to stern like open sardine tins. It has to pass through several rapids, encountering first an oily stillness, then a quick swirl of whirlpools, until with a thunderous roar of ancient engines it cuts its way through the agitated water. Passing beneath the Roc Mountain range, through the Great Vine Gorge and past the Jade Sands, it finally emerges in a landscape of rounded karst hills similar to those admired from the Li River by half a million tourists a year. Only a few adventurous backpackers ride the Flying Leap.

The hills around Wuxuan have also attracted legends as colourful as those of Guilin. They include the Immortal's Hill, celebrated by the Tang dynasty poet Liu Zongyuan, and the Eight Fairies' Pool. (The fairies bathed by night in its tempting waters. Caught by daylight, they turned into stones which still lie there.) In 1986 the discovery near Wuxuan of a 2,000-yard cave filled with fossilised remains was reported by foreign news agencies – the only time that the county was mentioned abroad until Zheng Yi's revelations. The cave contained fossils of more than 30 species of animals including the stegodon, an elephant-like mammal that lived more than 10,000 years ago. Wuxuan's important early associations with the Taiping rebellion are almost unknown. A new road is now being driven across the mountain to Jintian in neighbouring Guiping County where the rebellion began. Yet Guiping itself still awaits tourism on any scale, although local officials place their hopes on the Wuzhou-Nanning trunk road now under construction.

New roads bring progress but they also encourage unsettling contrasts with more favoured towns and counties. Old Wuxuan behind the covered markets has hardly changed since the horrors of 1968. But the sons and daughters of those involved emulate an entirely different lifestyle in the dingy dance halls, karaoke bars and hairdressing shops of new Wuxuan. At weekends they can now reach Liuzhou City in less than three hours by bus, along the new highway between Liuzhou and the booming coastal city of Beihai far to the south. Liuzhou bustles by day with private entrepreneurs, and swarms by night with smartly dressed young people, enjoying the neon lights, jewellery shops, fast food stalls and night clubs. Cultural innovations come to Wuxuan by the same route. On the police station wall in the old part of town, during my visit to Wuxuan, the following cautionary tale was displayed:

> In the evening of 2 August 1993, opposite the bus station in the 'Basement Video Parlour' run by the Wuxuan County Cultural Palace, more than 200 local young men crowded in the flickering light. At first, the screen echoed with the noise of gun fights, martial

arts and explosions. Some of the audience stayed put and others walked to and fro but none could bring themselves to leave.

At 1 am, the young men outside all flocked back in, and the iron door clanged shut. Then on the silver screen there appeared a sight not meant for human eyes: the image of a man and women engaged in intercourse! In a moment the whole hall was silent. Some young men even let their lighted cigarettes burn their fingers without noticing.

At 1.20 am, a car containing public security officers left the city gate police station for the Basement Video Parlour. Its unguarded iron door was forced open according to law. There was confusion inside and the original film of shooting and fighting was quickly substituted for the one being shown. After the audience had been evicted, the County Middle School student Li Jian was searched according to law. Three yellow films were found on his person, including the one just shown: 'The Nun Sister Discovers the Joys of Love.'

The police bulletin, written in the journalistic style now used by the popular broadsheets, ended with a warning to the 'gentlemen' responsible for peddling pornographic videos. If they persisted, it concluded rather weakly, they would certainly end up in jail! In spite of repeated campaigns and exemplary punishment, the trade appears unstoppable everywhere in China. Guangxi has a particularly bad reputation for the kidnapping of women to be forced into prostitution.

City pleasures reach Wuxuan more easily than rewarding work for its youthful labour force (half the population here, as elsewhere, is less than 20 years old). Across the Qian River by the bridge which carries the new Liuzhou-Beihai road, one reaches a vacant site on waste ground displaying the sign 'Wuxuan Technology Development Zone'. In 1993 it was still – like most county-level development zones in the interior – empty of new industry. Unless it can deliver jobs, Wuxuan's young people will become increasingly frustrated with their lives. On a wall next to the market on National Day, the county's exam results for college entrance are pasted up on red honorific paper, anxiously studied by candidates from the town. The Confucian temple may be derelict, but graduating from high school to college elsewhere remains the only sure route to a better career. In the town's karaoke bars, every youth whom I questioned has only one ambition: to escape from Wuxuan. The county is by no means exceptionally disadvantaged. It is in the middle range of the Guangxi statistics: in the nationwide directory it is classified as 'hilly' rather than 'mountainous' (where the worst cases of poverty are found). These anonymous counties are rarely visited or studied, yet they are a significant test for the reforms. How many other Wuxuans are there in Guangxi, or in China?

IX

China's New Frontier

I climb into my lonely pavilion and gaze towards the
  imperial capital;
Even a bird would take half a year to fly such a
  distance;
Rivers and mountains must terrify the man who makes
  the journey,
Circling this way and that a thousand times, winding
  from town to town.

(Li Deyu, written in exile on Hainan, AD 849)

Hainan province is an island of misty mountains, coconut
palms, sandy beaches, tropical rain-forest, and – in recent
years – a booming, entrepreneurial urban economy which
operates on the fringes of legality. In imperial times Hainan
was the final destination for exiled officials who had offended
the emperor. Though almost as large as Taiwan, it remained
in recent times virtually unknown, regarded on the mainland
as 'the end of the earth', excessively hot, filled with snakes and
populated by wild aborigines. After 1949 it was still distant
and obscure for most Chinese, though it was becoming an
important base for the People's Liberation Army (PLA) to

defend China against the US policy of 'containment' (and later to support Hanoi in the Vietnam War). Though Hainan was no longer a place for penal exile, migration was highly organised and most of those who went there had little alternative. In the 1950s, the majority were ex-soldiers and their families, economic migrants who were settled on state farms to open up the land.

A decade later in the Cultural Revolution, a new wave of political migrants arrived: young Red Guards who had volunteered, or been persuaded, to 'go down to the countryside'. There they cut down Hainan's forests to plant new rubber plantations with great enthusiasm but disastrous results for the environment. In the 1980s Hainan at last became such a desirable gaol that entrance to it from the mainland had to be restricted. 'Opened' to the outside world in the early 1980s, it was soon well known throughout China as a place where, it was said, the enterprising or the unscrupulous could prosper. Designated a Special Economic Zone in 1986, it attracted thousands of investors and job-seekers from all over China, flourishing in spite of a succession of financial scandals to become China's wild southern frontier. Hainan's new voluntary exiles from the mainland were soon testing, to the criminal limit and beyond, the post-Mao policy of allowing those with entrepreneurial ambitions to 'get rich first'.

As I travel around Middle China in the early 1990s, it sometimes seems as if everyone is heading for Hainan in the hope of making their fortune. The trains travelling south through Guangxi carry hopeful young entrepreneurs with their street-stall profits as capital. In the grey oil port of Zhanjiang just into Guangdong province, they are surrounded by touts at the railway station offering bus-boat tickets to the southern tip of the Leizhou peninsula, then across the straits to Hainan's capital Haikou. They waste no time as if every hour counts. Why are they going? The answer, with a laugh, is to *zhuangqian* – earn good money.

More circumspectly, junior civil servants and employees from government-owned industry on the mainland may announce that they are visiting Hainan 'for a holiday', nothing more. All their colleagues know that are were really going there to check out the prospects – but without smashing their state-provided 'iron rice bowl' in advance!

Under the arches of a new fly-over in Haikou, I find rows of mainland peasants squatting in the shade and waiting patiently. Some clutch a fret-saw to signify that they can do carpentry. Others just hold up their bare hands, offering their unskilled labour for hire. The fortunate among them will be taken on by the day to do the dirtiest jobs needed to underpin Haikou's construction boom. Excavating foundations by hand is regarded as slightly less filthy than digging gravel out of the river bed. Many spend the night too under the arches, in the same clothes which they have worn over on the ferry from Zhanjiang. Some are rounded up by the police and sent back to the mainland, to return as soon as they can. Only the luckiest ones manage to buy illegal *hukou* – residential permits. More than 20 per cent of these peasant migrants – some 80,000 out of 400,000 in Haikou in 1992 – have come from the deprived rural areas of Sichuan province alone.

The rush to Hainan swelled early in 1992 when Deng Xiaoping's 'southern expedition' gave a new boost to the economic reforms. In February, while he was visiting Shenzhen, 167,000 mainlanders applied to enter Hainan legally. Only 8,000 were turned away. Hainan's population of five million in 1988 had grown to seven million in five years. Its reputation was now well established as the 'most special' of the Special Economic Zones, with fewer restrictions than those on the mainland. Economic crimes, said the chief procurator in July 1991, were 'rather rampant'. A stock market, illegal at that stage, opened in the autumn. A housing boom developed in which 40 separate new property companies bought and sold land speculatively. Haikou soon became known, in the words of one Hong Kong newspaper, as 'the haven of smugglers, gangs, guns and girls'.[1]

Hainan was one of two provinces singled out in 1992 by the Ministry of Public Security in Beijing for an intensive anti-gun drive – the other was drug-laden Yunnan on the border with Burma. The Chinese press, in an unusually explicit account, reported the public destruction of arms and ammunition a year later. Since Hainan became a province in 1988, a police official explained, there had been a massive increase in the 'illegal manufacture, sale and private collection of arms' and in armed crimes. During the crackdown, the police claimed to have destroyed nearly 200 'dens' where arms were made or stored, and to have arrested more than 650 'gangsters'. Unfortunately the effort had to be repeated just one year later but made little difference. In the next official figures for January–June 1994, the authorities claimed to have arrested 5,500 criminals, broken up 318 criminal gangs and discovered 525 criminal hide-outs, and captured 2,556 guns including 199 combat weapons.

Prostitution in Hainan is widespread and unchecked, and the 'lemon tea-time' at the Haikou Hotel has become a tourist attraction. Most of the women come from Guangzhou, Guangxi or Shanghai, a few from the north-east. They wear expensive white slacks, pink or yellow silk blouses and have elaborate hairstyles. Protective young men in expensive leather jackets keep a watchful eye. The 'chickens' chat among themselves or peer, looking for customers, into powder-compact mirrors. The whole café is raised on a carpeted dais in the hotel foyer: 'chickens', clients and spectators are all together on the stage. There is a piano with a crimson cover on a green pedestal for use in the evening. Local waitresses, laughing a little, take orders for lemon tea – the signal of willingness to do business. 'The police never enter hotel rooms here,' a resident explains, 'unlike Guangzhou where they do so from time to time and levy fines by credit card. Here it is all arranged through the hotel security guards, who then pay off the police. They have become very wealthy men.'

Until the 1980s, Hainan was the last destination in China to which anyone would wish to migrate voluntarily. From ancient times it had been dimly perceived as an island buffeted by typhoons, inhabited by aborigines, far from Chinese civilisation and one's native home, traditionally the destination not for migrants but for exiles. Edward Schafer, one of the few Western scholars to study Hainan, has written:

> Through the ages Hainan has been regarded as the ultimate place of exile. It was horrible enough to be sent to live out one's days in misery in the fearful jungles of Annam beyond the Gate of Ghosts, but the passage of the strait that separated the island from the continent symbolised a divorce that was even more to be dreaded – the transit marked a sort of spiritual death. Even in modern times Hainan has been seen chiefly as a sink of desperadoes and outlaws . . . So worthless was it for the purposes of decent men that Sun Yatsen (according to one report) wished to sell it to a foreign power for fourteen million dollars.[2]

The poet Su Dongpo (whom we last met in fear of his life heading downstream through the Yangzi Gorges) would have agreed. The most famous of many officials exiled in classical times, Su spent three years in Hainan (1097–1100) near the end of his life. Writing in the 1940s Su's modern biographer, the author Lin Yutang, reflected the general attitude. Hainan was 'all but uninhabitable from the Chinese point of view. The climate was very damp, oppressive in summer and foggy in winter. During the autumn rains everything grew mouldy, and Su Tungpo once saw a great number of white ants dead on his bedposts . . . "How can a human being, who is not made of rocks or metals, stand this for long?"'[3] Su's philosophy of life, much influenced by Buddhism and Daoism, helped him to make the best of Hainan. Driven out of the house where an indulgent local official first allowed him to stay, Su built a shanty in a palm grove on the edge of the forest and made drinking friends with neighbouring families of the non-Chinese Li (or Loi) people.

> Half-sober, half-drunk, I call on the Lis;
> Bamboo spikes, rattan creepers tangle every step.
> Following cowpats I find my way back –
> Home beyond the cattle pen, west and west again.[4]

Su's western exile was physically hard to endure, and at times he had nothing to eat but vegetable soup. Even rice had to be imported from the mainland. 'We eat here without meat,' he wrote, 'get sick without medicine, seek shelter without houses, go out without friends, go through winter without charcoal, and through summer without cold springs. I cannot enumerate all the things we have to do without.' Finally reprieved in 1100 by the new emperor Hui Tsung of the Song dynasty, Su wrote another quatrain to celebrate his escape from Hainan (not knowing that he would die the next year).

> I thought I'd end my days in a Hainan village
> But God sent Wu Yang* to call back my soul.
> Far, far, where the sky lowers and eagles pass from sight:
> A hairbreadth of green hill – there is the mainland![5]

> [*the sorcerers who rescued the soul of the poet Qu Yuan]

Five other righteous officials, exiled for proferring unwelcome advice at court during the Tang and Song dynasties, are remembered locally in Haikou's 'Five Officials' Memorial Temple'. The most famous was Li Deyu, chief minister under two Tang emperors who, like Su after him, was banished first to Guangdong and then – to complete the humiliation – across the straits to Hainan. Li built a small pavilion where he sat and gazed back at the mainland, writing the lines quoted at the start of this chapter.[6]

Hainan's society has been formed by exile and migration over several thousand years. Until recent times the population was to a large extent stratified by race and location. The coastal lowlands were inhabited by ethnic Chinese who had migrated over many centuries from different parts of southern China creating an exceptional degree, even by Chinese standards, of linguistic confusion. Dialects of Mandarin, Fujianese, Hakka and Cantonese can still be found within a few miles of one other. After they were formed many of these communities in turn sent out new migrants, joining the outflow of Overseas Chinese into south-east Asia in the later nineteenth century: the coolie ships from Guangzhou stopped in Haikou harbour on their way to Malaya or the Dutch East Indies. Inland from the ethnic Chinese, non-Chinese Miao from Guangxi lived in the foothills of Hainan, while the mountains beyond them were occupied by the aboriginal Li or Loi. These are related to the Tai race of Indochina but have been domiciled in Hainan for three thousand years. The Chinese divided the Li into those communities which had been semi-sinicised – known as the Tame Li – and, beyond them, the Wild Li who lived in and around the peaks of the Five Finger Mountains. Until well into this century these inland parts were visited only by a few Chinese traders, and a small number of Western missionaries and naturalists. Hainan's most famous native son, the scholar-official Hai Rui of the Ming dynasty, had put forward a 'crossroads proposal' to build two roads across the Li territory, but nothing had been done. The botanist explorer B. C. Henry was told that 'to cross the island . . . directly through the centre was a feat which even the Chinese had never accomplished'.

Together with a Danish missionary, Henry almost managed to complete the crossing, but was frustrated as he reached the heart of the island by a Chinese trader who frightened the porters with false tales of bandits ahead. Henry described the fertile vegetation and mountain scenery in lyrical terms, offset only by reference to the frequent rain and to the leeches which attacked without mercy. In the valleys there were 'cat-tails in great abundance, covered with flowers like large yellow, purple-centred cups, ferns of great variety and grace, and, not the least attractive, vining bamboos, climbing over the larger trees, and stretching in graceful masses over the narrow ravines'. He saw mountains completely covered with heavy forest, and 'many fine ravines and wild gorges' cut in the side. The great Five Finger Mountains were shrouded in mist throughout his travel – as they usually are (the first European only reached the summit in 1922). As well as practising slash-and-burn agriculture, the Li traded in rattan, deer-horns, dried mushrooms, fragrant wood, hides and other minor articles for the Chinese market. Henry drew a favourable contrast between the local Chinese and the indigenous Li, and his advice to future travellers among the Li was 'to avoid, as far as possible, all dealings with the Chinese who live among them'.

> The contrast between them [the Li villagers] and an ordinary Chinese crowd was most evident. They kept at a respectful distance, unless encouraged to come near, and in their curiosity showed not the slightest rudeness ... It was a pleasure to gratify their curiosity. Our watches and alarm clock greatly astonished them. The texture of our sleeping rugs, and the gay colours of one of them, especially attracted them. They seemed possessed of an innate gentleness and politeness towards strangers that divested all their actions of rudeness.[7]

In modern times Hainan remained remote and poorly explored even though it was almost as large as Taiwan and lay on the main shipping route down the South China Coast to Indochina. Haikou had become a 'treaty port' in 1858, but was only fully opened to foreign commerce 20 years later. Its small Western community rarely travelled outside Haikou. When Henry visited Haikou in 1882, it had one principal street and a foreign population of a dozen. The trade of the port, he noted, had hardly realised the expectations awakened at its recent opening. Sugar, oil and live pigs were the chief exports but the island was already flooded with opium, the principal import trade, 'which comes in legitimately through the European houses' or was smuggled in by Chinese 'under foreign names'.[8]

A standard guidebook, Carl Crow's *Handbook for China* published in 1933, described Hainan as a 'little-known part' of Guangdong province whose central and southern parts were covered 'with densely wooded hills inhabited by aborigines'. Crow observed that there were 'great opportunities for development here, but efforts in that direction have been retarded by the climate of the place, its lack of communications, etc'. It was believed, he added prophetically, that rubber would thrive (and also camphor which however has not become one of modern Hainan's cash crops). The British Admiralty handbook, compiled from 1930s data, described Haikou port as 'poorly equipped'. The town had been modernised with concrete streets, but sanitary arrangements were 'primitive' and there was little industrial development.[9]

Yet Hainan was not too remote to suffer together with the mainland from warlord struggles, corrupt Guomindang rule and Japanese occupation. The Hainanese people did not endure passively but their resistance was ferociously suppressed. It has been calculated that over 17 major civil disturbances took place between 1895 and 1939, an average of one every two and a half years. Local warlords and

Guomindang governors levied extra-legal taxes, particularly on the Li people. The roving American traveller Harry Franck reported in 1925 that Hainan was politically 'in a mess' and mainly in the hands of local military dictators. The air was full of stories of the 'ruthless rule' of the most prominent of them who held Haikou.

> Within the week he had ordered five men shot for quarrelling in a gambling-place; another was executed for taking both the ten-dollar bill he had stopped to change into 'small money' at an exchange shop and the 'small money' itself, quite possibly by mistake. Long careful trials were not to the taste of the Hoihow [Haikou] dictator. A day or two before, several men had been brought to the yamen charged with some petty theft or misdemeanor. The dictator sent out to ask how many men there were; someone said nine, and nine were shot. A little later it turned out that two of the men were coolies who had just brought in loads for the yamen residents. But there was probably no prick of conscience or loss of sleep on the tyrant's part . . .[10]

After the ousting of the warlords on the mainland by the Nationalist army in 1927, followed by Chiang Kai-shek's suppression of the Chinese communists (destroying the 'united front' which Sun Yat-sen had formed with them), communist-led guerrilla groups emerged in Hainan. They seem to have shown great bravery but suffered enormous losses. In June 1928, a force of 3,000 men was reduced to just 130 who fled into the mountains. In 1932 these lost contact with the mainland communists and were blockaded on Mount Anrui in the centre of the island. 'They tried to flee one at a time,' says a history of the Red Army, 'but found no way out or back. They were short of food, clothing and medicine and were often caught in enemy ambushes, so that their life was desperately hard.' Finally breaking out after ten months, their numbers were now reduced to just 26 officers and men. The decimated movement struggled on, picking up to about 300 guerrillas by 1939 when the Japanese Army occupied Hainan.[11]

Three decades later, their exploits put Hainan on the map for the entire population of China through the ballet *The Red Detachment of Woman*. Set during the revolution in the Five Finger Mountains, it was one of the eight officially approved theatrical works staged under the direction of Jiang Qing (Madame Mao) in the Cultural Revolution. It tells the story of the daughter of a poor Hainan peasant, beaten by an evil landlord, who escapes and joins the guerrillas. When the group attacks the landlord's stronghold, in her anger she gives the signal prematurely and the enemy escapes. Later the guerrillas' mountain base is surrounded and the handsome Communist Party cadre in charge is captured and executed. Finally the uprising succeeds: the heroine personally kills the landlord and submerges her grief by becoming the new women's leader. The ballet offers idyllic views of Hainan's coconut groves and mountain peaks. 'Fleecy white clouds dot the clear blue sky,' reads one stage direction, 'coloured flags flutter in the breeze, songs fill the air. A lofty kapok tree is in bloom with a profusion of red flowers.' Peasant girls with straw hats and baskets of lichees form the *corps de ballet* and the revolutionary fighters quench their thirst with coconut milk: otherwise there is no attempt to portray Hainan's minority culture. The ballet did nothing to improve mainland understanding of Hainan. The island was merely the exotic location for a stereotyped revolutionary tale.[12]

It was in the end the hated Japanese occupiers who took the first serious steps to develop Hainan's economy during the Pacific War, building new ports, roads, a railway, and investing in mineral extraction and tropical agriculture. Conditions improved further after the 1949 Liberation, but Hainan was at a disadvantage in being subordinate to the provincial government of Guangdong. The opportunity to open up to the outside world in peacetime conditions was also denied. Hainan was in the 'front line' of China's southern defences and its life and economy were dominated by the PLA. This at least meant final completion of the Central Highway proposed by Hai Rui five centuries before. The only voluntary visitors were those Party cadres and trade unionists – and a few foreign residents in Beijing – rewarded for their work by a holiday on the southern beaches at Sanya. Hundreds of thousands of long-term migrants came to Hainan after 1949: whether they were exiles or volunteers was not so easy to tell.

In the 1950s groups of mainland PLA soldiers were demobilised and settled in Hainan, together with some ex-students and Overseas Chinese. Many of the soldiers belonged to the army which had originally liberated the island – and some to the Nationalist army which had been defeated. After the Korean War they were joined by a whole division. By 1958, these migrants totalled 39,000, of whom most were employed to open up the new rubber plantations.[13] China was effectively cut off from importing rubber – the nearest source would have been Malaya – by the Western embargo on strategic goods imposed during the Korean War, and was desperate to grow alternative supplies. Hainan's rubber production increased from nearly 200 tons in 1950 to 750 tons in 1957. A new drive was launched during the Great Leap Forward which elevated the goal of 'self-reliance' in rubber production to a new height. Here the figures for immigration become confused, perhaps not by accident. One Chinese source claims that between 1959 and 1962 a total of 300,000 mainlanders, 60 per cent of them ex-soldiers, arrived to open up more plantations.[14] The most authoritative survey of China's population shows nearly 190,000 arriving in 1959 while over 137,000 left. The same survey then claims that the statistics are missing for 1960. The next four years (1961–64) continue to show large movements of population in both directions – more than 463,000 coming in while over 597,000 left during the period. It offers this brief explanation:

> In 1961–64 outward migration was higher than inward migration. This was a period of bitter hardship for Hainan. Against the special background of three years of economic difficulties, the first wave of immigrants felt particularly unsettled, and the phenomenon of movement in the reverse direction suddenly appeared. The cumulative net outflow in these four years was 134,000 people, with an average each year of 33,600. 1962 was the high tide of emigration with a net outflow of 58,613 people.[15]

We can only guess at the human suffering and organisational confusion reflected in these bare figures (and concealed by those missing for 1960, the worst year throughout China for what were euphemistically known as 'economic difficulties'). In each year between seven and eight and a half per cent of the island's population left or arrived – an exceptional turnover which must have increased the chaos. Yet unlike everywhere else in China, there was no dramatic decline of population even in 1960. The younger age profile of the migrants and their above average physical fitness meant that in Hainan fewer people died of starvation or, in the official phrase, 'ahead of time'. Many of the migrants from this period who stayed and survived still live to this day on state farms in remote villages with few amenities, a forgotten generation for whom life has not greatly improved.

The road from the central highlands descends beneath the peaks of the Five Finger Mountains, where some scraps of the island's primeval forest still survive, past clearings where the mud-walled dwellings of Li or Miao farmers are thatched almost to the ground. It continues through the foothills towards Haikou, past a succession of state farms still known by their original military names. A small signpost is the only pointer to the 'No 10 Battalion Farm'. The side-road is metalled as far the 'Battalion headquarters' – now the main village building housing the farm's management office, school and other amenities. The farm managers welcome the unexpected visitor, switch on the electric generator which sparingly supplies the village with power, and discuss their problems over a meal, specially cooked in my honour, of snake. If only I could reciprocate with some good advice on how to solve their economic difficulties!

The chief manager (equivalent to a rural district head) is responsible for a community, scattered in small hamlets, of several thousands. 'Now we have to balance our own books,' he explains. 'The army or the state no longer supports us. We can't rely only on rubber. The yields of most of the old trees are falling off, and we cannot hurry the new ones. Now we are experimenting with growing avocadoes. Last year the market was good but this year we have to compete with the produce from Malaysia. We would like to set up some rural industry, but we need to find investors from outside.'

We rattle off in a bone-shaking jeep to visit one of the hamlets, an original settlement from the 1960s. It is ten kilometres down a muddy track barely negotiable after just a light rain. The inhabitants of the small community are at the end of the track up against the hillside which they terraced long ago. The deep shade of the rubber trees blocks out almost all the light, but four-fifths of those planted higher up the hill in the 1960s, they say, never survived. Now an ageing population, they live in old barracks split up into family units, or in cottages whose walls are lined with paper to keep out the damp. Incomes here are exceptionally low, still around the 30–40 rmb per month level which has not been an adequate wage since the 1970s. For food or entertainment they must walk all the way to the Battalion headquarters. These ageing exiles have a single, justified complaint: 'We made our sacrifice for the motherland. Why have we never been given our reward?'

The figures for migration to and from Hainan are again missing for the first three years of the Cultural Revolution (1967–69), but this period saw the beginning of a remarkable influx of new settlers. For the next two years alone, the figures show a net arrival of more than 200,000, increasing the island's population by five per cent. They were mostly ex-Red Guards and other 'educated youth' from the mainland, the majority from mainland Guangdong although some came from as far north as Beijing. After two years of 'making revolution', China's youth had been personally ordered by Mao to cease political struggle and go to the factories or countryside to 'learn from the workers and peasants'. The PLA moved in to schools and colleges, now no more than living quarters for the Red Guard factions, to enforce Mao's will. Most of the youth had no choice – except perhaps to be sent to a labour camp nearer home. 'There was never any thought in my mind of volunteering to go there,' one of them later recalled. 'In the first place who wants to leave Canton? And Hainan had a reputation as a dead-end place . . .' He tried to hide out in Guangzhou but was caught. 'Finally I was told bluntly that it was either Hainan or Yingde [labour camp] . . .' He went to Hainan and stayed for seven years. There were real volunteers as well. An Overseas Chinese girl, 15 years old at the time, joined a group in Beijing. 'We were very enthusiastic; we went there to carry out Chairman Mao's instructions and help the people of Hainan. Mao had said that the countryside was a great new world from which we should learn!'[16]

In the summer and autumn of 1968, foreign tourists returning by boat from Macao to Hong Kong often crossed the path of an identical elderly steamer heading from Guangzhou to Haikou (both vessels had belonged to the same shipping company before 1949). The decks of the Hainan-bound boat were lined with the fresh faces of young men and women – more often just boys and girls – wearing army-style caps and jackets decorated with Mao badges. Framed against the rich crimson sunset over the hills of Guangdong, it was a rare glimpse of the closed world of the Cultural Revolution. Though briefly within waving distance (and some did wave), the passengers of each boat inhabited such different worlds – colonial Hong Kong and revolutionary Hainan – as to be incomprehensible to the other group.

Arriving the next day at Haikou, most of the youth were placed on trucks and driven to one of Hainan's 120 state farms, deep in the countryside. Few would see Haikou again until they left the island. It was a rare event to visit the nearest county town for a political meeting or film. It was an effort even to walk on their Sunday off to the principal village where the state farm had its headquarters. The roads were unpaved and the hillsides thickly wooded: their job was to clear the forest and establish new rubber plantations. Everywhere the posters proclaimed: 'vigorously develop rubber production'. The saying was attributed to Mao's 'chosen comrade-in-arms' Defence Minister Lin Biao (until he was disgraced after his mysterious death in 1971). The state farms were under army control from 1969 to 1974. A village was a company; the farm became a battalion. Yet the army officers were generally popular among the sent-down youth, treating them fairly and insulating them from the political purges which continued on the mainland. Students sent to Hainan's self-contained state farms were less likely to become disillusioned with rural life than those on the mainland who were quartered in the people's communes, sharing directly in the peasants' rural poverty. One participant estimates that about one-third were happy and many married and settled down permanently. Twenty-five years later, the Overseas Chinese girl from

Beijing still recalled her time on Hainan (the average stay was three to five years) with affection.[17]

> It was the happiest time of my life. I knew nothing of the outside world; every day we spent up in the mountains felling trees, then back in the evening to read about [model soldier] Lei Feng. We worked very hard, up to 16 hours a day. We were told: 'Make revolution to defy death; defy death to make revolution'! We believed in it and tried our best.
>
> At first we drank water from the river. It was boiled but still made us ill. There were a lot of skin diseases and even snake bites. We had to cut down trees to build our hut and dragged them out by ox. There were accidents when trees fell on people. The hut was very simple, boys in one half, girls in another and a screen in between. We were quite innocent but sometimes people did go into the fields: the army officer in charge criticised us for yielding to the 'wind of impropriety'.
>
> We ate rice with some oil or soya bean; if we had egg we were very happy. Meat was supplied only on New Year's Day and National Day, and then everyone got diarrhoea. At one time we were not allowed to grow vegetables, told that it was capitalist to do so, but the Li people in the next village traded with us. Once someone caught a big snake which could not move fast enough because it had swallowed a small goat. We were all very pleased and said 'Tonight we'll have some extra dishes' – meaning the goat as well as the snake!

The long-term effect on the students of being sent down to Hainan may have been mixed: the immediate effect on the island's environment was disastrous. The American geographer Catherine Enderton conducted field research in 1980 and talked with many ex-Red Guards who had returned to Guangzhou University. She concluded that their efforts had been 'in large part economically counter-productive and environmentally destructive'. The official emphasis upon rubber production led to over-planting and overtapping. Under army leadership, the advice of expert local settlers was rejected. Saplings were planted on steep slopes vulnerable to erosion and there was insufficient water to nourish them. Trees were tapped when too young, and the mature ones were tapped too frequently. The pace of deforestation of Hainan was accelerated – Enderton estimates that the island's forest cover decreased by 50 per cent from 1950 to 1980. By 1984 265,000 hectares were planted with rubber against only 2,000 in 1950. The students themselves observed the speed with which the land deteriorated:

> Under the PLA we opened up too much land too fast, planted too many rubber trees and didn't consider the need for a labour force to care for the new trees. When we returned to the newly cleared areas the following year we couldn't even see the rubber tree saplings amid the weeds and brush. The mountain had reclaimed the land. The deer and the buffalo ate the saplings. The ones that survived grew crookedly, which would make them too difficult to tap.[18]

The Li minority were discouraged from their traditional slash-and-burn agriculture, but clearing the hillsides for rubber destroyed far more of the secondary forest. At the height of the Cultural Revolution, local Chinese peasants were also obliged to change their farming habits. They were prevented from rearing pigs for family use, and forced to grow rice instead of the familiar crops of sweet potatoes and peanuts.

Like all frontier regions, Hainan always carries the prevailing trend even further. Deng Xiaoping's 1980s policy of encouraging people to 'get rich first' was embraced by the Hainan leaders with the same enthusiasm of the earlier campaigns to 'Defend Hainan' and 'Plant More Rubber'.

It was encouraged to do so from Beijing where the reform faction saw the island as a useful laboratory for testing its 'open door' and 'socialist market' policies. At such a distance from the capital, Hainan was politically safer too if the experiment went wrong. In 1988 the Party Secretary-General Zhao Ziyang labelled Hainan 'more Special than the Special Economic Zones [SEZs]'. Hainan officials claimed to have his authority for the island to exercise 'more independent powers and more preferential treatment', freer entry and exit policies for foreigners, and a more relaxed foreign exchange administration. In May of the same year Vice-premier Tian Jiyun used a speech in New York to make a special selling pitch for Hainan:

> China has decided to make Hainan Island an independent province and the country's largest SEZ, with policies that will give foreign investors even more preferential treatment than those pursued in other SEZs. Foreigners will be allowed to invest in real estate, to repatriate their profits without restrictions, and to be exempt from import tariffs. Foreign insurance companies will also be allowed on the island.

Meanwhile Hainan had already become 'more special' in a notoriously different way. In the single decade of 1985–94, Hainan was the scene of some of the most famous (and widely admired) financial scams of the Deng reform era. The top leadership of the island had to be changed three times, on each occasion in dubious circumstances. Created an SEZ in 1988, Hainan quickly attracted the attention of far-sighted operators who understood that the island would be allowed more latitude and would be less easily controlled than the much smaller mainland zones. Local Party and government officials quickly shed their inhibitions about engaging personally or through their families in the pursuit of wealth long before this became tacitly accepted on the mainland. Hainan regulations also permitted officials to retire directly from public service to enter private business.

The first episode was the most celebrated: the great automobile scam in which tens of thousands of foreign cars and trucks were imported in the space of one year, were granted relief from import duty and were then improperly re-exported to the mainland. (It was never clearly established whether the re-export actually broke Chinese law or simply exploited a loophole). Estimates of the number of vehicles range between 50,000 and 85,000. Hainan officials also approved the import of 2.8 million television sets, 250,000 video recorders and 122,000 motorcycles between January 1984 and March 1985. At its height, nearly 900 companies including 88 Hainan government departments were involved in the mainland resale of imported vehicles fetching double or three times their original price. The most notable feature of the affair was the open encouragement it received from the island's top Party and military officials. Navy boats and airforce planes were used to ferry the re-exported items to the mainland, continuing to do so even after an investigation team was sent down from Beijing. The prime mover was none other than Lei Yu, Governor of Hainan, who was sacked in 1985.

Lei Yu, unlike most of his officials, was never accused of profiting personally from the trade. He had deliberately encouraged it as a means of raising large sums from the mainland to boost Hainan's tentative economic development, becoming a hero to the Hainanese. At the end of the decade, young entrepreneurs still recalled those exhilarating months and regarded Lei Yu with affection. 'Lei Yu didn't waste time talking,' explained one. 'If you had a good idea, he just let you make money. And he had the whole army, navy and airforce out delivering cars.' Although demoted, Lei Yu received light treatment from Beijing. Within three years he was appointed a deputy mayor of Guangzhou with the recommendation that he was 'receptive to new things . . . familiar with economic affairs . . . and enjoys considerable prestige among cadres and people'. In 1992 he was promoted to neighbouring Guangxi in charge of plans to 'open up' the region, and was soon seen in Hong Kong enthusiastically promoting its interests.

Lei Yu's successor Liang Xiang also learnt fast on the job. He was in charge of transforming Hainan into an independent province, free from the oversight of Guangdong which – the Hainanese claimed – had held their island back since Liberation. Liang gave numerous interviews to the foreign press on Hainan's 'more special' status and its 'avant garde' economic reforms. The biggest lure was a complete absence of import quotas and the right to secure land on long leases. To no one's surprise, the first foreign missions came from Japan. An initial outline agreement was quickly signed with the Hong Kong subsidiary of the Japanese conglomerate Kumagai Gumi to develop the new port of Yangpu, with provision for a 70-year lease of the land site. Liang Xiang was forced to defend himself publicly against the charge that Chinese sovereignty had been diminished by this deal. The Chinese flag would still fly over Yangpu and Chinese laws would still apply, he insisted. Besides Yangpu was nothing more at present than 'a stretch of wasteland'.

Liang already had five years' experience as a top official in the pace-setting Shenzhen Economic Zone but soon ran into trouble in Hainan. Although the island was now independent, local Hainan officials were suspicious of his past links with Guangdong province. Hainan began to boom under Liang, with hot money flowing in from Hong Kong, Taiwan, and the richer mainland provinces, but most of it was invested in speculative enterprises: in particular, property deals and trading in import licences. Liang himself was accused of allowing his own wife to speculate in land, after she sold two new villas in Haikou for 400,000 renminbi profit. Liang was quite unashamed in flouting national policy.

'What's the purpose of central planning and approval?' he once said. 'Those with bundles of money will call the shots.' But he also sought to buy Beijing's political support by inviting the offspring of high-ranking officials to sit on the boards of Hainan-based state trading companies. This proved a serious mistake. The most prominent high-ranking 'prince' from Beijing was Zhao Erjun, son of Liang's patron in Beijing, Party Secretary-General Zhao Ziyang. The son of a former Guangdong Party boss, Ren Zhongyi, became chairman of another trading group. With little sensitivity for recent history, Erjun's Hua Hai Company was granted the monopoly for importing foreign cars![19]

The political downfall of Zhao Ziyang in June 1989 after he had shown sympathy for the students in Tiananmen Square left his provincial supporters exposed to reprisal. Zhao's reputation abroad was enhanced by his opposition to martial law and the suppression of the democracy movement. Yet it must be remembered that his family's business ventures topped the original lists posted by the students in their denunciations of corruption in high places. His son Zhao Erjun was also attacked because of the close links developing between Hainan and Japan – believed to have been encouraged by his father – which touched a familiar patriotic nerve. Liang Xiang, recalled to Beijing, was accused of 'abusing power for personal gain', and dismissed from all his Party and government positions – a severe punishment by the more lenient standards usually accorded to transgressing Party officials. Liang Xiang had 'forgotten his fundamental task: to *wholeheartedly serve the people*. He relaxed his vigilance in carrying out reform and opening to the outside world,' the official Chinese news agency proclaimed, 'and he was unable to resist the decadent thinking of *putting money above all else*. All our comrades must take warning from this!'[20]

Now under a new governor, Liu Jianfeng, Hainan kept its

head down in the cooler political and economic climate of 1990. But the pressure for a new boom was already building up before Deng Xiaoping signalled the new, more radical, economic 'opening up' of 1992. Several hundred thousand migrants had crossed from the mainland in the previous year while the flow of hot money into the Haikou property market resumed. Soon there were more than 400 property companies grabbing land earmarked for luxury housing, golf courses, hotels and industrial development zones. Most of the industrial sites remained empty while they were being sold and re-sold, but new estates of luxury villas were built in the suburbs of Haikou. They were advertised for China's new rich and Overseas Chinese with such desirable features as patios, private gardens, Spanish-style verandahs, Swiss-style spiral staircases, full air-conditioning, satellite TV and the unheard luxury of three toilets in one house. They sold for at least half a million renminbi (US$100,000).

Liu Jianfeng lasted three years. As governor of Hainan, committed like his predecessors to 'opening up', he was constantly in conflict with the senior Party man, the provincial secretary Deng Hongxun who wished to keep the brakes on. Their feud soon bred bureaucratic conflict at lower levels of the administration. The solution, in January 1993, was to replace them both with a new leader, Ruan Chongwu, who would combine the two jobs. (A year later, a high official in the Hainan government was accused of 'forging evidence' to frame Liu.) Ruan had been picked by the national Party leader Jiang Zemin under whom he previously worked in Shanghai. Jiang now visited Hainan to demonstrate his personal backing for the new governor. The local paper reported in heroic language how he had 'braved the hot weather to inspect Hainan's new tourist spots'. With an indirect glance at the 'chickens' in the Haikou Hotel and other disreputable features, Jiang announced that Hainan needed 'wholesome [tourist] attractions . . . The more that we open to the outside world, the more we should build up our Spiritual Civilisation!' This was a ritual injunction: Hainan's boom now resumed with new and untrammelled energy. In July 1994 Governor Ruan at a meeting on public security called on the police force to 'maintain its political integrity and professional competence' and to 'mobilise the masses to prevent crime'. A month later, the public procuratorate announced that it had filed 99 corruption cases for investigation since the beginning of the year and 66 cases of economic crime.

When Deng Xiaoping had come south to re-launch the economic reforms in 1992, hopeful officials prepared a suite for him in Sanya's luxury Luhuitou hotel – 'where Jiang Qing used to holiday'. Deng stayed on the mainland, but his initiative had rekindled the Hainan spirit. His new lieutenant Vice-premier Zhu Rongji, specially charged with promoting the reforms, described Hainan as a 'Special Economic Zone with Hainan characteristics'. This was a revealing adaptation of the usual formula about China practising 'Socialism with Chinese characteristics'. Hainan's characteristics clearly had nothing to do with socialism at all.

A mood of new optimism was encouraged by booming statistics. No one queried their accuracy or the probable effect on inflation. Hainan reported a real growth rate in its 1993 gross domestic product of 22.8 per cent. The output value of its industry – where the growth rate was an amazing 38.9 per cent – for the first time exceeded that of agriculture. Licences had been granted for no less than 2,400 new foreign-funded firms to set up in Hainan. Hainan officials now wooed potential clients in Hong Kong and Taiwan with the promise that 'we let foreign investors make their own decisions according to market conditions'. Before his removal, governor Liu Jianfeng explained that 'we shall accelerate our development by going beyond conventional means'. The tendency for the southern coastal provinces to ignore Beijing's restrictions was carried even further in Hainan. In April 1992 the island opened a stock exchange without permission – the third in China after Shenzhen and Shanghai. Zhu Rongji flew from Beijing to warn his protégés that they would upset too many people on the mainland but Liu Jianfeng told the exchange to 'keep going'. Many local officials were already trading privately in mainland stocks. One explained to me that permission could not be withheld for long. 'You have to give a baby a ration-book even if its parents have exceeded the one-child policy. This baby has been born and they can't kill it off.' Hainan's entrepreneurial focus was shifting to the financial sector and China's biggest futures exchange was soon under construction in Haikou. In mid-1993 Beijing launched a national austerity drive to try to cool the country's overheated economy. The new governor Ruan Chongwu gave a long reassuring interview in a Hong Kong newspaper. The austerity policy would have 'little impact' on Hainan and he dismissed rumours that the island's prosperity was only 'a castle in the air'.[21]

Hainan also defied Beijing over new environmental regulations to ban the wasteful use of agricultural land for golf courses. Hainan argued that these were an essential tourist attraction: 15 were approved in 1993 and more were being laid out without approval. Among Hainan's new rich, a futures market had even developed in membership cards for golf courses still under construction. Hainan also distinguished itself by producing what was described as China's largest case of embezzlement and graft since the 1949 Liberation. Five local bank officials were executed in September 1993 for misappropriating 33.4 million renminbi of public funds (though there were suspicions of a cover-up for higher authorities).[22]

* * *

Will Hainan really become another of East Asia's 'little dragons' within the next two decades along with Singapore, Hong Kong, Taiwan and South Korea – the goal set by Governor Ruan? Or will it become the sleazy southern frontier of Chinese crypto-capitalism, lurching between boom and bust and from one scandal to another? A large part of the answer lies in the Yangpu Free Port Project which is now the flagship for the island's future development. The potential of this excellent natural deep water harbour on the north-west coast was identified long ago by Sun Yat-sen, and again in the 1970s by Zhou Enlai. The scheme was first approved in 1988 by Deng Xiaoping but was delayed for four years by political objections. Interviewed in 1992 when it finally went ahead, Kumagai Gumi's managing director C.P. Yu was quite frank about the reason: 'There were complaints in the National People's Congress that Yangpu would mean "surrendering Chinese sovereignty to Japan". The problem was mainly [Premier] Li Peng really. He wanted to cut the zone down to six square kilometres but that wouldn't make sense.' A clause in the draft lease would have allowed the Hainan government to veto any project within the zone. This, said Mr Yu, would now be removed after the intervention of Zhu Rongji. 'You will really be able to call it a free zone. I won't have to defer to the Hainan authorities for anything.'[23] But it proved much harder to remove the disputed clause from the document: the politics of leasing sovereign territory are still extremely sensitive.

When I visited Yangpu in 1992, the designated area was mostly scrub and cactus outside a small quay and warehouses. A new road had been completed from the main western highway further inland. Animals were strictly forbidden to use it: this did not seem to deter buffaloes, goats and one very pregnant sow. At the perimeter an arch over the road proclaimed with coloured flags: 'Welcome to Yangpu Free Trade and Economic Development Zone'. As with every project in China, the first new building was a hotel and karaoke bar. The quay was empty but for a pile of wood chips waiting shipment. Outside the Yangpu Development Office ragged children peered through the windows. The visitors from Hong Kong tried to match the Outline Development Strategy Plan, complete with Passenger Railway Station, Landscape Buffer Area, Flatted Factories and Neighbourhood Centre, to the barren waste around them. In a small village nearby, barefooted fishing families wove nets and dried a poor catch of sprats, while chickens scratched over muddy paving. One of Yangpu's advantages, Mr Yu had told me, was that the villagers would be 'easy to move'. They spoke an almost incomprehensible dialect: a guide from Haikou tried in vain to interpret. With great effort a young fisherman was found to answer one simple question: 'What language do you speak?' 'We speak Danzhou words,' he replied.

This part of the coast facing the mainland has been known as Dan for over 2,000 years. In Chinese the word means 'to carry ear-ornaments on the shoulders', perhaps describing the ornament-weighted earlobes of the aboriginal inhabitants. The people now living in Dan County are mainlanders who arrived just a thousand years ago, speaking a Mandarin which has long ago diverged from other dialects. It has always been a remote and poor area. This is where the poet Su Dongpo was exiled to in the 11th Century. 'Heaven curses your soil,' he wrote, 'No wheat, no millet!'

The zone was formally opened in September 1993 with a ground-breaking ceremony for its power plant, the first essential step in development. The outline development plan included building a new town as well as the port and industrial facilities. It looked ahead to a population in the next century of 250,000 residents, with work for 150,000 more outside the zone, and specified in detail the design of residential estates with parkland, play areas and provision for a range of sports from skating to five-a-side soccer. But this Hong Kong-style development depends on the success of Yangpu's main aim: to attract foreign investment to a free port offering cheap migrant labour, tax concessions and a lack of bureaucratic controls. Most early purchasers of industrial space were mainland Chinese firms, many of whom seemed more interested in speculative investment than development.

Yangpu's problem is that of the whole of Hainan's SEZ. As quasi-capitalist reforms spread elsewhere in China, does Hainan offer enough special concessions to offset its geographical remoteness and reputation for lawlessness and confusion? In mid-1994 the Hong Kong *Far Eastern Economic Review* reported that foreign business was beginning to suspect that 'this sort of gold-rush capitalism can "move" things only so far . . . lack of a strong legal framework deters many foreign investors'.[24]

Hainan's other saleable asset is tourism. The island is, in the not entirely fortunate phrase of the provincial tourism bureau, China's End of the Earth. It is not yet such a familiar location in the global travel business as Taiwan or Cyprus or the Seychelles but it does deserve to be better known. Water buffaloes and straw-hatted peasants amble across the new straight roads built under the regime of Governor Lei Yu. Roadside stalls sell coconuts, mangoes, wild birds and snake. The eastern island route from Haikou to the port of Sanya plunges through deep green paddy and groves of coconut palms – half a million in one plantation. The western route crosses the wilder flatlands past Dan County and Yangpu. The most interesting road, recommended so long ago by Hai Rui, climbs through the central valley into mountains where some virgin forest has survived the Red Guards. There are thatched Miao villages with yellow walls of adobe and brushwood stockades for the livestock and, in the foothills of the Five Finger Mountains, old Li women with black shovel hats.

'Tourism will be the motor for economic development', I was told by optimistic planners in Sanya. The town has a hundred miles of beaches, ten fine bays, many rocky promontories with interesting names, and a new airport able to handle Boeing-747s scheduled for completion by 1995. A new highway was also being built from Haikou which would reduce the six-hour drive by half. In 1992 city officials were sitting until late at night awarding contracts and handing out hotel concessions. Land prices had already multiplied six times in the last two years. Though the aim was to attract foreign investment, most funds came from the mainland. One hotel was owned by the tourism bureau of Nanjing in central China, another by the Tobacco Corporation of Yunnan province.

The goal of attracting large numbers of foreign tourists may also prove elusive. Hainan officials say that the island's beauty should make it the Hawaii of the East, but 90 per cent of tourists in 1993 still came from the mainland. Most of those classed as foreign were Hong Kong or Taiwanese 'compatriots'. Large travel operators from Japan, the US and Europe remained wary of the uneven quality of tourist amenities. Hotels were too often poorly maintained and isolated beaches could still be polluted. Parts of Sanya were still occupied by the Chinese army, and new projects (some with army money behind them) were being built with little regard for environmental effect. By 1994, several international chains were said to have bought land or shown interest though none had actually begun building a hotel. One of the front-runners was Club Med, which planned a joint-venture resort including a golf course, marina and casino. The Las Vegas casino company MGM Grand Inc also signed an agreement to explore the development of two 'entertainment complexes' near Haikou and Sanya. Both would include casinos – although gambling was still officially banned in China.[25] Will this then become the most notable feature of the island's 'more special' status – the freedom to allow casinos as well as brothels to flourish unimpeded? Hainan is still China's wild southern frontier, but it would be unrecognisable to the exiles of the past.

X

The Guangdong Experience

In the surging tide of reform and opening up, Guangdong
has been the trailblazer, fighter and leader, and the
remarkable progress and vitality of the economy in the
south of the province has captured attention at home
and abroad! (Xinhua News Agency, 25 March 1992)

So far we have concentrated on Middle China and its
problems of economic, political and cultural 'backwardness'.
Now we turn to the 'advanced' China that the outside world
knows best, with particular reference to the province of
Guangdong. Once part of the same central-south region as
the five provinces already studied, Guangdong's fortunes
ascended rapidly in the 1980s, leaving Middle China far
behind. It is now top of the statistical tables for foreign
investment, personal incomes, entertainment, infrastructure
– and corruption and crime. Where Guangdong has led,
Beijing and the other large cities have already followed.
Once the nation was urged to Learn from the Model Brigade
of Dazhai, deep in the hills of Shanxi, and from the heroic
workers of the Daqing Oilfield in the frozen north–east.
After Deng Xiaoping's famous Southern Expedition early in
1992, the model was Guangdong province with the Shenzhen
Special Economic Zone (SEZ) at its core. What then are the

characteristics of this 'advanced experience' which the rest of China is supposed to emulate?

It was above all the 'entrepreneurial spirit' of southern China which Deng admired on his 1992 visit, especially in Shenzhen which, he said, had 'blazed the trail and experimented boldly'. Eight years previously when he last visited Shenzhen, Deng recalled, it was still a small country town with ponds, mud-paths and old cottages. Now anyone who owned a plot of land could turn it into gold and buy his own house and car. The bicycles and hand-trucks had disappeared from Shenzhen's new roads, now lined with factories, science parks, curved-wall apartment blocks and clusters of luxury villas behind marble-faced walls. (The sheds with matting on the roofs for construction workers from the countryside were out of sight.)

From a revolving restaurant at Shenzhen's International Trade Centre, Deng surveyed with child-like enthusiasm the 'wide boulevards and high-rise buildings'. He visited the new tourist attraction at Splendid China, a theme park with the Potala Palace, the Great Wall and other famous sights in miniature from every Chinese province. He rode around the park in a golf buggy and was photographed by foreign tourists – a subtle way of leaking the news of his initiative to conservative critics in Beijing, mistrustful of the new economic reforms. (In theory Deng was in retirement so his utterances could not be reported in the official press until the Beijing leaders had approved.) This was real progress, he pronounced, surveying the frenetic Shenzhen scene. Never mind if mistakes were made: reform and 'opening up' to the world could never be entirely foolproof. 'If we do not have the courage to try, we cannot achieve anything'. He urged the rest of China to get on with it, faster.

Guangdong province wants to catch up with Asia's four little dragons [South Korea, Taiwan, Hong Kong,

Singapore] in 20 years, but it can catch up with them sooner if it speeds up its development. Shanghai is completely capable of achieving faster growth, and the four Special Economic Zones, the Yangzi River Delta, and even the whole country will be different if everyone makes an effort to catch up. We must speed up the reforms, starting now.[1]

Deng had three clear goals in his carefully staged Southern Expedition. The first was consistent with the views which he had urged during his struggle with the Gang of Four in the last years (1975–76) before Mao's death. It was to put economic development in first place and use all available means to transform China from a 'backward' to an 'advanced' nation. The new element in his thinking now was to accept the general trend in the world economy in favour of the market mechanism and reduce the role of planning. In this area above all others it was wrong, Deng argued, to 'surname' one technique as capitalist and the other as socialist. Some capitalist countries had partially planned economies. Why should not socialist countries use the market? Second, Deng made explicit his strategy since the Beijing Massacre to divert popular anger and the pressure for political reform by producing real economic benefits and opportunities. 'Why has our country been very stable since 4 June [1989]?' he asked. 'Because we have been pursuing reform and opening up, have promoted economic development and the people's livelihood has improved.' Deng's third goal was to ensure that China did not fall behind the rapid development of neighbouring Asian economies. Indeed, with its vast reserves of cheap labour, land and natural resources China should instead seek in time to dominate the region.

Guangdong province had already led the way since the early 1980s with the Shenzhen and Zhuhai SEZs as the cutting edge of modernisation. Hong Kong manufacturers had by 1993 set up more than 30,000 enterprises in the province, employing three million workers – mostly ex-peasant women or migrant labourers – to assemble goods previously made in Hong Kong. Guangdong's successes had previously caused jealousy in Beijing which blocked efforts by the provincial government to gain more autonomy in making foreign deals and retaining a reasonable share of its revenues. Deng's visit gave Guangdong an important boost: governor Zhu Senlin quickly announced that Deng had 'approved of our work and expressed great hope and confidence in our future'. Guangdong now had the green light to 'become affluent ahead of other provinces' – and the other provinces were now at liberty to try to emulate what became known as 'the Guangdong Experience'.

Deng Xiaoping was legitimising a model established over the previous decade. The Guangdong experience – and particularly that of the SEZs within the province – had already attracted ambitious young men and women and investment capital from all over China. Historically Guangdong had been China's doorway to foreign trade and technology. It had been the first port of call for Western traders since the 18th Century and before. It was also far enough away from Beijing so that it could be regarded, if necessary, as an exception to a more general closed door policy to the outside world. In more recent times the rapid development of Hong Kong gave Guangdong better access than anywhere else in China to new ideas and techniques in business enterprise, management and the technologies to go with them. In the economic reforms which Deng had begun to introduce in the late 1970s, Guangdong was therefore allowed to take the lead: 'to walk one step ahead' as the slogan put it.[2]

The essence of the Guangdong experience was an export-oriented strategy backed by a considerable degree of provincial autonomy. Increasingly Guangdong was allowed to retain more of its foreign earnings and to make investment decisions without depending on Beijing's approval. It was 'one step ahead' of the rest of China in experimenting with price reform (which meant reducing subsidies and letting prices rise), giving factory managers freedom from political control, allowing foreign banks to set up, and embarking on large, ambitious infrastructural projects in telecommunications and transport. Guangdong was ahead too in its more permissive attitude towards fashion, lifestyle – and sex. It also became a front-runner in the growth of crime which often involved the revival of old-style secret societies.

'Is Guangdong still a province of China,' asked *Newsweek* reporting on Deng's southern expedition, 'or has it become a colony of Hong Kong?' Fleets of lorries crossed the border daily with components or semi-finished products to supply the enterprises set up in the towns and villages of the Pearl River delta. By this time nine out of ten delta families (one-third of Guangdong's total population) had a fridge, TV – within viewing reach of the Hong Kong stations – and a washing machine. Over 80 per cent of foreign investment in Guangdong industry came from Hong Kong, and only three per cent of total investment came from Beijing. Hong Kong's investment over the 1980s was estimated to total more than 16 billion US dollars. More than five million farmers had become factory workers and another two million joined the service and distribution sectors. Their average wages were between 400 and 500 rmb– five times the rate in Hunan province. Several million peasant migrants from inland – particularly from Guangxi, Sichuan and Hunan – came in at the bottom of the employment ladder, doing the worst and dirtiest jobs in farming (or what survived of it as more land was covered by concrete) and the booming construction industry.[3]

Dongguan County in the Inner Delta was the classic case of a rural area transformed by its success in export processing for Hong Kong. The area had two advantages: it was on the main Shenzhen–Guangzhou road relatively close to Hong

Kong, and many of its former residents now lived in Hong Kong – some 600,000 including their families. About half of the investment came from these migrants. By the mid-1980s simple workshops had been built in nearly all of Dongguan's 33 townships and most of the roads were paved. Local peasants, particularly young women with deft fingers and good eyesight, provided the labour for the cutting up or assembling tasks required. A typical sight in the village square would be a knot of migrants, from neighbouring counties or further afield, sitting in the dust in the hope of casual employment. As indigenous peasants became industrial workers or entrepreneurs, their fields were rented (technically 'assigned' because the land legally still belonged to the collective village) to the migrants. Local cadres would allocate land for factory use and then become managers, working for the Hong Kong boss with whom they had set up the deal. A fleet of 700 trucks crossed the border daily with components and finished goods. By 1987, out of a county population of 1.2 million, over 150,000 were employed in the export processing industry. Over the previous eight years Dongguan had earned nearly 400 million US dollars in foreign currency. The demand for cheap labour continued to grow and by 1989 Dongguan had 300,000 migrant workers.[4]

Dongguan County now acquired city status and a modern urban environment to go with it. It was the first rural town in China to install an optical fibre telephone system. Dongguan peasants could dial directly to the outside world when citizens of Beijing or Shanghai were still queuing for public telephones. Dongguan now became a model of township and village enterprise with which to impress official visitors from Beijing and abroad. One was the Governor of Hong Kong, Sir David Wilson, who saw the link between Hong Kong capital and Guangdong labour as one of the most encouraging signs for the territory's future. In a glowing article on the Pearl River Delta, the People's Daily reported that those visiting for the first time 'could not help sighing: "It is really like visiting abroad!"'. It singled out Dongguan for special praise, and quoted the Secretary-General of the city Party committee as predicting that by the end of the century Dongguan would have become 'the Los Angeles of the East'. One of his colleagues, Deputy mayor Yuan Lisong, had already taken this literally. Using public funds, Yuan had set up a company in Hong Kong which then re-invested in Dongguan, thereby avoiding taxes for up to five years and gaining other concessions. He was also the part-owner of a 500-room hotel in Los Angeles. The legal basis for these transactions might be dubious, but Yuan insisted that it was all done 'for the Party and the people!'.[5]

Dongguan also became a pace-setter in the less desirable consequences of rapid rural industrialisation. It was one of the first cities in Guangdong – after the provincial capital of Guangzhou – to experience a serious drugs and crime problem. In May 1991, it was also the scene of a catastrophic factory fire, one of many reported among the new industries where safety standards were appallingly low and scarcely monitored. At least 60 workers were killed and more than 70 others injured when fire swept through a raincoat factory. The victims were trapped 'because exits were blocked by stockpiled goods'. This was an all too familiar tale in the new sweatshops of South China.[6]

By the early 1990s, Guangdong authorities were admitting that industrial accidents had become 'seriously out of control'. In 1992, the rate of deaths increased by more than half throughout the province – a total of over 1,300 in factories and mines. Particularly alarming, said the official Party newspaper, was the even sharper increase in what it called 'economically developed areas'. Shenzhen City, pride of Mr Deng's open door policy, had the most shameful record of all: deaths were up by over 170 per cent compared to 1991. Shenzhen was about to experience an even more dreadful year.

In April 1993, eleven people were killed in the suburban town of Huanggang when a building that housed quarry workers collapsed. In June a makeshift workers' dormitory collapsed under heavy rain, killing 17 and injuring 20. In August a chemical blast in the Qingshuihe industrial complex spread to neighbouring warehouses storing inflammable goods. The series of explosions, heard in Hong Kong, was compared to a string of giant firecrackers. At least 15 died and 200 were injured. The original blast had occurred in a warehouse storing dangerous goods which was owned by the People's Liberation Army. Military influence had been used to procure its location in close proximity to other warehouses including a timber-yard and a storage plant. Finally in November, 80 were killed in a fire which swept through a toy factory. Guangdong radio broadcast a vivid account:

> When we rushed to the scene at about midnight, we saw only the cement skeleton of the three-storey factory, and found a strong scorching smell around the site . . . The building used to have three doors, but the two doors facing north were entirely blocked by the factory management. Originally, there used to be 20 huge windows on each floor; nevertheless, the management had them all sealed with strong wire netting. Consequently, when the fire broke out yesterday, there was no way for the workers to escape via the windows. In a panic, they all swarmed into the passage leading to the only exit. As the stairway was blocked by thick smoke and fire, many workers were trapped in the building and suffocated to death . . . All but one of the victims was female, and it was estimated that most of them were from Sichuan.[7]

These were just the most conspicuous disasters (more easily monitored from Hong Kong than those further inland) in one year in Shenzhen. In December another disaster further up the coast in Fuzhou (Fujian province) finally forced the government in Beijing to react. In one of many Taiwan-owned factories, workers at the Gaofu textile plant had continued to staff their deafening assembly lines while some 60 co-workers were burnt to death in their beds as fire swept the floor above. The fire had been started by a young woman with a grudge after she had been sacked for theft, but this did not excuse the over-crowding and lack of safety measures. 'Why must these tragedies repeat themselves again and again?' asked the *People's Daily*. Across China, 11,600 workers had died in industrial accidents in just eight months. But attention was focused on the high proportion of accidents in factories under foreign control. 'The way some of these foreign investors ignore international practice and our own [safety] rules, and act lawlessly and immorally, and lust after wealth, is enough to make one's hair stand on end,' lamented the *Economic Daily*. Unusually, Chinese trade unions were urged to stand up for their rights. Some criticism of foreign investors was justified, but the outrage was selective. Local officials who turned a blind eye to violations were equally to blame, and conditions were just as bad in many Chinese-owned factories.

At least six million Chinese workers, it was now estimated, were employed in some 130,000 companies set up with foreign investment. Deng Xiaoping's signal to speed up the pace of economic reform in 1992 had led to fierce competition to attract foreign capital. Local authorities at province, town or even rural county level were allowed to offer many of the tax advantages previously confined to the coastal Special Economic Zones and a few big cities. Within months of Deng's southern expedition, this had led to what became known as the 'development zone fever'.

By September 1992, nearly 2,000 new development zones had been approved throughout the country, occupying more than 15,000 square kilometres. They covered an area equal to the size of one average county – and usually took up good arable land. Local officials bought land from the peasants, enclosed it with a wall or barbed wire, and then in many cases left it unused. The *Economic Daily* complained that:

> It's very easy for government departments simply to issue an order, hold a news conference and establish a development zone or an industrial zone. Real estate tycoons can also just speculate on land prices as if land were like stock certificates. But 'development' will be just a dream if enterprises and businessmen don't put their money on real construction. You can map out the land, repair the wall, but inside there will be no activity going on.[8]

Ceremonial arches announcing the construction of 'X County Technology Development Zone' became a frequent sight on country roads. Local officials set up development zone offices with their own budgets: peasants complained that these were frequently spent on banquets or 'investigation' visits to Shenzhen. The officials were also able to divert bank funds and state investment into the zones, making it even harder for peasants to raise loans for improving their land. Hunan province alone had 111 development zones at the county or township level. Within the year, orders had been issued to crack down on unauthorised zones and to examine the plans of the others more carefully. But with the right connections in the provincial government, it was not difficult to escape the prohibition.

Strictly speaking, what was sold was not the land but the 'land-use right'. Except for private housing, the ultimate title to land continued to be held by the municipal government in urban China, and by the residual collective structure in rural China. Thus it became a land market, but remained in 'socialist' hands. This made no real difference except to ensure that local officials had to be cut in on most deals. The first land auction had only been held in Shenzhen in 1987. By 1992 it was proudly claimed that a new 'real estate fever' was sweeping China in every province except Tibet, and that more than 4,000 real estate companies had been set up. In theory the aim was to raise funds for local government, and to bring unused land into productive use. The funds were certainly raised, but not so certainly spent on suitable public purposes. Much of the land, when put into use, was developed for prestige commercial buildings and Hong Kong-style luxury housing. For a while the Chinese press was dazzled by the statistics even when they reflected a purely speculative market. The example of Hainan, where land prices tripled in January–June 1992, was particularly admired.[9] The market for luxury housing within reach of Hong Kong soon became saturated. Hong Kong newspapers were filled with full-page colour advertisements showing villas with mock-European architecture, fountains, landscaped gardens and wrought-iron decoration. But low prices compared to those of Hong Kong could be deceptive. Boom turned to bust in the town of Danshui when living conditions proved to be less than secure and local secret societies took control, smuggling luxury cars from Hong Kong.[10]

Guangdong had the highest incomes in China; the Shenzhen SEZ had the highest incomes in Guangdong – workers in SEZ factories earned up to three times the rates elsewhere in the Delta. Guangdong also had the highest crime rates in China – a State Statistical Bureau survey for 1991 listed the province as 'worst in terms of public order', followed by Zhejiang, Liaoning, Guangxi and Beijing; and Shenzhen had the highest crime rates in Guangdong.[11] The detailed statistics were chilling. In 1992 there were some 700 cases of murder, rape, looting and serious robberies, an increase of 37 per cent over the previous year. Seventy per cent of all offenders convicted of crime were minors: this was not so surprising in a zone where the average age was only 28 years old. There were also over 100 cases of official corruption and bribery. The overall crime rate was four times higher in Shenzhen than throughout the province.[12]

Guangdong was also one of the first regions to be affected by the revival of drug traffic. This had been stamped out after 1949 but reappeared in border regions as China began to 'open up'. One drug in particular, opium, has a special significance in Guangdong's history. In 1839 the imperial commissioner Lin Zexu had forced the British traders at Guangzhou (then Canton, to which foreign trade was confined) to hand over their stocks of opium. More than 20,000 chests of the drug were mixed with salt, lime and water and then destroyed near the river mouth. (Lin had first written an apology to the Sea Spirit, warning him that his waters were about to be polluted.) A century and a half later, drugs were openly burnt on the outskirts of Guangzhou for the first time since before 1949. The number of identified drug addicts had risen from five thousand in 1991 to eight thousand in 1992. Drug processing plant was destroyed in several counties including Dongguan, and some traffickers sentenced to death. Shenzhen already had dozens of addicts and its own rehabilitation centre.[13]

In spite of rapid development, Guangdong still has its own rural poor. Almost 70 per cent of the province's territory is mountainous or hilly, and some remote villages still have no road access. The construction boom in the Delta brought money to some mountain areas supplying building materials. Mountain youth also formed a large proportion of the migrant workers in Shenzhen and other Delta towns. Though the economic reforms also raised incomes in these backward areas, the improvement was uneven. In the new entrepreneurial climate, mountain counties had more difficulty in attracting investment and some factories which had been located there in the 1960s closed down. They also had to rely more on their own resources to fund education and other public services.[14]

In 1987 a new poverty programme (part of a wider national effort) was launched to help the poorest counties. New roads, communications and power projects were started and loans were given for new agricultural techniques and afforestation. The number of very poor was reduced from six to four million by 1992, but there was still a long way to go. A quarter of a million were still defined as 'not having enough to eat and wear'. Grain production fell for three successive years (1991–93) and farmland was swallowed up alarmingly for construction. The equivalent of a whole medium-sized county disappeared in 1992. Two years later it was reported that 'rural instability' was a serious problem, with 'a sharp decrease in farmland and a rapid increase in population'. Guangdong agriculture generally – not just the poorest areas – suffered from the slowing down of rural development and the widening income gap with the cities.[15]

It is the cities of Guangdong province, not its rural interior, which excite the attention of the Chinese press and the aspirations of the emerging Chinese middle-class. The symbols of modernity are the shopping mall, the luxury apartment block, the family car – and the skyscraper. On National Day, 1994 the official *Beijing Review* was euphoric about the changing urban skyline in booming urban China. 'From now to 2001,' it boasted, 'skyscrapers will mushroom all over East Asia, especially in major Chinese cities. Before the 20th Century fades, the tallest buildings in the world will loom over the skylines of China . . .'[16]

China's seriously rich can now take refuge in these sky-scrapers where China's first business clubs have started to appear. The lifestyle of these new millionaires does strain the theory of combining socialism with a market economy to the limit. 'Some people have become rich through inglorious means', admits the *China Business Times*. But it quickly adds that 'their spirit of enterprise is first class ... We should respect these people of the new generation, they represent a force in the nascent socialist market economy'. It applauds the fact that in the Shenzhen SEZ it is now possible not just to 'get rich first' but to do so 'overnight'.[17]

Not everyone shares this undiluted admiration for entrepreneurial ability. Some of the collective ethic of the Maoist decades still survives, particularly among older people and in inland areas less affected so far by the consumer values of the coast. Deng Xiaoping's thesis that techniques of economic development should be judged by whether they succeed — not by whether they are 'capitalist' or 'socialist' — has been challenged too. A school of 'neo-conservative' thought is emerging among some Chinese intellectuals (backed for political reasons by Party leaders opposed more generally to reform) which warns against allowing free play to market forces. The debate is much less advanced in China than in many developed countries where the social and environmental costs of the 'successes' generated by unfettered free market economics are now more critically weighed. Yet doubts are voiced and the mixed consequences of market reforms in Russia and Eastern Europe also provide some useful warning signs. China in the mid-1990s displays an ill-assorted mixture of naive enthusiasm and uneasy questioning about its future. As interested observers, we too may ask the same questions. Will the dream deliver 'prosperity' to more than a minority of China's vast population? How can a society whose value system has been turned upside down so rapidly maintain the 'stability' which the leadership demands? Can the Chinese learn from the evidence elsewhere and perhaps preempt some of the serious problems which now afflict Western societies? Is any of this possible without political as well as economic reform? As we complete our plunge into Middle China, it is time to consider where the country as a whole is heading.

XI

Where is China Heading?

In this book I have focused on some of China's 'inner' problems, both in a geographical and in a more profound human sense, in the hope that these will throw more light on the prospects for China's development. The pace of the economic reforms and the social revolution which goes with it is not denied, nor am I attempting to suggest some crude division between a prosperous coast and an impoverished interior, even though the disparities are considerable (and probably widening). But China's development is unbalanced and barely controlled, making great gains but also incurring considerable negative costs culturally and socially and for the environment. Standards of health, education and public order still compare favourably with many other developing countries, though here too the reforms have brought an adverse trend. In the political field, there has been almost no progress in the first half of the 1990s, and indeed significant retrogression since the Beijing Massacre. Here China already lags a long way behind most comparable countries, including in Asia where states such as Taiwan and South Korea (and more tentatively Indonesia) are moving away from authoritarian rule. This peculiar Chinese mix of chaotic economic change and deadening political immobility, in a vast country which is hard enough to manage at the best of times, increases the risk of an unexpected explosion in Chinese society or, at best, the tailing off of the 'economic miracle' into a much more messy process of uneven and unequal development, creating dangerous new internal tensions.

To understand where China is heading we need to ask first where it thinks it is heading; yet at all levels in China it is extremely hard to find a coherent answer, other than a vague aspiration for the country as a whole to become 'better off'. This was not always so. For 30 years every Chinese learnt at secondary school how the country was proceeding through a 'socialist transition' which would lead in time to the new golden age of communist society. This goal is only mentioned now on the most formal Party occasions. The steps by which it might be achieved – the expansion of socialist 'relations of production' including collectively-run agriculture and the dominance of state-owned industry – have been explicitly repudiated. No alternative set of steps has been suggested. For a brief while in the early 1980s, some attempts were made to justify the economic reforms as another, more authentic, route towards socialism. In the countryside, it was suggested, the semi-privatisation of land would create new conditions in which more 'genuine' forms of collective agriculture could emerge. The intellectual debates of the mid-1980s sought to harmonise reform – both economic and political – with a broader structure of social (if not exactly socialist) values. These efforts were extinguished by the 'conservative' backlash which led up to the Beijing Massacre and the exile of most independent-minded thinkers. Since then ideology has become the preserve of a small number of dogmatic theoreticians, who use the defence of socialist values as a polemical weapon against those promoting economic reform. Elsewhere there is little interest in political theory: business studies and management techniques appear much more attractive to the ambitious young graduate. At the end of 1994, the Academy of Social Sciences in Beijing closed down its 40-year-old Institute of Marxism and Leninism (plus Mao Zedong Thought, added 20 years ago). Instead the academy will shift its focus to research into finance, budget, foreign trade, agriculture and the 'socialist market economy'. When asked what the adjective 'socialist' denotes in this context, public explanations are limited to stressing the need for overall state control of the economy. (There is some dispute as to whether the state still needs to control the major part of economic activity, or only a number of critical areas.) The most common answer given in private is that 'it means the Party stays in charge, that's all'.

The Party, Mao used to say during the revolution, swims among the people like a fish in water. It was overwhelmingly a peasant revolution, mobilising rural volunteers to fight for a cause which promised them land and liberation. Not a single town was captured in the civil war until a year before the 1949 victory. China is still predominantly a nation of peasants: their absolute numbers continue to rise even while the urban sector expands. China's future still depends upon satisfying the expectations of this vast population or at least on maintaining the promise of better things to come. Yet in large parts of the countryside the gains of the 1980s' reforms have not been maintained. Urban development has sucked in funds which should go there, and manufacturing prices have risen faster than peasant earnings. By 1993 average peasant incomes were less than 40 per cent of those for urban families and the ratio between rural and urban income had widened since 1984 from 1:1.7 to 1:2.5. It is true that peasant incomes have always lagged well behind those of urban dwellers, but many expenses now borne by the individual peasant family were previously paid for by the community. Official figures concede that the rise in average peasant incomes has almost come to a halt: for a significant number conditions have worsened. In 1994 the State Statistical Bureau finally admitted what was long obvious (although not to those too eager to find confirmation of the 'economic miracle' in official statistics). Local officials, the Bureau said, often over-state peasant incomes to conceal their failure to improve living standards and cover up for the levying of illegal taxes. The famous 'township and village enterprises' (TVEs) also inflate their production figures to avoid being closed down, or because their managers earn bonuses based on output.

Behind the figures lies a fundamental change of attitude towards the peasants and their relationship to the national project of modernisation and change. It is true that from 1949 onwards the agricultural surplus had been largely used to fund national development in ways which favoured urban China. Chinese rural economists acknowledge that 'the countryside was often sacrificed to save the city'. No one died in the cities during the years of hardship after the Great Leap Forward, though millions starved in the villages. Yet huge efforts were made – as through the Second North-South Trunk Line – to open up the rural areas, and even the policies which went most disastrously wrong were designed not to exploit the peasantry but raise it to new heights. (The contrast between ideal and reality in Shaoshan, as we have seen, was too painful for Mao to contemplate in June 1959.) The Party remained to a large extent a peasant Party. Peasant values and virtues were widely extolled, becoming part-reality part-myth in Chinese political culture. Yes, the peasants were (in Mao's famous words) 'poor and blank', but could not one write the most beautiful words on a blank sheet of paper?

Today the peasant is seen very differently. In the country-side itself, as we have also observed in Henan (in the Lingxian documents), the Party fears it has 'lost control' over a rural population which defies political authority. Millions of peasants believe, on the contrary, that the Party's control has become more oppressive. Local cadres and their families no longer feel inhibited by 'revolutionary morality' from engaging in blatant corruption. The assets of the old people's communes were cornered by the cadres instead of reaching the market. Buying and selling the right to farm the land is still circumscribed by arbitrary regulations. Peasants in the disadvantaged areas of Middle China get the worst of both worlds: the rural reforms have stopped half way between socialism and capitalism.

In the cities much less is heard about peasant values, much more about their threat to stability. Rural migrants are blamed for clogging the railways and pushing up the crime figures. There is little understanding of real conditions in the countryside. Business people in Chengdu in 1993 were hardly aware of the rural riots in Renshou County less than a hundred kilometres away. 'Ignorant' peasants are regarded with suspicion or contempt by the new urban entrepreneurial class. It is true that rural educational standards are declining. Schools charge higher fees and have difficulty in attracting good teachers. Sons may be withdrawn from school at an earlier age to maximise labour power in the fields. Some daughters may not be sent to school at all. Young peasant migrants, dazzled by urban riches, may indeed turn to crime which offers such lucrative possibilities that the risk of being caught and executed seems worth taking. That is why in spite of exemplary executions, numbering several thousand every year across China, there are always new cases of 'railway and highway bandits'.

There is an 'authoritarian' school of thought among Party intellectuals which openly argues that the peasants are a threat to Chinese stability and must be tightly controlled until the distant future when they too may enjoy a reasonable standard of living. In 1994 this was argued in a book called *China Through a Third Eye* whose authorship was obscure but was widely believed to have been encouraged by a faction in the leadership. Urban China cannot decide whether to impose new restrictions to keep the peasants out, or ease residence requirements to allow them to settle. Peasant gangs were recruited in earlier times to provide 'contract labour' for urban projects and for massive public works such as the Second North–South Trunk Line. But these did not lead to structural changes either in the countryside or the towns. Now the two most dynamic sectors of the Chinese economy – the construction and foreign export industries – could not function profitably without abundant supplies of cheap peasant labour over the long-term. This is rationalised by Chinese economists as a 'division of labour' from which both sides will gain. Rural China does now benefit considerably from the inflow of migrant earnings, but in this process the relationship between town and countryside has worsened. In Maoist terminology, the Party has become divorced from the masses. The masses turn instead, as we have seen from Henan to Guangxi, to new inspiration in the images of popular (sometimes pornographic) films and magazines, and for a growing minority, in superstitious cults and religion. The models they seek to emulate no longer contribute their labour zealously to socialism, but strive to become successful enterpreneurs by methods which in the old days would have been criticised as 'exploitation'. When the Gallup Organisation carried out its first consumer poll in China, 68 per cent of those questioned said that the phrase 'Work hard and get rich' summed up their personal philosophy. Only four per cent cited the Maoist aspiration to 'Never think of oneself, and serve the people'. Many thoughtful Chinese have begun to ask whether this is a satisfactory replacement for the old values, and whether it will unify society or create new divisions.

Even without the migrant influx, urban China is already in a state of uncertain transition, with entirely new social forces – they can even be called classes – beginning to emerge. We find, at one end of the economic scale, international hotels, shopping malls, housing developments, night-clubs, gold shops, modern factories funded largely by foreign investment, Development Zones, High Technology Zones, new roads and airfields. Capitalism in all but name is much further advanced in the towns than the countryside. There are private schools and universities, private commercial ventures, and a host of nominally public enterprises whose profits enrich their managers as effectively as if they were shareholders or owners. Speculation in land is no longer confined to the Special Economic Zones and Shanghai, whether conducted privately by house-owners who managed to retain title to their land or have it restored after the Cultural Revolution, or by state companies manipulated for personal advantage. Official forecasts that the rich–poor divide will widen further are largely based on the assumption that land will appreciate in value. Foreign investment drives up prices further, and creates new opportunities for Chinese middlemen and 'fixers' of services: these play a role not dissimilar from the 'compradores' of old treaty ports. In the widening interstices of the 'socialist economy', we may conclude, a capitalist class is rapidly emerging in urban China with a distinct lifestyle emulating that of other urban Asian centres. Its wealth may be based on entrepreneurial activity, or on actual ownership of land and other assets, or more frequently on the ability to *use* and exploit such assets.

Meanwhile what of the Chinese worker? As the dissident journalist Liu Binyan has observed, workers in China have received curiously little attention over the past 40 years. In spite of the slogan that 'the working class is the master of the country', they never acquired anything like the emblematic identity of the Chinese peasant and displayed much less enthusiasm for the 'socialist revolution'. But workers enjoyed one great advantage over the peasants. The unit – factory or commercial enterprise or transport organisation – which employed them was obliged to provide a complete welfare package of housing, education and health. It was this 'iron rice bowl' which usually managed to secure at least their passive loyalty if not their enthusiasm. It is this same bowl which the industrial reforms of the mid-1980s onwards have explicitly sought to crack. The result was the appearence in Tiananmen Square in May 1989 of the first organised independent workers' movement. Many believe it was this phenomenon, so threatening to the Party leadership in the light of East European experience, which led to the armed suppression of the student democracy movement.

At the other end of the urban spectrum, we find serious overcrowding in colourful but unmodernised lanes and alleys, sweatshops and back-street factories which are frequently ill-lit and unsafe, an array of small peddlars and street stalls reflecting considerable underemployment, and a new underclass composed of migrant workers (of both sexes), part-time or professional criminals, beggars and even street-children (now estimated to total at least 200,000 throughout China). Foreign travellers are now regularly advised to avoid certain areas of Beijing and other cities after dark, and also to be careful on public transport at night-time. Not since the early 1960s have beggars been seen on city streets or young and old scavengers searching the litter beside railway lines and on rubbish dumps.

Job creation is now by far the biggest problem facing urban China. To the numbers of unemployed – mostly young people coming on to the job market for the first time – must be added those who have been 'stood down' (or *xia gang*) as in the case of many Wuhan factories. Such workers only receive a proportion of their pay and are not required to report to work. While remaining on the books of their original work unit, they have no guarantee of staying there for ever. In 1994 Shanghai recorded a total of 150,000 fully unemployed: but more than twice as many workers (318,000) had been stood down. Wuhan's problems continued to worsen as Mayor Zhao Baojiang announced that 15 per cent of its state-owned enterprises would be declared bankrupt or auctioned off in 1995, and a further 50,000–60,000 workers would have to be 'resettled'. There are no reliable national figures for urban unemployment, but the official rate of 2.8 per cent is a serious underestimate. Including stood-down workers, the real rate may be as high as 15–17 per cent.

Urban China's second most serious and fast worsening problem is air and water pollution. The effect of double-digit industrial growth, with inadequate and easily evaded pollution controls, has been intensified by a rapid increase in motor transport of all kinds. According to China's National Environmental Protection Agency director, half of China's rivers are contaminated with industrial waste and almost one-third is affected by acid rain. Beijing, Shenyang, Xian, Shanghai and Guangzhou are listed as among the world's ten worst cities for air pollution. The problem is not confined to the large industrial centres. Some of the worst offenders are older industries located in Middle China in the 1960s and 1970s as part of the strategic 'Third Line'. The infilling of Jingzhou City with relocated industry from Shanghai has created a pall of choking smog over its fine city walls. The visitor to Fenghuang in western Hunan will find a floating scum on the Yuan River where Shen Congwen, playing truant with his friends, used to swim. Pollution has increased in the countryside as traditional labour-intensive farming practices requiring collective organisation are abandoned, and chemical fertilisers are used widely and often wastefully. Natural resources, land, water and forest have all come under greater pressure while conservation controls are too easily evaded by bribery or official apathy. Massive schemes to alter the physical landscape such as the Three Gorges Dam are likely to have unanticipated effects on the environment. China is also expected to become one of the world's largest car markets within the next decade. Hainan island's great car scam was an early indicator of the huge demand for this form of transport. The use of an official car has been prized for decades as the ultimate indicator of political and social status, with chintz curtains (or more recently tinted glass) to protect the privacy of the occupant. Now, as it begins to come within the reach of China's new rich, foreign manufacturers are being encouraged to compete for a market forecast to number tens of millions. China produced 230,000 passenger cars in 1993: annual demand is predicted to rise to 1.4 million cars by the year 2000 and almost to treble again by 2010. These figures may be exaggerated, but the construction of motorways is becoming a fashionable necessity in provincial infrastructural planning. There is no indication yet that Chinese planners have learnt any lesson from the adverse effects of the private car economy elsewhere.

The economic and social problems which China now faces are exacerbated by the absence of a political atmosphere in which they can be clearly analysed and openly discussed. China's political stagnation is all the more striking when contrasted with the pace and variety of economic change in the mid-1990s. It is easy to forget that serious efforts were made throughout the 1980s to discover and promote forms of political change which would keep pace with economic developments. There was an unbroken thread of political activism outside the Party, from the Democracy Wall of 1979–80 (which briefly served Deng Xiaoping's purpose as he challenged the post-Maoist leadership for power), through various provincial initiatives in the mid-1980s to the Democracy Movement of 1987–89 which culminated in the Tiananmen protests. Many of those taking part were ex-Red Guards who had been radicalised by exposure to real life in the countryside during the Cultural Revolution. The tradition of activism dated further back still to the Hundred Flowers movement in 1956–57. Too often, Western observers belittled the serious character of this movement: even in 1989 it was often said that the students 'don't know what democracy means'. A lack of political sophistication was entirely understandable in a political culture which had been deprived of debate for so many years. It did not lessen the political challenge which it posed to the regime. This was perhaps better understood by foreign diplomats and business leaders, anxious lest democratic agitation should disturb China's 'stability' and hinder the expansion of market opportunities for foreign investors and traders. Their influence helped ensure that Western governments barely allowed the question of human rights and democracy to influence their policy towards Deng's China until compelled, for a time, to do so after the Beijing Massacre. (This was very different from the policy of linkage adopted towards the Soviet Union. The West could live with the Chinese but not the Soviet Communist Party.)

Deng Xiaoping himself had stimulated some discussion within the Party on political reform, although intermittently and in ambiguous terms. A number of reform-minded social scientists and economists had been enlisted by him to demolish the arguments of Mao's immediate successors. They continued with some encouragement from Hu Yaobang, the Party's Secretary-General who stated in December 1984 that Marx and Lenin 'cannot solve China's problems', and in spite of recurrent bouts of criticism from the Party dogmatists. 1986 saw a theoretical offensive by the reformers with sympathetic support in some official newspapers. There were calls for free discussion of policy issues before these were decided by the Party, and for open debate within the Party and a real choice of candidates. Similarly, the 'masses' should enjoy in reality the right to criticise and supervise their leaders which only existed on paper. The reformers also sought to understand the causes of popular alienation from the Party, and the persistence of authoritarian habits of government. They blamed much of this openly on the system of 'feudal autocracy' which Mao had perpetuated. Their criticism of Mao went far beyond the narrow limits laid down by Deng.

In the final struggle of the 1980s, Hu Yaobang was sacrificed by Deng during a counter-offensive by the Party conservatives, and it was his death two years later sparked the national protest which led to the Beijing Massacre. During these final months, the non-Party activists had finally joined forces with the internal reformers, forming a much more threatening combination which was soon augmented by the emerging independent workers' movement. The bloody suppression of June 1989 was followed by two years of stagnation and a widespread sense that the regime now had no long-term future. This was the mood so brilliantly reversed by Deng in his 1992 Southern Expedition to launch the new economic revolution. The fierce repression of 1989 had already driven nearly all dissidents who escaped arrest either underground or into exile. With no audible voice, the concept of political reform now seemed to have become irrelevant. Favourable comparisons were drawn with other Asian regimes whose economic take-off had been based upon authoritarian government – ignoring the fact that such countries as Taiwan and South Korea were now becoming more democratic. The lesson of the former Soviet Union, where the collapse of communist power had led to the break-up of the Union itself, also seemed to argue against radical change. Yet by the end of 1994, new concern about the prospect of Deng's death combined with the evidence of greater social instability and the effects of inflation and corruption to prompt a new interest in politics. In spite of the recent chorus of uncritical foreign enthusiasm for the Chinese market and for Deng personally, economic reform – it now appeared – could not by itself solve China's problems any more effectively than Marx and Lenin.

What does Middle China offer in this age of new uncertainty? Sadly for China, it is so impoverished in political knowledge and understanding that it can have very little to contribute. The main international events are reported on television, usually in the form of brief Western reports (British or American) with a Chinese language voice-over, but there are no documentaries on current affairs abroad – only the occasional travelogue. Domestic news is still presented either as political ritual (reports of conferences and speeches) or as optimistic assertion (news of economic successes). Some social issues may be discussed more freely on the new-style chat-shows – such as problems in the workplace, differences between young and old and changing moral attitudes. One or two documentaries have looked exceptionally at the problem of rural poverty, but in general television provides little more than entertainment and sport. Most Chinese are far better informed about the state of British football than that of their own politics. The programmes of provincial or city stations are even more limited. Local newspapers rarely contain more than four pages and their coverage has hardly widened over the past 15 years. The most significant change is the increase in the number of advertisements and the inclusion of stock exchange prices.

Popular tabloids, weekend supplements and illustrated magazines offer a more colourful diet of crime reports (often with a strong sexual element), romantic stories, news of film stars, general interest tales from abroad, and household advice. The covers are lurid and the headlines sensational: the object of these new media is to make money. Political gossip about past upheavals – including as we have seen innuendo about Mao's sex life – may occasionally appear but current topics, with rare exceptions, are avoided. There is no point in risking confiscation of an issue or withdrawal of a publication licence.

Occasional broadsheets do appear with more political content, but they have nothing in common with the 'democracy posters' and dissident magazines produced during the 1980s. On long train journeys and in public parks, illegal broadsheets (carrying counterfeit licence numbers) can sometimes be bought for less than one rmb. These carry snippets of current political news, usually attributed to foreign papers and agencies or to obscure Chinese journals whose names are probably invented. They may deal very crudely with rumoured conflicts between national leaders and the fortunes of their privileged 'sons and daughters'. They also offer banal revelations on military matters and national security – together with more conventional advice on how to improve male potency! These are ephemeral publications, untrustworthy and empty of argument. Their main purpose too is to make money.

We must be careful not to conclude from the absence of visible argument or challenge to political orthodoxy that Middle China lacks any potential to generate it. Human rights organisations have recorded a number of cases of dissident activity and many more will have escaped attention. Most of these stem from the events of May–June 1989. The only evidence of independent action since then is found in the uncoordinated protests of peasant communities (as we saw in the village of Wangyan Shitun) and in labour protests. Educated urban youth in the mid-1990s are less likely to mobilise for the same aims as their predecessors in the late 1980s. Although official corruption has grown since then, so has access to entrepreneurial opportunities and the freedom to move around China in search of new openings. There is a small core of critical intelligentsia, particularly among some younger journalists, social scientists and members of the new legal profession. But they still have to operate within a system which is not only dominated, as before, by the Party bureaucracy but which has been enriched by the economic reforms and is now closely meshed with the expanding entrepreneurial interests of the armed forces.

Let us conclude by asking some final questions about China's future.

Will there be more Tiananmen Squares? After the great demonstrations of 1976 and 1989 (with several smaller events in between), Tiananmen Square has acquired powerful symbolism. If a new Chinese leadership fails to grasp control coherently and a sense of vacuum at the centre is created, then it is quite possible that the crowds will drift back to the Square – if only out of curiosity.

However, Tiananmen Square's real significance in the 1990s is its position at the top of the list of episodes requiring a 'reversal of verdicts'. No convincing progress can be made towards more democratic or responsive government unless this and other black spots in recent history are dealt with. The Party's own chance of survival will largely depend too on its ability to clear the historical slate. It is, as we have seen in Hunan province, a long and difficult task which was started but then aborted during the Deng regime. It will be hard enough to resume the critique of Mao, let alone begin to re-evaluate Deng's own role in previous events including the 'anti-right' witch-hunt of the late 1950s. If the Party is overthrown, then history will indeed be 'reversed'. The practice in Chinese historiography has always been to praise the new and condemn the old – when it is safe to do so. This would be equally unsatisfactory. China has to come to terms with the decades of Party rule, not condemn them to oblivion.

Will China break up? Will the regions or provinces defy Beijing? This is a subject, like so many others, on which Western opinion has swung wildly between extremes. The uncritical praise for China's 'economic miracle' in the early 1990s was accompanied by loud assertion that China, unlike the Soviet Union, would never break up. Deng's hopes of allaying unrest by the promise of general prosperity was taken at face value. By 1994–95 a far more critical view had emerged as Deng's health faded and the structural problems underlying the famous miracle were revealed. A report from the International Institute for Strategic Studies warned that China faced a crisis of self-definition and that 'the very fabric of the Chinese state' might be in jeopardy. Another report from the Pentagon forecast a 50 per cent chance that China would disintegrate, and that local regimes could emerge with the backing of regional military leaders.

Such analyses pointed correctly to the tensions created by the economic reforms, the widening gap between rich and poor and the crisis in rural unemployment. But the consequences of these problems are much more complex than in the past and historical analogies with periods of national division and warlord rule are misleading. Certainly the difference in average incomes between the coast and the interior is striking, but it conceals wide variations within the provinces of Middle China. The main urban centres may duplicate many of the features of Hong Kong or other Asian cities which provide a model for the aspirations of the new middle class, even though on a much smaller scale. The real interior is their own countryside. Even here, as we have seen in Guangxi, levels of development can differ considerably between one rural county and the next. Schemes of inter-provincial cooperation also help to break down the geographical barriers between provinces which protected the warlord regimes of the 1920s. Though these schemes may be more grandiose on paper than in reality, infrastructural elements such as new roads and railways can have a dramatic linking effect.

A weaker regime in Beijing would allow a greater degree of provincial autonomy, but the threat of separation will be confined to the border regions where the aspirations of non-Han Chinese (Tibetans, Uighurs and Kazakhs, and Mongolians) will be revived – as they have historically whenever the centre appeared to be losing its grip. Even here the separatist thrust will be blurred by the large number of Han Chinese migrants, and by closer economic links with the rest of China.

Can the Party survive? Predictions that the Party was too discredited by the Beijing Massacre to survive for long were mistaken. Instead it strengthened its monopoly of government and retained ultimate authority over the economy even while devolving important areas into foreign or private hands. The economic reforms have actually increased the opportunities for bureaucratic control and enrichment: but they have also created a need for more modern institutions staffed by competent managers, financial experts, lawyers, journalists and other professionals. Most belong to the Party because it is a requirement of their jobs, but they form a new and potentially more progressive stratum. A few of the most outspoken (particularly in the legal profession) have managed to expose cadre corruption. A new more open-minded leadership at the top could call on their support in its inevitable struggle against Party conservatives. The dissident movement abroad, which itself has become divided, for the most part seeks the reform of the Party rather than its overthrow. A post-Deng transition to more liberal policies could secure the return of many exiles including thousands of students with newly acquired skills from abroad. Yet this will require careful handling in a political atmosphere inside the Party where factional fighting has become a way of life. (As its veterans observe, 'the Party swings from side to side as regularly as the waxing and waning of the moon'.) The Party's loss of rural control in many places – except by coercion and extortion – is a further threat. Periodic campaigns against corruption have intensified, with occasional death penalties handed out against high-ranking provincial offenders. Yet official statistics admit that the number of cases has increased steadily since the 1980s.

Can China find a way forward? China's ability to develop its economy and evolve politically is critical for the world of the 21st Century. Whether it can manage to do so is problematic but not completely impossible. By 1995 some of the problems described in previous pages have been officially acknowledged and a few are being tackled, at least by official pronouncement. They include: persistent poverty among up to 100 million people; dwindling arable land and the 'real estate fever'; bureaucratic restraints on more efficient farming; the burden on students of new educational fees; declining standards of health provision; falsified statistics; illegal taxes and numerous other forms of corruption; urban unemployment and under-employment; social alienation and the search for new faiths; exploitation of women and children; crime and the revival of secret societies; rapid ecological degradation; worsening urban pollution; widening gaps of income and living standards between different sectors of society and different areas of the country.

These problems are the dark side of the bright picture of economic transformation which has become the organising principle of Dengist ideology and attracted so much admiration abroad. Many Chinese, starting with Deng himself, have put their faith in rapid economic growth: here was a new 'magic weapon' to replace those proffered in the past such as collectivisation, class struggle, and the Thought of Mao Zedong. The Three Gorges Dam is the supreme example of this approach, a grand scheme to transform the future of the whole Yangzi valley, ultimately affecting one in five of all Chinese. A more sober approach has to recognise that while the economic changes are impressive and far-reaching, the ideology of growth creates as many problems as it solves. The strategy is also based to a very large extent upon seeking foreign investment and allowing foreign business to exploit China's main asset of cheap labour. New growing cities such as Shashi in Middle China will seek to undercut the coast in attracting investment and offering their own cheaper labour. The enthusiastic participation of the Overseas Chinese has so far helped to make this a succcess but it places China's own future health at the mercy of changes in the international economic climate.

China surely needs a more rounded and flexible strategy to take account of its diverse conditions, as well as a more mature political system which can implement it. All the problems described above are painfully familiar in large areas of the developing world. In the past China offered a different approach which avoided – or at least postponed – many of these problems. Dogmatically preached in a hostile international climate, Chinese self-reliance never had a chance. Now China's approach is essentially the same as that preached by international orthodoxy to developing countries the world over. Post-communist Eastern Europe barely paused before rejecting the possibility of an alternative. China still has, in theory, the possibility of learning from all the lessons, positive and negative, and charting a different course. There is no possibility of Middle China becoming, as Deng Xiaoping proposed, 'like Hong Kong'. The whole country is more likely to become, on a vastly larger scale, another Third World country where city is ranged against countryside, wealth against deprivation, and technological wonders mask deep social ills. China has a very short time left to find a third way.

China's provinces

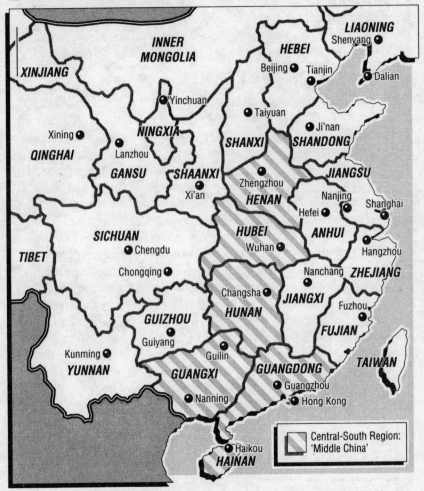

INNER MONGOLIA

XINJIANG

LIAONING
Shenyang ●

HEBEI
Beijing ● Tianjin ●
Dalian ●

Yinchuan ●

Taiyuan ●

Ji'nan ●

Xining ●

NINGXIA

SHANXI

SHANDONG

QINGHAI

Lanzhou ●

GANSU

SHAANXI

Zhengzhou ●

JIANGSU

Nanjing ●

Shanghai ●

Xi'an ●

HENAN

Hefei ●

SICHUAN
● Chengdu

HUBEI
Wuhan ●

ANHUI

Hangzhou ●

TIBET

Chongqing ●

ZHEJIANG

Nanchang ●

Changsha ●

JIANGXI

HUNAN

Fuzhou ●

GUIZHOU
Guiyang ●

FUJIAN

Kunming ●

Guilin ●

YUNNAN

GUANGXI

GUANGDONG

TAIWAN

● Guangzhou

● Nanning

● Hong Kong

Central-South Region: 'Middle China'

● Haikou
HAINAN

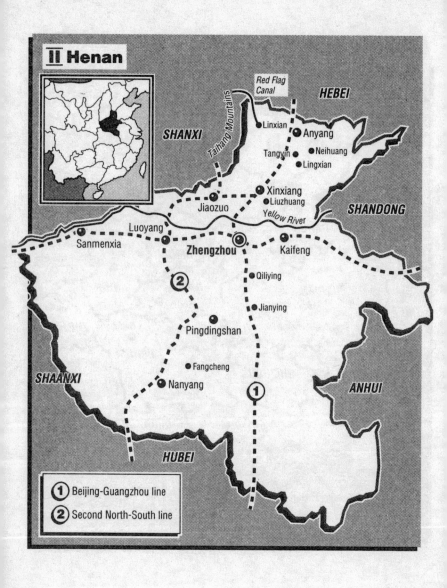

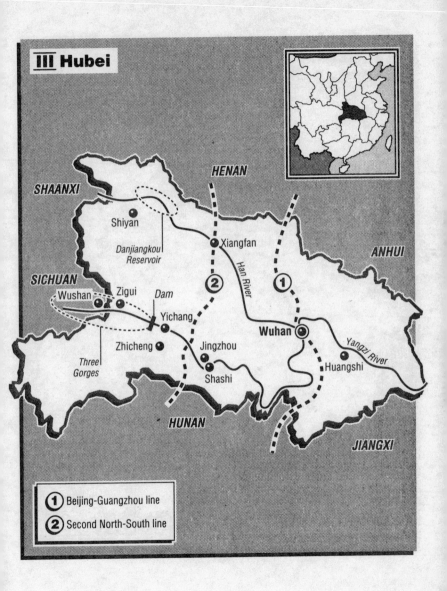

III Hubei

SHAANXI

HENAN

Shiyan

Danjiangkou
Reservoir

Xiangfan

ANHUI

SICHUAN

Han River

Wushan

Zigui

Dam

②

①

Yichang

Zhicheng

Jingzhou

Wuhan

Yangzi River

Shashi

Huangshi

Three
Gorges

HUNAN

JIANGXI

① Beijing-Guangzhou line

② Second North-South line

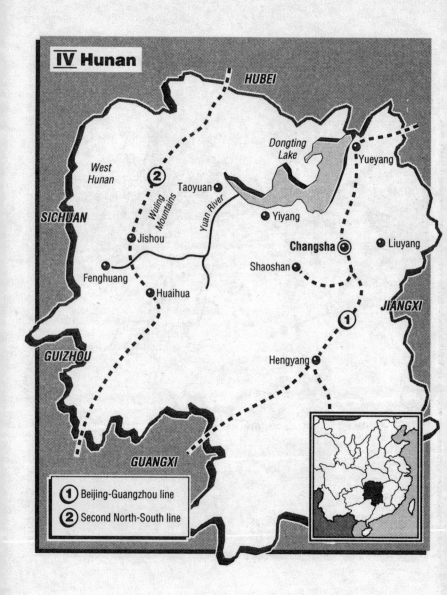

IV Hunan

HUBEI

West
Hunan

SICHUAN

Dongting
Lake

Yueyang

Taoyuan

Yiyang

②

Wuling Mountains

Yuan River

Jishou

Changsha ◎

Liuyang

Shaoshan

Fenghuang

Huaihua

JIANGXI

①

GUIZHOU

Hengyang

GUANGXI

① Beijing-Guangzhou line
② Second North-South line

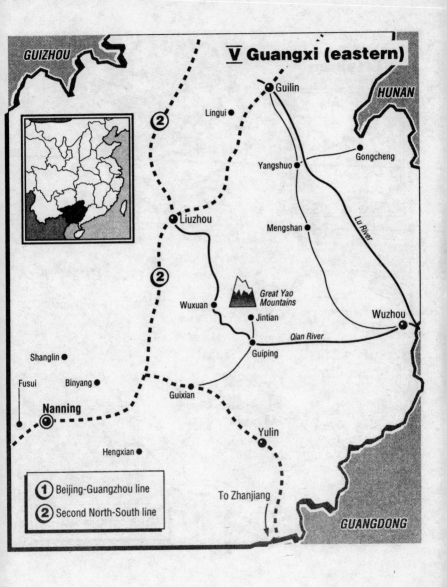

V Guangxi (eastern)

GUIZHOU

HUNAN

Guilin

Lingui

Gongcheng

Yangshuo

Liuzhou

Mengshan

Lu River

Great Yao Mountains

Wuxuan

Jintian

Wuzhou

Qian River

Guiping

Shanglin

Binyang

Fusui

Guixian

Nanning

Hengxian

Yulin

To Zhanjiang

① Beijing-Guangzhou line

② Second North-South line

GUANGDONG

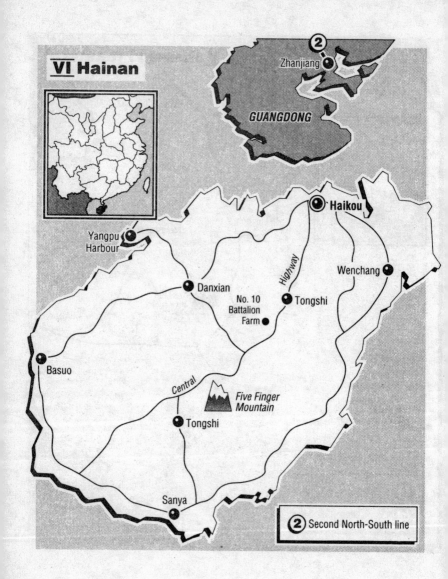

VI Hainan

GUANGDONG

Zhanjiang

Haikou

Yangpu
Harbour

Danxian

No. 10
Battalion
Farm

Tongshi

Highway

Wenchang

Basuo

Central

Five Finger
Mountain

Tongshi

Sanya

② Second North-South line

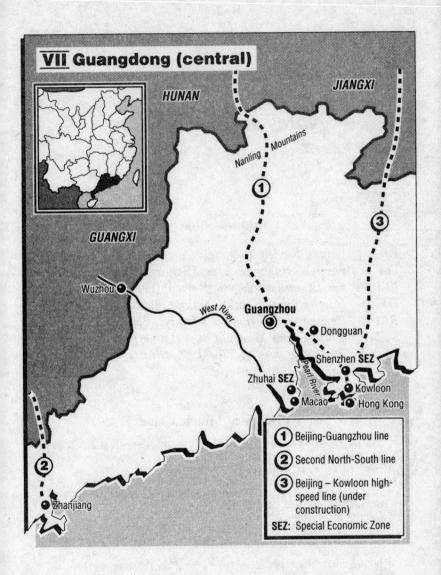

VII Guangdong (central)

HUNAN

JIANGXI

Nanling Mountains

GUANGXI

(1)

(3)

Wuzhou

West River

Guangzhou

Dongguan

Shenzhen **SEZ**

Zhuhai **SEZ**

Pearl River

Kowloon

Macao

Hong Kong

(2)

Zhanjiang

(1) Beijing–Guangzhou line

(2) Second North–South line

(3) Beijing – Kowloon high-speed line (under construction)

SEZ: Special Economic Zone

Notes and References

Abbreviations

BR   *Beijing Review* (Beijing)
FLP   Foreign Languages Press (Beijing)
FEER   *Far Eastern Economic Review* (Hong Kong)
IHT   *International Herald Tribune* (Paris)
RMRB   *Renmin Ribao [People's Daily]* (Beijing).
SCMP   *South China Morning Post* (Hong Kong).
SWB   BBC *Summary of World Broadcasts: Part III, The Far East* (London)

I Journey to Middle China

1 Reuters (Beijing), 4 April, 20 September, 24 November 1993; *SCMP* (weekly ed.), 14–15 August 1993.
2 *Financial Times*, 29 December 1992.
3 *Asiaweek*, 23 January 1993; *Time*, 10 May 1993.
4 *IHT*, 21 May 1993; *World Economic Outlook* (Washington DC: International Monetary Fund, May 1993).
5 *IHT*, 19 May 1993.
6 *ibid.*, 16 June 1993.
7 'China's consumer markets: here comes the boom', *DRI News Service* (London), 10 October 1994.
8 Li Chengrui, *A Study of China's Population* (FLP, 1992), pp. 163–4.
9 I have avoided the use of the terms 'outer' and 'inner' for 'Western' and 'Eastern' China since these can lead to confusion.
10 For different definitions of Middle China see the 'Middle Zone' defined in the Tenth Five Year Plan (1986–90), and the modified version in G. J.

R. Linge & D. K. Forbes, *China's Spatial Economy* (Hong Kong: Oxford University Press, 1990), p. 69.

11 On regional policy see Linge & Forbes, *op. cit.*; Terry Cannon & Alan Jenkins, eds., *The Geography of Contemporary China* (London: Routledge, 1990); Gerald Segal, *China Changes Shape: Regionalism and Foreign Policy*, *Adelphi Paper 287* (London: Brassey's UK, 1994).

12 China News Service (Beijing), 5 April 1994.

13 *Zhongguo tielu jianshe* [*Chinese Railway Construction*] (Beijing: Railways Press, 1990), pp. 107–10.

II Peasants in Revolt

1 Amnesty International, *Appeal on behalf of Hu Hai*, London, June 1992.

2 Deng Liqun, *et. al.* ed., *Dangdai Zhongguo de Henan* [*Contemporary Henan*], vol. 1, p. 14.

3 Mo Qi, *Zhongguo renkou: Henan fence* [*China's population: Henan section*] (Beijing: China Finance Press, 1989), p. 32.

4 *Guangzhou ribao* [*Guangzhou Daily*], 6 February 1993, in *Inside China Mainland* (Taipei: Institute of Current Studies, April 1993).

5 *Zhongguo Qingnian Bao: Shehui zhoukan* [*China Youth Daily: Society Weekly*], 4 March 1993.

6 Executive Yuan Rural Revival Committee, *Henan sheng nongcun diaocha* [*Investigation into rural conditions in Henan*] (Shanghai: Commercial Press, 1934), pp. 94–5.

7 *Lingxian nongcun gongzuo xin zhixu* [*New order of rural work in Lingxian*] (Lingxian: Party Committee, January 1991).

8 Henan radio, 15 June 1989, in *SWB*, 28 June 1989.

9 Henan radio, 27 January 1991, in *SWB*, 1 February 1991.

10 'Pressed farmer takes own life', *BR*, 21–27 December 1992.

11 'A profound call: Oh where are you Party?' *Nongmin Ribao* [*Peasants' Daily*], 12 September 1988, in *SWB*, 1 October 1988.

12 Reports by Lena Sun, *Washington Post*, 20 and 22 June 1993.

13 *Fazhi ribao* [*Legal Daily*], 3 May 1994, trans. in *SWB*, 6 May 1994.

14 Qin Huailu, *Chen Yonggui fuchen lu* [*The rise and fall of Chen Yonggui*] (Xiyang County: private publication, 1991); a book with the same title, written by Wu En (Hong Kong: Cosmos Books, 1993), is a standard biography.

15 Lin Min, *Red Flag Canal* (FLP, 1974); *Nongmin Ribao* [*Peasants' Daily*] (Beijing), 2 September 1992.

16 Chu Li, *Inside a People's Commune* (Beijing: FLP, 1974); China News Agency (Beijing), 3 April 1990.

17 *Jingji Lanxun* [*Business Tribune*] (Beijing), 8 March 1994.

18 Lincoln Kaye, 'Ugly face of reforms', *FEER* (Hong Kong), 22 April 1993.

19 'Jinri ruhe zuo qianren' [How to make money today], *Beijing Qingnian Bao (Qingnian Zhoumou)* [*Beijing Youth News (Youth Weekly)*], 23 April 1994.

20 *Dangdai* [*Contemporary*] (Hong Kong), 15 April 1993.

21 Reuters (Beijing), 2 September 1993.
22 Xinhua News Agency (Beijing), 29 Junea 1993; China News Agency (Beijing), 7 September 1993.
23 *RMRB*, 17 December 1993; *Wen Wei Bao* [*Wen Wei Newspaper*], Hong Kong, 8 December 1993.
24 *BR*, 18–24 July 1994.

III The Religion Fever

1 *Liaowang* [*Outlook*] (Hong Kong), 17 June 1991, in *SWB*, 28 June 1991.
2 *Nongmin Ribao* [*Peasants' Daily*], 18 October 1989, in *SWB*, 26 October 1989.
3 *China Study Journal* (London: Council of Churches for Britain & Ireland), vol. VI, no. 2, August 1991, pp. 68–71.
4 My summary of scenes on a video produced in 1993 by the Revival Christian Church, Hong Kong.
5 A. J. Broomhall, *Hudson Taylor & China's Open Century: Assault on the Nine* (London: Hodder & Stoughton, 1988), p. 372.
6 Archibald E. Glover, *A Thousand Miles of Miracle in China* (Glasgow: Pickering & Inglis, 1904), pp. 272–3.
7 J. Dyer Ball, *Things Chinese* (Hong Kong: Kelly & Walsh, 1903), pp. x, 442–3.
8 G. E. Morrison, *An Australian in China* (Hong Kong: Oxford University Press, 1985), p. 5.
9 Robert Whyte, *Unfinished Encounter: China and Christianity* (London: Collins, 1988), p. 169.
10 Alan Hunter & Kim-Kwong Chan, *Protestantism in Contemporary China* (Cambridge: Cambridge University Press, 1993), pp. 126–35.
11 Xiao Zhitian, 'Changes in the framework of Christian religious activities over the last 40 years', trans. in *China Insight* (Littleton, Colorado: Overseas Missionary Fellowship), February–March 1993.
12 As note 3.
13 The survey is translated by Alan Miller in *China Study Journal*, vol. IX, no. 2, August 1994.
14 Michael Dillon, 'Muslim communities in contemporary China: The resurgence of Islam after the Cultural Revolution', *Journal of Islamic Studies* (Oxford: OUP), vol. V, no. 1, pp. 70–101.
15 On Buddhism in the 1980s, see Hunter & Chan, *op.cit.*, pp. 219–35.
16 *Nongmin Ribao* [*Peasants' Daily*], 17 April 1987, trans. in *SWB*, 29 April 1987. On the distinction between 'religion' and 'superstition', see Stephan Feuchtwang & Wang Ming-ming, 'The politics of culture or a contest of histories: Representations of Chinese popular religion', *Dialectical Anthropology*, (The Hague: Kluwer) No. 16 (1991), pp. 251–72.
17 As note 3, p. 72.
18 Dissident *qigong* account in the *Guardian*, 31 May 1990; Reuters (Beijing), 2 December 1992.

19 *China: Persecution of a Protestant Sect* (New York: Human Rights Watch/Asia, June 1994).

20 *SCMP*, 18 July 1993; *Wen Wei Bao* [*Wen Wei Newspaper*], 18 August 1993.

21 Associated Press (Beijing), 17 February 1994; Amnesty International, *China: Protestants and Catholics detained since 1993* (London, March 1994), pp. 6–7.

22 *RMRB*, 20 June 1994, in *SWB*, 14 July 1994.

23 Clarence Burton Day, *Chinese Peasant Cults: A study of Chinese paper gods* (Shanghai: Kelly & Walsh, 1940), p. 191.

IV Damming the Gorges

1 'Alarm at first entering the Yang-tze Gorges', in Arthur Waley, *170 Chinese Poems* (London: Constable, 1947), p. 151.

2 Statistics vary widely for the earlier years. Sources include *Dangdai Hubei jiben jianshe* [*Basic Construction in Contemporary Hubei*] (Wuhan: Hubei People's Press, 1987); Shiu-hung Luk & Joseph Whitney eds., *Megaproject: A Case Study of China's Three Gorges Project* (Armonk, NY: M. E. Sharpe, 1985).

3 Archibald Little, *Through the Yang-tse Gorges* (London: Sampson Low, 1888), p. 67.

4 Walter H. Mallory, *China: Land of Famine* (New York: American Geographical Society, 1926), p. 46.

5 O. J. Todd, *Two Decades in China* (Taipei: Cheng Wen Publishing Co., 1971 reprint), pp. 73–80.

6 Isabella Bird, *The Yangtze Valley and Beyond* (London: Virago, 1985 reprint), p. 81.

7 *ibid.*, p. 102.

8 John Thomson, *Through China with a Camera* (Westminster Press, London 1898), pp. 208–9.

9 Lin Yutang, *The Gay Genius: The Life and Times of Su Tungpo* (London: Heinemann, 1948), p. 43.

10 Cornell Plant, *Glimpses of the Yangtze Gorges* (Shanghai: Kelly & Walsh, 1926), p. 54.

11 Quoted in Frances Wood, *China (Blue Guide)* (London: A & C Black, 1992), p. 449.

12 Bird, *op.cit.*, p. 136.

13 He Yu, 'Geng li xi jiang shi bi, zai duan Wu shan yun yu' [Building a stone wall, slicing apart the clouds and rain of Mount Wu], in *Minzhu Zhongguo* [*Democratic China*] (Princeton, New Jersey), No. 18, November 1993, pp. 7–12.

14 *Mao Tse-tung: Nineteen Poems* (FLP, 1958), pp. 28, 35–8.

15 The essays edited by Li Rui in 1956 were republished as Li Rui et al., *Chang Jiang guihua wenti* [*Problems of the Yangzi River Plan*] (Beijing: Dianli gongye chubanshe [Hydroelectric Industry Press], 1957). The 1992 decision was justified in a series of *Beijing Review* features.

16 The late 1980s debate is documented in Dai Qing, *Yangzi Yangzi* (London: Earthscan, 1994), and Margaret Barber & Grainne Ryder eds., *Damming the Three Gorges* (London: Earthscan, 1993). See also Richard Edmonds, 'The Three Gorges (Sanxia) project: Panacea or plague?' *Britain–China* (London: Great Britain–China Centre), Winter 1992–93, pp. 9–13. The World Bank issued an internal report (No. 11641–CHA, 8 June 1993) on 'China Involuntary Settlement': see John Gittings, 'Homelessness in the name of aid', the *Guardian*, 18 March 1994.
17 *The Three Gorges Dam in China* (New York: Human Rights Watch/Asia, February 1995).
18 'Problems and solutions to public safety and security in the Three Gorges area' (document of Public Security Bureau, Wanxian), trans. by Probe International (Toronto), August 1994. For claims of success see *BR*, 10–16 October 1994.

V A Tale of Two Cities

1 *Hubei Ribao [Hubei Daily]*, 1 May 1994.
2 *ibid.*, 24 May 1994, translated in *SWB*, 2 July 1994.
3 Arnold Wright ed., *Twentieth Century Impressions of Hongkong, Shanghai, and other Treaty Ports of China* (London: Lloyd's Greater Britain Publishing Co., 1908), pp. 692–9.
4 Theodore White & Annalee Jacoby, *Thunder out of China* (New York: William Sloane, 1946), p. 53.
5 W. H. Auden & Christopher Isherwood, *Journey to a War*, revised edition (London: Faber & Faber, 1973), pp. 14, 40.
6 White & Jacoby, *op. cit.*, pp. 55–7.
7 *Hubei jindai lishi [Modern history of Hubei]* (Wuhan: Hubei People's Press, 1990).
8 Edgar Snow, *The Other Side of the River: Red China Today* (London: Gollancz, 1963), ch. 75.
9 Michael Shapiro, *Changing China* (London: Lawrence & Wishart, 1958), pp. 115–22.
10 Jim Abrams, 'Mountain hamlet becomes China's motor capital', Associated Press (Beijing), 16 May 1990.
11 Gordon White & Robert Benewick, *Urban government reform in China: the case of Wuhan* (Falmer: University of Sussex, 1993).
12 Linge & Forbes, *op. cit.*, pp. 80–1.
13 White & Benewick, *op. cit.*, pp. 26–9.
14 James McGregor, 'Wuhan sets role for itself as China's inland gateway', *Asia Wall Street Journal*, 12 January 1993.
15 'Hong Kong "plus plus" is a big hit in Wuhan', Associated Press, 21 December 1992.
16 Peter Woo, '"Do Something": The China Strategy of the 90s', speech in Singapore, 27 April 1993.
17 Associated Press, 26 August 1992.
18 Reuters, 10 November 1993.

19 Author's interviews in Wuhan and Hong Kong, May 1994.
20 Peter Woo, address to Chatham House, London, 1 June 1994; *Far Eastern Economic Review*, 10 November 1994.
21 As note 14.
22 *New York Times*, 6 May 1994.
23 SCMP, 13 July 1993; *Dangdai* [Contemporary Monthly Hong Kong], 15 April 1994.
24 Patrick E. Tyler, 'In China, corruption hits textiles', *IHT*, 26 May 1994.
25 Bird, *op. cit.*, p. 87.
26 *Yueyang Wanbao [Yueyang Evening News]*, 12 March 1993.
27 'Yangtze pearl foresees new century', *BR*, 12–18 September 1994; 'Huangshi: A new star rises on the Yangzi', *BR*, 6–12 December 1993.

VI The Legacy of Mao

1 Visitors' statistics from Wen Rexin, *Mao Zedong yu guxiang [Mao Zedong and his Native Home]* (Beijing: Police & Official Education Press, 1991), p. 162; Jiang Guoping, *Mao Zedong yu Shaoshan [Mao Zedong and Shaoshan]* (Beijing: China Youth Press, 1992), p. 269; and information gathered on the spot.
2 Zhao Zhichao, *Mao Zedong he tade fulao xiangqin [Mao Zedong and his family folk]* (Changsha: Hunan Literature and Arts Press, 1992), p. 503.
3 'Shaoshan revisited', in *Ten More Poems of Mao Tse-tung* (Hong Kong: Eastern Horizon Press, 1967), p. 4. My interpretation is supported by Su Xiaokang et al., *Wutuobang ji [Utopian Sacrifice]* (Beijing: China News Press, 1988), pp. 70–72.
4 The Dishuidong visit is described in 'Xifang shandong li de Mao Zedong' [Mao Zedong in a Western cave], *Zuojia Wenzhai [Authors' Digest]* (Beijing), 19 February 1993; and in the books by Jiang Guoping and Zhao Zhichao cited above.
5 Jiang Guoping, *op. cit.*, p. 163.
6 Letter of 8 July to Jiang Qing, *Issues and Studies* (Taipei), No. 9, January 1973.
7 The *Zuojia Wenzhai* account claims Mao's desire to die in Shaoshan was blocked by the Politburo. Zhao Zhichao, *op. cit.*, pp. 548–9, describes his nostalgia for his native home as he lay dying.
8 Portrait incident reports in *SWB*, 25 May, 4 July, 15 August 1989; *Anthems of Defeat* (New York: Asia Watch, May 1992), pp. 27–9; *Chinese Workers* (London: Workers' Autonomous Federation of China), No. 2, June 1993, p. 9.
9 *Zhongguo: Mao Zedong re [China: the Mao Zedong Fever]* (Beijing: Beiyue Press, 1991).
10 Quan Yanchi, *Mao Zedong, Man, not God* (FLP, 1992).
11 Liu Zhi, 'Mao Zedong de wannian beiju' [The tragedy of Mao Zedong's last years], *Zheng Da Zong Yi [True Culture]* (Inner Mongolia), November 1992.
12 Luo Bing, 'Fan Mao pai pi Mao si shenghuo' [Anti-Mao group

criticism Mao's personal life], *Zheng Ming [Contention]* (Hong Kong), July 1992.

13 'Deng Liqun on the Mao Zedong Fever', *Guangming Ribao [Guangming Daily]*, 26 November 1991.

14 Harrison E. Salisbury, *The New Emperors: Mao and Deng, a dual biography* (London: HarperCollins, 1992).

15 Zhisui Li, *The Private Life of Chairman Mao* (London: Chatto & Windus, 1994).

16 Li Rui, 'On Mao Zedong's thinking and practice in his later years', *Guangming Ribao [Guangming Daily]* (Beijing), 2 February 1989, trans. in *SWB*, 9 February 1989; 'Beiju: wannian Mao Zedong' [The tragedy of the last years of Mao Zedong], *Qiao [Bridge]* (Beijing), No. 1, 1993.

17 Associated Press (Hong Kong), 3 January 1995.

VII The Silent Writer

1 Shen Congwen, *Recollections of West Hunan* (Beijing: Panda Books, 1982), author's preface, pp. 14–15.

2 Jerome Ch'en, *The Highlanders of Central China: A history 1895–1937* (Armonk, NY: M. E. Sharpe, 1992), pp. 165–6, 191–9.

3 Shen Tseng-wen, *The Chinese Earth* (trans. by Ching Ti & Robert Payne) (London: Allen & Unwin, 1947), p. 7.

4 Yuan Chia-hua & Robert Payne ed., *Contemporary Chinese Short Stories* (London: Noel Carrington, 1946), pp. 10–11.

5 Shen Tseng-wen, *op. cit.*, pp. 174–6.

6 Huang Yongyu, 'My Uncle Shen Congwen', in Shen Congwen, *The Border Town & Other Stories* (Beijing: Panda Books, 1981), p. 194.

7 *ibid.*, p. 7.

8 *ibid.*, p. 184.

9 Ling Yu, *Shen Congwen zhuan [Biography of Shen Congwen]* (Beijing: October Literature & Art Press, 1988), pp. 441–2. The standard English-language biography is Jeffrey C. Kinkley, *The Odyssey of Shen Congwen* (Stanford: Stanford University Press, 1987).

10 *ibid.*, pp. 452–9; Shen Congwen, essays of May and July 1957, in *Shen Congwen wenji [The works of Shen Congwen]* (Hong Kong: Sanlian publishers, 1982–5), vol. x, pp. 189–96, 210–16.

11 Shen's experiences in the 1960s and 1970s are described in the works by Ling Yu and Huang Yongyu cited above.

12 Liu Yiyou, 'Shen Congwen xianxiang' [The phenomenon of Shen Congwen], *Jishou Daxue xuebao (shehui kexue ban) [Journal of Social Science of Jishou University]* (Jishou), No. 1, March 1989, pp. 1–20.

13 Fenghuang Branch of the Chinese People's Political Consultative Conference, *Huainian Shen Congwen [In memory of Shen Congwen]* (Fenghuang, December 1989), pp. 8–13, 'Two letters to a fellow-provincial'.

NOTES AND REFERENCES

VIII From Cannibalism to Karaoke

1 Writing Group for editing the main events of the 'Cultural Revolution', *Wuxuan xian: Wuchanjieji wenhua dageming dashijian [Main events of the Great Proletarian Cultural Revolution in Wuxuan County]* (Wuxuan, 28 May 1987).

2 Zheng Yi, *Hongse jinianbei [Red Monument]* (Taipei: Hua Shih Cultural Press, 1993).

3 Liu Binyan, 'An unnatural disaster', *New York Review of Books*, 8 April 1993.

4 Zheng Yi, *Lishi de yibufen [A Part of History]* (Taipei: Tianyuan Publishers, 1992), pp. 305–7.

5 *ibid.*, pp. 308–10.

6 Transcript of Mao Zedong and other leaders discussing national situation on 28 July 1968, in *Miscellany of Mao Tse-tung Thought (1949–1968)*, Joint Publications Research Service (Arlington, Virginia) vol. 2, February 1974, p. 481.

7 As note 2, pp. 92–3, 128–30.

8 Zheng Zhengxi ed., *Zhongda yundong ruhe ru Zhi [How to Enter Big Movements into Gazetteers* (Nanning: Guangxi People's Press, 1989); Stig Thogersen & Soren Clausen, 'New reflections in the mirror: Local Chinese gazetteers in the 1980s', *Australian Journal of Chinese Affairs*, No. 27, January 1992.

9 *RMRB*, 10 September 1984.

10 As note 3.

11 'Fengyang xian de siwang jilu' [Record of deaths in Fengyang County], *Kaifang Zazhai [Open Journal]* (Hong Kong), March 1994.

12 Key Ray Chong, *Cannibalism in China* (Wakefield, New Hampshire: Longwood Academic, 1990), pp. 46–54, 134–7.

13 P. Arens, *The Man-eating Myth* (New York: Oxford University Press, 1979), pp. 83–7.

14 Lu Xun, 'Medicine' and 'A Madman's diary' in *Selected Stories of Lu Hsun* (FLP, 1960); Wen Yuhong, 'The Mad City', in Henry Zhao ed., *The Lost Boat* (London: Wellsweep, 1993).

15 Wolfram Eberhard, *The Local Cultures of South and East China* (Leiden: Brill, 1968), pp. 170–73, 448–50.

16 MM. Callery et Yvan, *L'Insurrection en Chine* (Paris: Librairie Nouvelle, 1853), p. 46.

17 Leo J. Moser, *The Chinese Mosaic* (Boulder, Colorado: Westview Press, 1985), p. 227.

18 Tian Shulan, *Guangxi luxing ji [Travels in Guangxi]* (Shanghai: Chung Hwa Publishers, 1935), p. 248.

19 Xie Zhihong ed., *Guangxi zizhiqu jingji dili [Economic geography of Guangxi A.R.]* (Beijing: Xinhua Press, 1989), pp. 46–51.

20 Zhao Fulin interview, Guangxi radio, 16 September 1993, trans. in *SWB*, 23 September 1993.

21 Zhou Dingzhi, *The Beautiful Li River* (Changsha: Hunan Education Press, 1988).

22 T. Watters, *Guide to the Tablets in a Temple of Confucius* (Shanghai:

American Presbyterian Mission Press, 1879); *Guangxi lidai mingren mingsheng lu [Record of famous persons and events in Guangxi history]* (Nanning: Guangxi Nationalities Press, 1991).

IX China's New Frontier

1 *SCMP*, 20 July 1991.
2 Edward H. Schafer, *Shore of Pearls* (Berkeley, University of California Press, 1970), p. 85–6.
3 Lin Yutang, *The Gay Genius*, (London: Heinemann, 1948), p. 323.
4 Burton Watson, *Su Tung-p'o: Selection from a Sung Dynasty Poet* (New York: Columbia University Press, 1965), p. 130.
5 Schafer, *op.cit.*, p. 100 (adapted).
6 *Haikou wu gong si daoyin [Guide to Temple of Five Officials]* (Haikou museum), p. 8.
7 B. C. Henry, *Ling-Nam, or Interior Views of Southern China, including explorations in the hitherto untraversed island of Hainan* (London: S. W. Partridge & Co., 1886), pp. 415, 420, 469.
8 *ibid.*, pp. 333–4.
9 Carl Crow, *Handbook for China* (Hong Kong: Oxford University Press, 1984 reprint), p. 372; 'Admiralty: Naval Intelligence Division', *China Proper, volume III* (London: His Majesty's Stationery Office, 1945), pp. 237–40.
10 Harry A. Franck, *Roving through Southern China*, (New York: Century Co., 1925), p. 325.
11 Zhang Yangui & Yuan Wei, *Zhongguo Gongnong Hongjun shi lue [Brief History of the Chinese Workers' and Peasants' Red Army]* (Beijing: Party Materials Press, 1987), pp. 415–20; Gregor Benton, *Mountain Fires* (Berkeley: University of California Press, 1992), p. 428.
12 'The Red Detachment of Women', in Martin Ebon ed., *Five Chinese Communist Plays* (New York: John Day Co., 1975), pp. 119–53.
13 Huang Jiaju ed., *Hainan te qu fazhan zhanlue yanjiu [Research into the Development Strategy of Hainan Special Zone]* (Beijing: Electric Engineering Press, 1989), p. 4.
14 Shen Yimin & Tong Chenzhu, *Renkou qianyi [Population Movement]* (Beijing: Chinese Statistical Press, 1992), p. 178.
15 Zhan Changzhi ed., *Zhongguo renkou (Hainan fence) [China's Population (Hainan section)]* (Beijing: Financial Press, 1993), pp. 87–8.
16 B. Michael Frolic, *Mao's People: 16 portraits of life in revolutionary China* (Cambridge: Harvard University Press, 1980), p. 198; author's interview, May 1992 (Overseas Chinese).
17 *ibid.*, p. 206; Overseas Chinese recollection as above.
18 Catherine Schurr Enderton, *Hainan Dao: Contemporary Environmental Management and Development on China's Treasure Island* (Los Angeles: University of California, dissertation, 1984), p. 295.
19 Julie Leung, 'Hainan pays price for laissez-faire fling', *Asian Wall Street Journal*, 24 November 1989.

20 Xinhua News Agency (Beijing), 14 September 1989, in *SWB*, 19 September 1989.
21 *Da Gong Bao* [*Da Gong Newspaper*] Hong Kong, 30 August 1993, in *SWB*, 23 September 1993.
22 Xinhua News Agency (Haikou), 28 September 1993, in *SWB*, 30 September 1993.
23 Author's interview, May 1992.
24 Karl Huus, 'One province, no system', *FEER*, 2 June 1994.
25 *FEER*, 5 August 1994; *Asian Wall Street Journal*, 10 August 1994.

X The Guangdong Experience

1 *SWB*, 11 March 1992; Deng's remarks were toned down in the edited version, *Selected Works of Deng Xiaoping: volume III* (FLP, 1994), pp. 363–64.
2 This slogan provides the title of the authoritative study of Guangdong's reform policies in the 1980s by a Western scholar with unique access to the province and its officials: Ezra F. Vogel, *One Step Ahead in China: Guangdong under reform* (Cambridge, Mass: Harvard University Press, 1989).
3 'China's fastest-growing region looks to the future', *Newsweek*, 17 February 1992; Associated Press, 29 March 1992; *Financial Times*, 16 June 1992; Lena Sun, 'South China drives boom region', *Washington Post*, 2 December 1992.
4 Vogel, *op. cit.*, pp. 175–181; 'Dongguan, the road to wealth by peaceful transformation', *Jiushi Niandai* [*The Nineties*] (Hong Kong), December 1991.
5 *RMRB*, 8 June 1992; John Pomfret, 'Mayor of boom town has feet in two worlds', Associated Press, 25 September 1991.
6 Associated Press, 31 May 1991.
7 Guangdong radio, 20 November 1993, in *SWB*, 22 November 1993.
8 *Jingji Ribao* [*Economic Daily*], Beijing, 25 January 1993, quoted in Reuters (Beijing), same date.
9 'New real estate industry craze', *BR*, 9–15 November 1992.
10 Louise de Rosario, 'House of cards', *FEER*, 14 July 1994.
11 China News Agency (Beijing), 12 May 1993, in *SWB*, 24 May 1993.
12 Carl Goldstein in *FEER*, 8 April 1993.
13 Arthur Waley, *The Opium War Through Chinese Eyes* (London: Allen & Unwin, 1958), pp. 42–6; *Wen Wei Bao* (Hong Kong), 12 November 1993.
14 Vogel, *op. cit.*, ch. 8: 'The mountain counties'.
15 Governor Zhu Senlin, quoted by Guangdong radio, 19 October 1992, in *SWB*, 5 November 1992; *Wen Wei Bao* (Hong Kong), 23 February 1994, in *SWB*, 10 March 1994.
16 'Heading for the 21st century', *BR*, 26 September–2 October 1994.
17 John Kohut, 'The China clubbers', *SCMP* (international weekly), 22–23 October 1994; 'China salaries mimic those of capitalist West', Reuters, 18 September 1994.

Index